His and Hers

His and Hers

*Essays in Restoration and
Eighteenth-Century Literature*

Ann Messenger

THE UNIVERSITY PRESS OF KENTUCKY

Copyright © 1986 by The University Press of Kentucky

Scholarly publisher for the Commonwealth, serving Bellarmine
College, Berea College, Centre College of Kentucky, Eastern
Kentucky University, The Filson Club, Georgetown College,
Kentucky Historical Society, Kentucky State University, Morehead
State University, Murray State University, Northern Kentucky
University, Transylvania University, University of Kentucky,
University of Louisville, and Western Kentucky University.

Editorial and Sales Office: Lexington, Kentucky 40506-0024

Library of Congress Cataloging-in-Publication Data

Messenger, Ann, 1933–
  His and hers.

  Bibliography: p.
  Includes index.
    1. English literature—18th century—History and
criticism. 2. English literature—Early modern,
1500–1700—History and criticism. 3. English
literature—Women authors—History and criticism.
4. English literature—Men authors—History and
criticism. 5. Women in literature. 6. Feminist
literary criticism.   I. Title.
PR448.W65M47   1986   820'.9   86-7803
ISBN 0-8131-1575-2

for Bill
my mainstay

and for my students
who come and go
but leave their marks

CONTENTS

ACKNOWLEDGMENTS

SHORT VERSIONS OF CHAPTER 1, "A Problem of Praise," and Chapter 8, "Choices of Life," were published in the *Transactions* of the Samuel Johnson Society of the Northwest, volume 13 (Calgary, 1982) and volume 14 (Calgary, 1983), respectively; I am grateful to the society for permission to reprint.

An earlier version of chapter 3, "Selected Nightingales," was published © 1980 by the Association of Canadian University Teachers of English. It is reprinted from *English Studies in Canada,* vol. 6, no. 2 (Summer 1980), pp. 145–53, by permission of the association. Again, my thanks.

I also thank the Library of the University of British Columbia for purchasing at my request a microfilm of *The Female Spectator.* And I thank the Province of British Columbia for a Youth Employment Programme grant (summer 1983) to compensate a research assistant—and to Diana Relke, who did the job so well.

On the personal side, I am grateful to many colleagues and friends for their interest and support, especially at those times (not infrequent) when I felt like a voice crying in the wilderness. Heartfelt thanks to my parents for a lifetime of love and encouragement. My dedication says the rest. Among the students, I am particularly indebted to Barbara Arnason, Janet Giltrow, Anna Jean Mallinson, Juliet McLaren, and Diana Relke; it has been a privilege to work with them.

His and Hers

... one part of the critic's function, when he is not just pontificating, ... is to act, more humbly and usefully, as a sort of caretaker for literary reputations. In this capacity he can at least open the front door for visitors, see that the rooms are kept dusted and ventilated, and, if need be, comment on the exhibits if any visitors arrive.

—James Sutherland

... one main concern feminist critics have is to retrieve the extensive body of women's literature and art that has been neglected in the past—not only to retrieve it but to integrate it into the canon.

—Josephine Donovan

RESTORING THE PICTURE

IMAGE ONE OF THOSE LARGE, busy, eighteenth-century paintings, a battlefield or a ballroom, a marketplace or a madhouse. For generations it hung in a London mansion, smoked by sea coal, stained by damp. One day, a Victorian heir of the family, rather low on funds and caring little for art, sold it to a museum, where it attracted much attention, despite its poor condition. For certain figures stood out, remarkable in their workmanship, some elegant, some majestic. Scholars came to study them, amateurs to admire. The murkiness of the background called forth occasional deploring comments, while some half-visible figures attracted a few who liked problems and puzzles and murk. But the clearest figures were so fine that they absorbed almost everyone's attention.

Then one day a new science was born, the science of the Art Restorer, and one of these new scientists took a great interest in the murky painting. The Art Restorer gathered together a team of specialists and persuaded the museum authorities to let them try to clean the painting. The authorities were reluctant, for there was an element of risk—might not the fine figures lose some of their luster in the process?—and besides, the painting was interesting and popular enough as it was. But the Art Restorer finally persuaded them, promising that the painting would be even more popular and that the famous figures would suffer no diminution of their glory. They might even gain in stature when seen in their proper relationship to the obscurer figures around them. (The Art Restorer was very canny.) For the Restorer wanted to see the whole picture: clear figures and dim, great figures and small, colors subtle and true, balance and composition not distorted by accidental highlighting. Perhaps a perfect job was more than could be expected, but surely something closer to the original scene could be achieved.

And so the painting is being cleaned—slowly, for it is a delicate and extensive task. Some of the Art Restorer's team have become so fascinated by the recovered figures that they have created a vigorous new branch of scholarship as they publish their findings about what had been hidden. Many of the traditional scholars continue their work on the familiar figures, ignoring the new revelations or nodding politely in their direction now and then. Some content themselves with the dim figures they had already perceived. And a few, defecting from the ranks of the traditionalists or extending the boundaries of the restoring specialists' skills, have become fascinated by the relationships between the old, known figures and the new ones. As the cleaning progresses, those relationships are appearing in all their subtlety and bewildering variety. Here a great figure is seen to crush a small one; there a small one gives a great one a push or a pull. Here a formerly invisible one appears, not so small, a figure of considerable size beside or behind a familiar one, revealing a balance, a complementarity in the composition. There a group of new ones huddles, dwarfed by the increased majesty of a great one. A gesture gains meaning—one can see what the finger points to; an expression becomes understandable—one can identify the suppliant, the partner, the admirer, the tormentor. The relationships vary endlessly, but always both old figures and new, both familiar and unfamiliar, cast some light on each other. The picture grows more true.

To drop the image, the following essays are a contribution to the task of revising the history of English literature. The task is not really a new one—scholars rediscover writers and revise the reputations of familiar ones as part of their traditional labors—but it has recently turned in new and significant directions. Critics are asking, what *is* literature? What kinds of writings make up that amorphous entity? On what grounds do we assess importance and quality? We are paying increasing attention to genres that used to exist only on the fringes—letters, diaries, journals, sketches, fragments. We are looking at written manifestations of "popular culture," a term once pejorative, now not always so. We are recapturing ephemera, writing that for one reason or another—social, political, moral—was allowed to slip into oblivion. We are questioning the familiar categories of "major" and "minor" authors. And we are paying more and more attention to literature written by women.

My image of the Art Restorer and the painting says nothing about sex, and clearly literature written by both men and women is being resurrected and reassessed in the process of restoring the picture. Yet the dim and invisible figures are more often women than men. The men are better known, even those of lesser stature, and generally require only the sort of gentle custodial care that James Sutherland described in his essay on John Gay, from which I took my first epigraph. The women, especially the women who wrote before Jane Austen, are much less known. As Josephine Donovan wrote in a debate on feminist aesthetics, their work needs to be retrieved and made part of the canon. This task is quite different.

My commitment to this task began with a mild curiosity about the poetry of Anne Finch, Countess of Winchilsea, the only woman represented in the eighteenth-century anthologies from which I received my traditional training. Although she was there, we did not spend much time on her; Dryden, Swift, Pope, and Johnson were the major figures, the mainstream, the canon. I did devote my first sabbatical year to Lady Winchilsea, but returned to the great figures and the standard anthologies with hardly a qualm. On my second sabbatical, though my announced plans were quite different, I began to look about to see if there were by any chance any more women writing in the Restoration and eighteenth century besides Lady Winchilsea— and Aphra Behn, of course, whom everybody had heard of though few had read. I knew that the nineteenth century had produced many women writers and the twentieth was chock-a-block with them. But the eighteenth? The seventeenth? By the time that sabbatical was over, I had found the women writers and I had found the task.

Such an excursion into autobiography as I have just committed is not uncommon among female critics, for we come to the study of female authors by many different paths, and descriptions of those paths help to explain what kind of feminist criticism we practice. (Many younger scholars began as feminists; those of my generation more often have become feminists.) In fact, I was somewhat surprised to discover that I *was* practicing a kind of feminist criticism in the essays in this collection. My impulse had been not to plead a case for my own sex but to redress a balance, to restore a picture. To my delight, I discovered that that is one of the things some professed feminists do.

Although feminist criticism is a fairly new discipline, it has already produced overviews, surveys, and codifications in an attempt to define itself and its work. These attempts usually conclude that feminist criticism is wide-ranging and multifarious, that it overlaps and draws on other schools of literary criticism, that it impinges on philosophy, anthropology, economics, history, and just about every other conceivable discipline, that it is "ultimately cultural criticism."[1] Among its central issues is the question of a female tradition in literature: do women writers have a tradition of their own, and if so, is it enclosed within the male tradition, separate from it, or partially overlapping?[2] Does the female writer have a "gender-specific" voice, or is her voice androgynous?[3] Is a woman's language different from a man's?[4] And does a specifically female sensibility and hence a female aesthetics or poetics exist?[5] Do women "encode" their meaning in their writing in a way specific to their sex, especially autobiographical meaning?[6] As for the critics of literature written by women, should they prescribe or describe?[7] Should they be more ideological or less ideological?[8] Should they function separately from men and the patriarchal tradition in criticism, or is such segregation undesirable?[9] And should they take cognizance of literature written by men—their writing in general or their images of women—or devote themselves entirely to that written by women?[10]

Some call it betrayal of sisterhood and some call it breaking out of the ghetto, but a few voices have been raised calling for critical studies comparing the writing of men and women, to which I add my own. Such comparisons serve many purposes, among them to determine what is "*distinctly* female" in writing by women (which assumes that some element or elements are so), and to illuminate more fully and clearly the writing of both sexes.[11] Katharine M. Rogers states the case straightforwardly: "Women authors must be evaluated as men are—in the context of their period and the mainstream of literature—not isolated in a literary ghetto with its own separate standards. . . . Only then will it be possible to make sound generalizations about the differences between women's work and men's and the particular contribution of women to the tradition."[12] This is the position which makes the most sense to me. And there are other considerations. Writing by men exists—lots of it—and while it may be true that women have a specifically female tradition, they nevertheless have "two lines of inheritance," according to Elaine Showalter; as she explains, although Virginia Woolf says in *A Room of One's Own* "that 'a woman writing thinks back through her mothers,' . . . a woman writing unavoidably thinks back through her fathers as well."[13] Men's writing cannot be ignored. Besides, one of the main modes in which the human mind functions is the comparative mode: we think about things and come to understand them by putting them next to other things.[14] In the essays in this book, therefore, I have put works by men and women side by side, in order to shed some light in both directions.

For a variety of reasons, making comparisons and exploring

other linkages between men's and women's writing have not been central to feminist criticism. Some of these reasons are strategic and ideological: women writers have been discriminated against and generally neglected for so long that they need disproportionate attention now to make up for it; only women critics can fully understand women writers and ought therefore to devote all their efforts to the study of their sisters. These convictions, both stated and unstated, underlie much feminist criticism. There is also the highly important fact that, for most feminist critics, nineteenth- and twentieth-century literature, whether they acknowledge it or not, is the "norm," the base of operations from which critical principles derive and to which they most directly apply.[15]

Many other assumptions lie buried in this one, assumptions which have profoundly influenced feminist criticism in most of its various manifestations. First, the idea that the mind of the individual artist is of central interest in the work of art is a Romantic and ongoing, post-Romantic idea—the source, I believe, of the feminist dictum that women always encode autobiographical meaning in their writing. Obviously, all writers exist in their writing to some extent, but the Augustans were not usually confessional or self-absorbed. Although one can find some concealed and encoded autobiography in their work, their voices, male and female, were more often public than private. Next, that the artist is an isolated, misunderstood outcast is similarly a Romantic and post-Romantic idea;[16] one has only to look at Dr. Johnson's claim that poets are the legislators of mankind and Shelley's that poets are the *unacknowledged* legislators of the world. Feminist critics, building on the idea of the isolated and unacknowledged artist, often say that women artists are doubly isolated, by their sex as well as by their profession, as indeed in the nineteenth century they were. One thinks of the poems and novels emanating from a remote corner of the Yorkshire moors or from an invalid's couch, and one thinks of the women hiding behind male pseudonyms when they published their work. One may even think of Jane Austen slipping her manuscript pages under the blotter on the desk when someone came to call. Aphra Behn, on the other hand, far from concealing her work, often wrote in a room full of visitors. Later eighteenth-century female novelists were immensely popular, so much so that male novelists, trading on this popularity that grew as lending libraries grew, sometimes masqueraded under female pseudonyms. And the greater number of eighteenth-century writers, men and women, lived at least part of the time in the bustle of London. They were not isolated outcasts.

It is probably also true that women lived apart from men in a "homosocial" world in the nineteenth century more than they did in the seventeenth and eighteenth.[17] Such a community makes more valid the idea of a culture, including a literary culture, exclusive to women, and justifies the study of women's literature in isolation from men's. But in the earlier periods, life was different. As the massively documented (if sometimes debatable) studies by Lawrence Stone, Keith Thomas, and others show, much that we take for granted about our sensibilities only gradually came into being in the eighteenth century.[18] Life— thinking, feeling, behaving, relating to other human beings and to oneself—was different. For instance, it was not necessary to kill the angel in the house, because she wasn't quite there— yet.[19] Feminist criticism, with its norms in the nineteenth and twentieth centuries, often fails to take these differences into account. A case in point is the important and influential *The Madwoman in the Attic,* by Sandra Gilbert and Susan Gubar, which has been rightly said to exclude history.[20] However valuable it may be in its chapters on nineteenth-century writers, it distorts the picture of eighteenth-century writers badly by pushing them under the same critical umbrella.

A sense of historical differences is necessary. In the seventeenth and eighteenth centuries, men and women writers were not cloistered in a monastery and a nunnery at either end of town. Nor were they scattered one by one in remote corners of the kingdom. Their world was relatively small, they knew each other, and for the most part they conceived of literature as public utterance. They addressed each other in verse epistles. They satirized each other, imitated each other, plagiarized from each other, edited and criticized and wrote sequels to each other. Dr. Johnson gave a party for Charlotte Lennox when her first novel was published and wrote part of a crucial chapter in her second, *The Female Quixote.* In her autobiography, Laetitia Pilkington recorded some of the most peculiar peculiarities of her good friend Jonathan Swift. Pope published a congratulatory poem by Lady Winchilsea among the prefatory materials to his collected works. It was a community.

Communities, of course, are not always made up of congenial and like-minded people. And I do not at all deny that discrimination against women writers existed. The cries of despair are there in their writing—Anne Killigrew's "Upon the saying that my Verses were made by another," Lady Winchilsea's "Introduction," Aphra Behn's pleas in prologues and prefaces that she be allowed to exercise her "masculine part," her literary talent. Men schemed against women playwrights in the theater, heaped abuse on learned ladies in scurrilous satires, and sneered at sentimental novels and romances, especially if an author's virtue was questionable. Some of the women retaliated: Aphra Behn attacked Dryden as a turncoat, Lady Mary Wortley Montagu anatomized Pope as a hunchbacked Cain. All was certainly not sweetness and light in the community.

Nor are some of my earlier generalizations about the period entirely valid. Lady Winchilsea wrote most of her poetry in relative isolation in the country, while in the homosocial nineteenth century Christina Rossetti had close connections for some time with the Pre-Raphaelite Brotherhood. Some of Anne Killigrew's poems are profoundly private and confessional and hence un-Augustan. And women writers did have some sense of a separate tradition of their own: Anne Killigrew and others write of Katherine Philips, Lady Winchilsea of Aphra Behn; later in the century, the Bluestockings, though they admitted men to their soirées, forged strong bonds among themselves, as their letters show. Romantic isolation, the confessional mode, and female community were not unknown.

Yet female community was far from universal. Laetitia Pilkington, who rhapsodized about Katherine Philips ("... dear *Orinda!* gentle Shade! sweet Poet! Honour of thy Sex!"),[21] turned up her nose at Eliza Haywood: "Her *Female Spectators* are a Collection of trite Stories, delivered to us in stale and worn-out Phrases ..." (2:293). Anna Laetitia Barbauld rejected the idea of collaborating with other women on a literary paper in no uncertain terms: "There is no bond of union among literary women any more than among literary men; different sentiments and connections separate them much more than the joint interest of their sex would unite them."[22] Fanny Burney, in her unpublished play *The Witlings* (1779), and Susan Ferrier, in her novel *Marriage* (1818), skewered Bluestocking hostesses and their coteries mercilessly. And, although Lady Winchilsea mentioned Aphra Behn, she chastised her foremother for writing "too loosly."[23]

What this scrambled account adds up to is a picture of literary life in the seventeenth and eighteenth centuries that no single critical or historical label fits. There were isolated, confessional, misunderstood, suffering women writers, and there were successful amateurs and professionals, welcomed and supported as part of the community. There were fighters and rebels who were writers, and there were contented wives, mothers, and Sunday school teachers who were writers. There was a sense of sisterhood, of a women's literary tradition, and there was overt rejection of the idea. The only truly valid generalization that can be drawn is that no truly valid generalization is possible.

For this reason, hoping to avoid what I perceive as the mistaken approach of some feminist critics, I have chosen to examine the work of a few women writers individually, without setting out to demonstrate a thesis. My purpose is to help to restore the picture, so I look at these writers in their various relations to other writers, the better-known ones of the opposite sex. I have chosen these eight women not because they constitute a historically representative sample, though they do range across the 140 years of the Restoration and eighteenth century, nor because their talents typify what women could and did do in the period. To show that, I would need many more novelists. Instead, I have chosen them because I think they are good—not the only good ones, by any means, but some of the good ones. They deserve to be retrieved and instated in the canon.

That statement raises two central, related critical issues: the question of "the canon" and the question of the grounds of judgment, of why a literary work is "good." These issues are as ancient as literary criticism itself, when the Greek audience threw rotten eggs at the stage if they didn't like the play and Aristotle set down the rules for tragedy. The canon and the grounds of judgment have varied over the centuries; they have also varied over recent decades, but not, despite some fluctuating reputations, by a great deal. A standard university anthology of eighteenth-century English literature looked much the same in 1980 as it did in 1930, and lecturers spoke clearly in both years about the test of time, about what has pleased many and pleased long, about the profound and the sublime, consistency and probability, effective metrics, and all the other criteria that live together in the grab bag of literary judgments. That is, they spoke of these things if they addressed the question of judgment at all. It is far easier and more common to be silent on the matter and simply to accept the works in the canon as great. We all do it.

But the contents of the canon, the very idea of a canon, and the grounds of judgment are growing increasingly unsteady. A symptom of the turmoil is the September 1983 issue of *Critical Inquiry*, devoted entirely to the question. It does not begin or end the debates but signals their vigor and importance. The canon is no longer seen to consist of those works which are most aesthetically pleasing. Instead, as the editor states, "canons are recognized as the expression of social and political power."[24] The old canon will no longer do, and "whether new canons, expressing as yet unestablished interests, ought now to be formed is an open question" (p. iv). In "Contingencies of Value" (pp. 1-35 in the same issue), Barbara Hernstein Smith addresses the question of evaluative criticism, which, though out of fashion, is practiced in the classroom and in scholarly journals. So evidently we support the idea of a canon, even the exploded canon, after all. Aesthetic value is not an entity in itself, she argues, but is contingent upon subject, political and social contexts, and other factors surrounding the production and judgment of literature. Only in Lawrence Lipking's article on Aristotle's sister (pp. 61-81), which attempts to formulate a feminine poetics, does this issue of *Critical Inquiry* address directly the question of literature by women in relation to the canon. But many of the arguments in other articles are obviously applicable.

That question is tackled directly by Lillian S. Robinson in "Treason Our Text: Feminist Challenges to the Literary Canon."[25] She surveys the territory thoroughly: the efforts to raise recognized women writers from minor to major status in the canon, the attempts to add unrecognized women to the canon, the creation of a female countercanon. And what is the canon, she asks, "the compendium of excellence or . . . the record of cultural history?" (p. 90). The stickiest question of all is aesthetic, and "We need to understand whether the claim is being made that many of the newly recovered or validated texts by women meet existing criteria or, on the other hand, that those criteria themselves intrinsically exclude or tend to exclude women and hence should be modified or replaced" (p. 88). Robinson also speaks of "the *agony* of feminist criticism, for it is the champions of women's literature who are torn between defending the quality of their discoveries and radically redefining literary quality itself" (p. 89).

As Robinson implies, the questions are unanswerable, the problems insurmountable. One can only choose a course of action, a line of criticism, knowing full well that it is personal and partial, that one is sidestepping some issues and taking debatable stances. Yet was not criticism ever thus?

When I argue for the inclusion in the canon of the eight women represented in this book on the grounds that their writing is good,[26] I endorse the idea of a canon based on quality that can, one way or another, be assessed. Our old friend "the test of time" will not do for the women, however, because so much of their work has not been available for such a long time. A few scholarly editions and a flock of facsimile reprints are now on the library shelves, but the reader who wants a comprehensive sense of writing by women before Jane Austen must still haunt rare book rooms, travel to major libraries, and crouch over microfilm readers. Even so, much is difficult or impossible to come by. The reasons for this state of affairs are many. Its consequence is that the test of time is irrelevant. One cannot judge the durability of the invisible.

Like most critics, I have a headful of rather muddled criteria—subjective and objective, self-contained and contingent, aesthetic and historical and psychological and generic, tragical-comical-historical-pastoral. . . . These, consciously or unconsciously, no doubt lie behind the rather simple basic criteria I have adopted in the essays in this book, namely, that a literary work is good if it stands up to careful and close reading, if it yields further facets of itself during repeated readings, and if it responds to a variety of approaches and grows in interest and fascination as the reader grows in acquaintance with it. This is to some extent New Criticism, that bogeyman to most feminists, yet I do not insist on paradox and irony and ambiguity, nor do I exclude history and biography. It is to some extent reader-response criticism, specifically the response of a female reader to texts by men and women, but I do not reduce the text, which is an artifact, to a process in my own psyche. Perhaps what I do can best be described as appreciation.[27] Mrs. Pilkington would have understood: "I always find in myself a strong Inclination to Criticism, and . . . I shall certainly indulge it: For my Part, let the World say what they please of Criticks, I esteem them as very useful Members of the Commonwealth of Learning. Whatever is well written will stand the Test of strict Examination, ay, and of Ridicule too; and when that is past, the Work appears like Gold from the Furnace, with ten-fold Lustre" (*Memoirs*, 3:32). I hope the work of these eight women will be buffed up a bit by what I have to say.

One further point remains to be mentioned in this rather lengthy introduction. Any writer, whether poet or critic, having decided what to say, must imagine an audience—general or specific, friendly or hostile, informed or uninformed. That audience will have a great influence on what the writer says and how he or she says it. My own imaginary or assumed audience is a diverse one. It will, I hope, include feminists, some of whom will be friendly to the endeavor as a whole, some hostile to the critical and ideological stances I take; I welcome such variety. But it will also, I hope, include senior scholars concerned with the seventeenth and eighteenth centuries, who probably know little of the women writers I discuss but know a great deal otherwise about the period. And I have in view beginning students, who know little or nothing about either the period or the writers, and of course students and scholars between these extremes. I have tried to keep my discussions comprehensible to beginners; I can only hope the novelty and interest of the material will compensate more advanced scholars for the simplicity of the critical appreciations. I hope too that some, wrestling with the fairly large quantities of summary and quotation that I include because the texts are so unfamiliar, will decide to turn their talents to the production of sound, scholarly editions of these and other neglected books.[28] Much needs to be done. Working together, we can make some progress in the job of restoring the picture.

ONE

A PROBLEM OF PRAISE

John Dryden and Anne Killigrew

IT IS EASY to dismiss Anne Killigrew's poetry as insignificant, as unworthy of attention, as poor stuff. When she died at the age of twenty-five, her father collected her entire output of verse into a slim volume one hundred pages long, fifteen pages of which are said to have been written by someone else.[1] A cursory glance through the volume reveals a longish, unfinished poem on Alexander the Great which the author "laid by" after she found the task too hard for her (p. 5); there are pastoral dialogues with the usual Alexis and Thyrsis, there are tributes to the virtue of the Queen, meditations on death and on the evils of gold, moral epigrams attacking atheism and cosmetics, a couple of songs and a couple of verse letters, and a couple of poems on the general miseries of the human condition. The topics are conventional, the genres already well worn, and the metrics—very occasionally—a little wobbly. Schoolgirl stuff, the cursory reader might say. Yet this is what John Dryden praised so extravagantly in his poem on her death, which stands as an introduction to the volume.

Dryden's praise stands, both literally and figuratively, between the reader and Anne Killigrew's poems. No one reads her poems without knowing Dryden's ode, and though her earliest biographers said that Dryden did not exaggerate her worth,[2] no poet can truly deserve the degree of praise he heaped upon her. Given this preconditioning, then, to attempt to demonstrate that there is quality in her work may seem to be an exercise in futility.

Critics of Dryden's ode have not made that attempt, although, with the exception of Ruth Wallerstein, who treats the ode strictly as an exercise in formal design, commentators on Dryden do seem to feel called upon to explain, or explain away, the extravagance of the praise, which they do in a variety of conflicting ways. On one point, however, they agree—that Anne Killigrew's poetry is insignificant. Sometimes that judgment is stated overtly, as when Judson Jerome dismisses her as "a mediocre poetess . . . not important in herself," indeed as the object of "gentle mockery," useful to Dryden only as an example or emblem of the death of innocence in a corrupt age. Arthur Hoffman takes the idea of innocence somewhat further, seeing Anne as a symbol, the very incarnation of poetry, a use for which she was appropriate because of her personal virtue and because of the high moral tone (not the quality) of her poems. David Vieth accepts this idea but finds in addition a consistent pattern of irony, qualifying and undercutting the praise, which produces an interesting tension in the ode. Reconsidering the problem, he concludes that the ode, like much of Swift's writing, exemplifies the Restoration structure of "extremes-without-a-mean" and that "Anne is portrayed in double focus as an ideal poet and painter but also, incongruously, as an ignorant, overzealous amateur." Robert Daly has questioned Vieth's first reading and proposed yet another—one which I find well argued: that Dryden believed all poets to be important, and hence worthy of praise, because of their function as teachers of moral truth.[3] Again, the virtuous content of the poetry qualifies the author for the near-divine rank that Dryden confers upon her.

It would seem that critics of Dryden's ode have not given Anne Killigrew's poems more than a cursory reading, if any reading at all. Had they done so, they would not—true enough—have discovered a neglected genius, a second Dryden or Pope just waiting to be brought out into the light of day. But they would have discovered a competent maker of poems with a remarkable and individual flair for handling images and allusions. They would have discovered how conventional sentiments about upright virtue can convey a unique sensibility. And, if the last three poems in the book are indeed by Anne Killigrew, they would have discovered how vividly a passionate young woman could express the depth of her love and the dark night of her soul.

My general sense of Anne Killigrew's poetry is that she deserves attention, but I differ somewhat from the very few modern critics who have indeed paid her some: Richard Morton, editor of the facsimile edition; Myra Reynolds, editor of the poems of Lady Winchilsea; and Elizabeth Hampsten. Morton notes "some forceful and startling images" in Anne Killigrew's poetry but decides that "The individuality of her works lies in their firm, evangelical, moral tone" (p. viii). Myra Reynolds finds "a vigor and a bitterness not to be looked for in a maid of honor. There is no hint of interest in nature, no tenderness, no lightness, almost no beauty or grace. The poems are marked instead by a crude virility." Both of these judgments are correct but incomplete. Morton's comment embraces only some of the poems and only at one level; Reynolds is saying essentially that Anne Killigrew's poems are unlike Lady Winchilsea's, indeed unlike what Reynolds in 1903 expected a woman's poetry to be. A more recent critic, Elizabeth Hampsten, essentially agrees with Reynolds when she says that the poems are "about violence and corruption" and that bitterness is their primary tone.[4] True again, but again incomplete—Anne Killigrew's range is wider. It is also noteworthy that these three critics who have read her poems, like Dryden himself and his critics, concentrate on what the poems say, paying almost no attention to the poet's artistry. Are we to infer, then, that they *all* find the poems to be poorly crafted stuff?

Three voices from the past give a complimentary view of the

poet's skill. The epigraph from Martial on the title page provides, albeit indirectly, a faint suggestion of a favorable judgment. When Anne's father or publisher chose the epigraph, he chose well: "To unwonted worth comes life but short, and rarely old age." Its meaning suits her virtue and her early death; furthermore, the boy being commemorated in the Latin shared other characteristics with her as well: "Pure was he in manners, of modesty unstained, *nimble of wit,* with charm richly blessed" (my emphasis).[5] More directly, "The Publisher to the Reader" tells us that Anne was not only a virgin and a beauty but also "a *Muse* for Wit!," and the English version of her Latin epitaph (both were published in her book), commends her "Beauty, Wit, Vertue Divine." However conventional, even ritualistic, these statements are, it is interesting that, directly and indirectly, she is repeatedly given credit for "wit," that multifaceted and extremely important Augustan quality.

In an attempt to demonstrate the existence of her wit, or that part of it which is artistic skill, I will discuss various elements in a number of poems, beginning with some of her notable images and allusions. To some extent, it is doing her an injustice to take lines out of context, because, like all good poets, she made her images and allusions integral parts of the poems in which they appear: allusion becomes image becomes poem. They are not separable decorations. But to begin to show her skill and also her individuality, I will separate and examine a few.

She praises the great virtue of Charles II's long-suffering wife in "To the Queen" (pp. 6-10), remarking not only on the Queen's superiority to the vicious world around her but also on the superiority of peaceful piety to the warrior qualities of the poet's first subject, Alexander the Great. Such heroes owe their glories to "ill Deeds," and they "build their *Babels* of Renown, / Upon the poor oppressed Crown. . . ." The idea that fame is simply words, voices, air, is commonplace; Anne Killigrew uses it again herself in "The Discontent" (p. 54), perhaps echoing Katherine Philips's "Greatness . . . whose food is air." "Fame is but the breath of the people" was proverbial in the seventeenth century.[6] Anne gives new substance to the usual breath, however, with the idea of the tower of Babel: an incomprehensible mishmash of languages would devalue fame even more seriously than the breath of a single people.

Another biblical image appears a dozen lines later in the poem (p. 8), a relatively unfamiliar one which demonstrates not only the poet's detailed knowledge of the Bible but also her diffidence in addressing her Queen:

> O that now like Araunah here,
> Altars of Praises I could rear,
> Suiting her worth, which might be seen
> Like a Queens Present, to a Queen!

In 2 Samuel 24, the Lord is chastising Israel with a pestilence, when King David has a vision of an angel "by the threshing-place of Araunah the Jebusite" (verse 16). Gad advised David to build an altar to the Lord at the threshing floor as penance for his sin and to avert the rest of the pestilence. When he explains his plan to Araunah, Araunah replies that he will give David the floor and the oxen and the wood for the sacrifice. "All these *things* did Araunah, *as* a king, give unto the king" (verse 23).[7] But David insists on paying fifty shekels, because an offering which cost him nothing would not be efficacious. In the poem, Anne Killigrew offers her praises to the Queen, the eighteen lines in quotation marks following the Araunah passage, "Like a Queens present, to a Queen." But neither Araunah nor Anne is a monarch. His offer is rejected, and hers, as the parallel modestly implies, will be too.

The passage of praise in quotation marks describes the Queen as a champion of persecuted Virtue, upholding her laws and tending her altar,

> "While impiously her hands they tie.
> [The Queen] Loves her in her Captivity;
> Like Perseus saves her, when she stands
> Expos'd to the *Leviathans.*"

Here the Queen, in one of the several transferences of sex in these poems, becomes the hero Perseus rescuing the innocent sacrifice, Andromeda/Virtue, from the sea monster sent by Poseidon to punish her father's profanity. There is more than a classical allusion in "the *Leviathans*," however. There is also Hobbes, whose ideas about human nature could be seen as a threat to the very existence of pure Virtue. But the Queen, with her active Christian piety, brings about the rescue.

It is difficult to see why, given the inventiveness and the ancient and modern learning displayed in these three images in "To the Queen," Dryden said,

> Art she had none, yet wanted none;
> For nature did that want supply:
> So rich in treasures of her own,
> She might our boasted stores defy. . . .[8]

Does knowledge of the Bible, of classical mythology, and of contemporary philosophical debate come from "nature"? This sounds dangerously like Dogberry's comment on the literacy of the Watch.

Yet another biblical image, again given a fresh turn, closes the poem:

> O that I once so happy were,
> To find a nearer Shelter there!
> Till then poor Dove, I wandering fly
> Between the Deluge and the Skie:
> Till then I mourn, but do not sing,
> And oft shall plunge my wearied wing:
> If her bless'd hand vouchsafe the Grace,
> I'th'Ark with her to give a place,
> I safe from danger shall be found,
> When Vice and Folly others drown'd.

Overwhelmed by the evil of the world around her, the poet seeks the champion and incarnation of Virtue, the Queen, and her protection. In the Bible, of course, the deluge cleanses the earth of sin, and the dove finally finds a resting place for the sole of her foot somewhere distant from the Ark (Genesis 8). Anne Killigrew, however, turns the cleansing floodwaters into "Vice and Folly," dangerous elements which drown the people around her. She seeks only safety in the Ark, one of the many images of enclosed space in her poems, the Ark which apparently will never find a viable Ararat. It is a gloomy vision, a strong and fitting climax to the argument of the poem.

Among other notable images is the conclusion to "On Death" (pp. 13-14), a poem which is a good example of the familiar argument that death is desirable as bringing rest to the afflicted, calm to the ambitious, repose to the despairing lover, and so forth. Yet people are unreasonably unwilling to die:

> Thus Childish fear did *Israel* of old
> From Plenty and the Promis'd Land with-hold;
> They fancy'd Giants, and refus'd to go,
> When *Canaan* did with Milk and Honey flow.

The repeated expletive "did," a usage Pope was later to condemn as "feeble," serves a useful artistic purpose here. Elsewhere in Anne Killigrew's poems it is sometimes simply crude and unsophisticated, as in "On the Birth-Day of Queen Katherine" (p. 47), but here the very lack of sophistication adds to the feeling that the Israelites are childish. Such a feeling is not present in the source (Numbers 13, 14) except in the familiar tag, "the children of Israel." Anne Killigrew has taken that tag literally and turned them into captious, stubborn brats, digging in their heels and refusing to enter the Promised Land.

A simile drawn from the *Odyssey* does good service in "A Farewel to Worldly Joys" (p. 18) in which the poet ties her will and fancy to the mast of reason, the usual threesome of seventeenth-century psychology, as Ulysses had his crew tie him to the mast; thus she passes safely by the sirens of worldly joys. A number of good images brighten "The Miseries of Man" (pp.

32-43); that poem ends with a notable one, the Platonic commonplace of the chariot of Reason pulled by unruly horses, but rather than just emotions and appetites as in the *Phaedrus,* this charioteer must control "Fierce Anger, boggling Fear, Pride prauncing still, / Bounds-hating Hope, Desire which nought can fill . . . hard-Mouth'd Horses"—and vividly particularized images.

A poet may be capable of producing good images and still not be able to sustain an argument, integrate sound and sense, capture the imagination and intellect of the reader—in short, write a good poem. But Anne Killigrew could. Using the most conventional of genres and models, the epigram, the pastoral dialogue, and Juvenal's tenth satire, she created, if not her three best poems, three among her best.

Her fourth epigram, "On Galla" (p. 17), demonstrates her skill with the form and also shows how devastating a quiet wit can be. The poem opens with a description of cold weather freezing the river and turning the lily-white and rosy-red of Corinna's complexion to pallor and purple. Everyone suffers, except Galla.

> *Galla* alone, with wonder we behold,
> Maintain her Spring, and still out-brave the Cold;
> Her constant white does not to Frost give place,
> Nor fresh Vermillion fade upon her face:
> Sure Divine beauty in this Dame does shine?
> Not Humane, one reply'd, yet not Divine.

Her make-up is unaffected by the weather. The point is subtle; like Jack Ketch, the poet has made the painted malefactor die sweetly. The idea may have come directly from Martial, whose Galla is similarly painted: "your face does not sleep with you," the poet charges.[9] The object of the satire is, of course, commonplace. The strategy is not unique: occasionally, Martial too plants the sting in the tail of an epigram, though not in the one on Galla's make-up. My point is not that Anne Killigrew's poem is unusual but that it accomplishes its purpose with skill.

"A Pastoral Dialogue" (pp. 11-13) is, like the epigram, conventional in form, with a shepherd and shepherdess exchanging four-line stanzas on the subject of love. The couplet rhymes are exact; the meter deviates from the regular iambic pentameter only for the occasional initial trochee. But the poem is not as innocuous as this description may make it sound, because it draws inferences from the discussion of love that are far from superficial. Also, in this poem the shepherdess, Dorinda, woos the shepherd, which is not quite the usual story. She begins by offering him "Sabaean Perfumes" from "fragrant Roses"; both her stance as the wooer and her reference to Sheba, a biblical land ruled by queens, make her a strong figure in the first stanza. Alexis replies politely:

> Immortal Laurels and as lasting Praise,
> Crown the Divine *Dorinda*'s matchless Laies:
> May all Hearts stoop, where mine would gladly yield,
> Had not *Lycoris* prepossest the Field.

The name "Dorinda" is an allusion to Katherine Philips, always called "the matchless Orinda"; it places the poem firmly in the tradition of women's literature and in the tradition of poetry about poetry.[10]

Dorinda goes on to take a bold step in the third stanza when she promises Alexis immortality in her poetry if he will respond to her love. Such a promise, though common in poetry written by men, is rare in that written by women. Perhaps because she had taken on, though a shade indirectly, the persona of Orinda for this poem, Anne Killigrew felt that she could make such an offer, such a claim to possess poetic skill and power.

Alexis replies politely again, complimenting her poetry but saying that the only immortality he needs is the inscription, "here doth lie / Lycoris's Love." Lycoris, whose name sounds dangerously close to "likerous," has had other loves, Dorinda replies pointedly. Alexis explains that that does not matter, because he "liv'd not then, but first began to be" when he and

Lycoris loved—a neat combination of sophistry and high romantic idealism. Responding to the idealism of his claim, Dorinda replies,

> Ah choose a Faith, a Faith that's like thine own,
> A Virgin Love, a Love that's newly blown:
> 'Tis not enough a Maidens Heart is chast,
> It must be Single, and not once mis-plact.

The implications here are curious. Because Alexis claims to have been born—and born for the first time—when he loved Lycoris, Dorinda says that he has a religious faith in love like her own. And yet the standards for behavior in love differ for shepherds and shepherdesses: the true maiden may never change her love, but Dorinda is asking Alexis to change his, which apparently would be acceptable. This may be merely self-interest, since she wants him and can't have him unless he does change, or it may be a realistic recognition of a double standard.[11] Alexis's scornful answer, the final stanza of the poem, moves the pastoral love debate to another plane of meaning:

> Thus do our Priests of Heavenly Pastures tell,
> Eternal Groves, all Earthly, that excel:
> And think to wean us from our Loves below,
> By dazling Objects which we cannot know.

Despite his romantic idealism, by now transparently sophistical, Alexis reveals himself here as a skeptic. Dorinda's "Virgin Love" is as much a myth as the heaven preached by the priests, he claims; it is a bribe which has no substance, a bribe that would "wean us from our Loves below." It is something, like heaven, "which we cannot know," he concludes. Yet real faith does "know" that heaven exists and pure love is possible. Dorinda does not need to reply to Alexis. Anne Killigrew has made Alexis condemn himself as a casuist in love and a skeptic in religion. The "religion of love" is conventional, of course, but she has used the convention to show the connection between libertine behavior and philosophical skepticism, both important issues in the Restoration. And the fact that Alexis has the last word, however wrongheaded it may be, gives a sense of the disturbing force and pervasiveness of that skepticism.

It was probably poems like this that Dryden had in mind when he described the purity of Mistress Killigrew's verse:

> Ev'n love (for love sometimes her Muse express'd)
> Was but a *lambent flame* which play'd about her breast,
> Light as the vapors of a morning dream:
> So cold herself, whilst she such warmth express'd,
> 'Twas Cupid bathing in Diana's stream.
>
> [ll. 83-87]

Vieth finds this passage ironic and Jerome finds it funny (p. 487); they agree that Dryden is saying that Anne doesn't know what she is talking about. Dryden's lines are an allusion to her poem "On a Picture Painted by her self, representing two Nimphs of Diana's, one in a posture to Hunt, the other Bathe-ing" (pp. 28-29).[12] But do his lines imply that she was igno-rant about love? True, the images stress her innocence, and throughout the ode Dryden was primarily intent upon demon-strating that the poet and her poems were virtuous. But in these lines Dryden does give her credit for being able to express "warmth"; and indeed there can be no doubt about Dorinda's feelings for Alexis, however decorously they are expressed, or about his feelings for Lycoris. Furthermore, the distinction that Dryden makes between the coldness of the poet and the warmth of the poems is not necessarily adverse criticism, though modern critics tend to read it that way. "Cold" sounds unattractive to the modern ear, and to the modern reader a gap between poet and poem looks like insincerity or perhaps, in this case, ignorance. But "cold" can mean simply "chaste," which is one of Johnson's definitions for it. Furthermore, the gap Dryden recognizes indicates not insincerity or ignorance but the Augustan ability to assume a persona or a rhetorical stance. In these lines, which are neither funny nor ironic, Dryden is praising both her virtue and her skill as a poet.

What neither Dryden nor the modern critics mention is the other plane of meaning in Anne Killigrew's love poems. In "A Pastoral Dialogue," as I have shown, she raises the issue of religious skepticism in the sophistical Alexis. A second "Pastoral Dialogue," that between Amintor and Alinda (pp. 57-62), also picks up a well-worn convention and gives it new depths. From Ralegh on, pastoral poets had been doubting if there was truth in every shepherd's tongue. Anne Killigrew's Alinda knows there is not, and cites a number of sad and even dead shepherdesses as her evidence and as reasons for her prayer, "My flocks from Wolves, my Heart from Love, defend." The two parts of her prayer are spoken with "equal Zeal," and the neat parallelism, especially in the words of a female character in a poem written by a woman, creates a remarkable depth of feeling. Not all of the poet's pastorals possess such a level of meaning and feeling, however. "The Complaint of a Lover" (pp. 19-22), in which an apparently male persona bemoans the disdain of his Rosalinda, has good landscape imagery but only competent commonplaces of sentiment to offer, perhaps because of the assumption of the male lover's point of view. (If the point of view is female, however, new questions arise, which I will consider later.) A third and longer "Pastoral Dialogue" among Melibaeus, Alcippe, Asteria, Licida, Alcimedon, and Amira (pp. 63-75) is heavily moralistic, dealing again with the dangers of love for the young virgin. Cupid bathes in Diana's stream in all of these poems, with an unvarying degree of purity, while the degree of significance varies. But the significance does exist, especially in the Dorinda and Alinda pastorals, where it is expressed with skill.

"The Discontent" (pp. 51-56; and see the appendix in this book) also belongs to a familiar genre, the double tradition of Juvenal's tenth satire and Ecclesiastes's cry against vanity, to which is added the conventional image of the painful and hazardous journey that is life. Anne Killigrew's poem begins with a good example of her power to control prosody in the service of meaning:

> Here take no Care, take here no Care, my *Muse*,
>   Nor ought of Art or Labour use:
>   But let thy lines rude and unpolisht go,
> Nor Equal be their Feet, nor Num'rous let them flow.
>   The ruggeder my Measures run when read,
> They'll livelier paint th'unequal Paths fond Mortals tread.

The line about ruggedness has rugged alliteration on the *r*'s; the line about rudeness has irregular meter. The line about equal and numerous feet has numerous feet in a punning sense (it is an Alexandrine) and regular iambics; here the effect is inverted, as the poet demonstrates that she can produce regular verse while disclaiming its validity in this context. In the last line quoted here the word "unequal" makes the line an Alexandrine, "unequal" to the preceding pentameter line with which it rhymes. Clearly, the poet was working on the same principles that Dryden was in his poem on Oldham's death when he made the sound echo the sense in "Thro' the harsh cadence of a rugged line" (p. 175, l. 16). Later in the first stanza, Anne Killigrew uses another Alexandrine for its long-drawn-out effect: "And headlong down the horrid Precipice they fall." The rest of the poem uses the varying rhymes and line lengths typical of the Pindaric form to good advantage for emphasis and to support the sense in other ways. There is less virtuosity to the performance than in the first six lines, but in those lines such virtuosity is most appropriate because prosody is itself the subject of the lines, as in Dryden's verses on Oldham and, later, Pope's on sound and sense. It all works very well indeed.

Prosody involves the term "feet" which "go" (in the sense of "walk"), "flow," and "run." Poetic feet are punningly linked with human feet in the first stanza. The fifth line, "The ruggeder

my Measures run when read," part of this pun, may be an allusion to the Old Testament prophet Habakkuk, who was commanded by the Lord to "Write the vision, and make *it* plain
upon tables, that he may run that readeth it" (2:2). The vision,
indeed the whole book of Habakkuk, is murky, to say the least,
but one can deduce that the prophet is distressed by political
and military oppression and by the general evil around him, and
that the Lord has commanded him to express himself on the
subject of the "iniquity . . . spoiling and violence" (1:3) that he
sees. "The Discontent" is a similar expression of distress.

The punning link between metrical and human feet connects
the opening lines on prosody with the image of life's journey
that dominates the rest of the first stanza and recurs in the last
to unite the poem. The image recurs frequently in Augustan
poetry. Some imitators of Juvenal's tenth satire suggest it; Roch-
ester began his "Satyr Against Mankind" (1679) with it; Paul
Fussell documents its ubiquity and its significance.[13] In Anne
Killigrew's version, hope makes the journey look easy, but soon
doubt and dismay perplex the travelers, who call upon reason
in vain as they fall down the "horrid Precipice" into the ocean
of despair: "My Muse pronounce aloud, there's nothing Good,
/ Nought that the World can show, / Nought that it can bestow."
Ecclesiastes was similarly gloomy. The poem goes on to argue
the evil and general unsatisfactoriness of gold, power, and fame,
three topics that Juvenal, Ecclesiastes, and their host of imitators all pay considerable attention to. Stanza 4 on Fame has
particularly painful overtones when one looks back at "Upon
the saying that my Verses were made by another" (pp. 44-47);
there the poet describes how she expected fame after she had
dedicated herself to the "Sacred Muse," but was denied it when
her poems were ascribed to an unnamed other. Despite the va-
garies of Fame—of the poet's reputation—however, poetry itself has value. To illustrate that value, in the fourth stanza of
"The Discontent" she turns to the tradition that music, song,
and poetry are interchangeable terms and claims that only the

strains of David's lyre could drive away Saul's evil spirit. The trumpet of fame failed to do so, but the lyre of poetry succeeded.

Unlike Juvenal and Ecclesiastes, Anne Killigrew concludes her list of the vanities with friendship, which pretends to be "of this Sad Journey, Life, the Baite," but which fails when friends grow cold or prove false or, as she claims is always the case, feel unequal flames. This emphasis on the failure of friendship may refer to the cult of female friendship enshrined in Katherine Philips's poetry, much of which is devoted to passionate and blissful friendships between the poet and other women and to the pain of breaking off such friendships. Rather than making a literary allusion, or perhaps in addition to doing so, Anne Killigrew could be revealing in general terms a disappointment in her own brief life. It is impossible to know, but the emphatic position of the subject in this poem and the profound sadness of tone suggest autobiography.

The poem concludes with the expression of a wish to retire to a land unsullied by humanity, its very air never breathed by "humane Breast," its soil never pressed by "Humane Foot." The miseries of the populated world are summarized: public and private jars, "Idle Stories" of fame, "Noysy-Glories," and subtle deceptions. The poet concludes:

> No Mundan Care shall more affect my Breast,
>   My profound Peace shake or molest:
> But *Stupor,* like to Death, my Senses bind,
>   That so I may anticipate that Rest,
> Which only in my Grave I hope to find.

Unlike Juvenal, who still found it worthwhile to pray for a sound mind in a sound body and for a stout heart, and unlike Ecclesiastes, who rested in the certainty of God's ultimate judgment of "every secret thing," Anne Killigrew seeks only the relief of oblivion, not death but a living stupor. Other writers have praised the comforts of nonbeing: Ecclesiastes suggests that the dead are better off than the living and that it is even better never to have lived (4:2-3); Prior, in Book 3 of *Solomon on the Vanity of the World*, makes his royal spokesman exclaim, "He alone is bless'd, who ne'er was born."[14] But the heartbroken cry—not even a prayer—for death-in-life is rare, perhaps unique, in the tradition; it makes a powerful conclusion to the poem. One hopes that the poem is *not* autobiographical.

Autobiography, however, though veiled in pastoral names and allegorical journeys, seems to me to be the only key to the last three poems in Anne Killigrew's book. These three are preceded by a note, presumably inserted by the publisher or by her father: "These Three following ODES being found among Mrs. Killigrews Papers, I was willing to Print though none of hers" (p. 84). Yet the style of the three, the level of prosodic skill, the tone, and a number of close verbal echoes all suggest that these poems came from the same hand as the rest of the volume. And George Ballard, in his *Memoirs*, lists the titles of all the poems in the book without distinguishing the final three in any way.[15] If these poems are indeed autobiographical, one can easily see why a discreet father or a cautious publisher would choose to disavow them, since they appear to be concerned with a tragic love for a woman and the poet's rescue from despair by another woman, who in turn practiced flagellation on yet another woman. Even if these poems were not Anne's, they were "found among [her] Papers," a circumstance significant in itself. The note implies that the poems had not circulated in manuscript, possibly because they were too personal. Why they were published at all is a mystery; perhaps her father had only the dimmest notion of what they were about, or perhaps he was unwilling to suppress a central and almost decently veiled experience in his daughter's personal and artistic life.

Any reading of Augustan poetry as autobiographical must be hedged about with cautions and disclaimers. One must consider the possibilities of persona and of rhetorical stance or even rhetorical exercise; one must consider the power of genre to control meaning; one must consider the influences of sources and analogues and conventions; one must consider the accepted idea that a poet is a teacher, a legislator, a public rather than a private voice. Certain more psychological, more twentieth-century cautions may also arise to further complicate any autobiographical reading. Do the poems deal with real people and real events or with projections, fantasies, parts of the self, desires acknowledged or unacknowledged by the conscious mind? In Anne Killigrew's case, one can say with certainty that she was sometimes autobiographical with no Augustan regard for persona or genre or any other such consideration, as witness "Upon the saying that my Verses were made by another," among other poems. Addressing more modern cautions, one can also say with certainty that she sometimes wrote about real people: the Queen, Lady Berkeley, Lord Colrane, and others were not fantasies or projections. And when she took a step or two beyond such literalisms, she still referred to real people: the Queen became Perseus and she herself became Dorinda/Katherine Philips, as I have demonstrated. Whatever fantasies she may be expressing are all attached to real experience. Taking all the cautions and disclaimers, then, as having been duly weighed, I suggest the following autobiographical readings of the last three poems.

"Cloris Charmes Dissolved by Eudora" (pp. 85-91; see appendix) records the poet's descent into the hell of despair, despair for which Cloris is responsible and from which Eudora rescues her. The poem is a "clue," a sort of guide or map, sent to Cloris so that she too may follow the same path. The poet begins by rejecting the possibility that Cloris could call her back from her despair; that is not the purpose of addressing her. Instead, she is to receive this "clue" in case she too must some day "Retire / To quench with Tears, thy Wandring Fire. . . ." (It is revealing that love, traditionally a "fire" or "flame," is here specifically a "Wandring" one, that is, straying from the usual heterosexual path.) The journey begins on a "Rocky Northern Shore," strewn with the bones and skulls of "the Robb'd, the Wrack'd, or Lost," the only people who cross that "Cursed Beach." The poet herself then has to be one of the robbed, wrecked, or lost. How she arrives at the beach we are not told. Neither are we told how Dante has come to be in the dark wood in which he awakes at the beginning of the *Inferno*. It is simply the starting point. The beach, horrendous enough with its bones, is rendered even more menacing by being described as "Northern," the north being traditionally associated with witches and evil in general as well as with the tangible miseries of cold. The journey takes the poet inland, past blasted trees and into a silent, dark "Grove of Fatal Ewe." A poisoned stream opens out into a "Floud," which is visited twice a day by a "Slave" who dips up water and carries it away. A murderer haunts a "Narrow Glade" in stanza 5, witches and fiends dance in stanza 6, and "the Shadow of a Man" cries ceaselessly in stanza 7 for a lost love. This is not a densely populated hell like Dante's. Instead, it is the hell of loneliness, with only a few solitary figures (apart from the witches and fiends) performing ritually repeated actions.

The moaning lover is the last figure we see before the poet reaches the center of her hell, a "Horrid Cliffe" with a creek below and a cave inside. The landscape here is similar to that at the beginning of "The Miseries of Man" (p. 32) and almost identical to that in "The Complaint of a Lover," where the "craggy Rock" hangs over "the swelling Main" and the hapless lover hides in a cave beneath the rock (p. 19)—similarities that strengthen the sense that the three poems are by the same hand. In the "Complaint," as I said earlier, the speaking voice is ostensibly male, or at least is that of a person who loves "Rosalinda"; if that voice is taken as female—and the poem does use the first-person pronoun—the ties to "Cloris Charmes" (and the probability of its authorship) grow even stronger. The speaking voice of "Cloris Charmes" is not actually identified as female, nor is it identified as male. The poet does use, again, the first-person pronoun, and does not use the language of conventional male love poetry. I see no reason to assume that a male persona is implied.

The cave, "Dreadful as Hell, still as the Grave," is inhabited by sea monsters and visited by the "Tide." When it is silent, "God-sleep might there reside," an image of utter nullity. But when "the Boysterous Seas ... resumes this Cell," it is filled with tempests, thunders, and echoes. "This is the place I chose," the poet says, "Changeable like my Woes...." The anatomical implications are inescapable: the womb/cave beneath the hill and next to the waters is governed by the monthly cycle of the tides. The emotional cycles parallel the physical: "Now calmly Sad, / Then Raging Mad...." The poet has chosen this place, has associated the core of her despair with the core of her sexuality. The description of the cave takes up three and a half stanzas, more lines than are devoted to any other feature of the allegorical landscape. There are bats and owls enjoying the "Eternal Night" of the cave. The only light afforded her, she says, has emanated from such appropriately gloomy sources as serpents' scales, fishbones, adders' eyes, and toadstones, though the context leaves it not altogether clear whether these are also in the cave.

The poet is conscious of her own emotional sickness. Withdrawn totally from the world, she has "lost the Sense, / Of all the hea[l]thful World calls Bliss." She finds beauty an "Offence" and absence of joy a joy, echoing her own "A Farewel to Worldly Joys" (p. 18). When she reaches this emotional nadir, suddenly "Celestial Strains did read [rend?] the Aire," and a divine and shining form appears, "As when Heav'ns Queen / In Hell was seen, / With wonder and affright!" Eudora, whose name means "good gift," has appeared, causing the whole landscape to alter. The sea monsters "fled for fear" from the cave, and the benign influence even "Dismantl'd" the "Terrors of the Cursed Wood" that lay far back near the beginning of the journey. Eudora, associated with the Virgin Mary in her miraculous and compassionate visit to Hell,[16] then sings to the poet:

> Dissolv'd is Cloris spell,
> From whence thy Evils fell,
> Send her this Clue,

'Tis there most due
And thy Phantastick Hell.

If one takes the line "'Tis there most due" as parenthetical, Eudora is commanding that not only the map of hell, the "clue," be sent to Cloris, but also the hell itself—that is, that when Cloris receives the poem she too will be plunged into the landscape of despair. And she deserves it. But perhaps Eudora is not quite so vindictive. Perhaps she is counseling the poet to send Cloris a copy of the poem simply for her information, as it were. But sending someone hell, however "Phantastick," sounds like a fairly serious proposition.

The simplest reading of the events in the poet's emotional life which this poem describes (if that is what it is doing) is that a friendship or love for one woman proved to be unhappy, even emotionally destructive, apparently the kind of unequal flame recorded in "The Discontent," and that another woman—not necessarily a lover but a woman possessing great power and authority (the Queen? Mary of Modena?)—brought the poet back to emotional health. This woman, Eudora, is also the central figure in the last two poems in the volume.

In "Upon a Little Lady Under the Discipline of an Excellent Person" (pp. 92-98), Eudora's role is less clear, however, than it is in "Cloris Charmes." "Upon a Little Lady" begins with the poet's puzzlement about the gloom which has suddenly darkened the morning sun. The little cupids are discontented, even "blubring in Despaire," and when the poet asks them why, one shoots an arrow at the source of the trouble. The arrow shoots itself back again and wounds the cupid, but the poet locates the source of the gloom: "A little Nymph whose Limbs divinely bright, / Lay like a Body of Collected Light," being whipped by a "Dame." The poet sees the Dame as a kind of Fury, and is about to heap curses on her when she discovers that the Dame is Eudora. She is profoundly shocked. She is speculating on the reasons for such mistreatment when suddenly the sun comes out, the birds begin to sing again, and she finds that the little

Nymph is smiling and singing with Eudora. "I then decreed no Sacriledge was wrought, / But neerer Heav'n this Piece of Heaven was brought," the poet decides; Eudora too seems as wonderful as she had done "When her soft Graces I did first adore":

> I saw, what one did *Nobly Will,*
> The other *sweetly did fulfil;*
> Their Actions all harmoniously did sute,
> And she had only tun'd the Lady like her Lute.

Whipping for sexual pleasure was practiced in the seventeenth century, as no doubt in every century; the word "discipline," which occurs in the title and in the poem, was used in the Restoration for sexual whipping.[17] To the uninitiated, like the poet, the sight is painful, but both the Nymph and the Dame come up smiling, and the poet is more than reconciled to what she has seen. Even the sun and the birds concur that all is well. And yet it is not entirely clear in the poem that sexual pleasure is the reason for the flagellation. The concluding lines imply that it is: the actions of the two women are "harmonious," and while one has willed the actions, the other "sweetly did fulfil," though it is a question which woman did which. Apparently the Nymph has not *submitted* to the whipping but has either willed it or "sweetly" fulfilled the Dame's desire for it. Other lines imply that moral correction is what is going on: the Dame "Now chastens Error, and now Virtue shews" as she administers "Words and Blows"; after the beating, the Nymph seems brighter: "Vertue darts forth a Light'ning 'bove the Skin." Still other lines could be read either way: the Nymph has been brought "neerer Heav'n" by the whipping, and she has been "tun'd like [Eudora's] Lute"; the heaven and the tuning could be either sexual or moral. It would take a very convoluted argument indeed to demonstrate that they could be both. Either the poem is about sexual flagellation, partially disguised as moral chastisement, or it is about moral chastisement which includes a probably unacknowledged sexual pleasure. I find it impossible to say which, though I lean toward the first reading when three further points are considered: "tune" was and still is a colloquialism meaning simply "beat"; Hamilton's Grammont gossips about a lesbian Miss Hobart in the court of Mary of Modena; and there existed in the mid-eighteenth century an explicit print depicting lesbian flagellation.[18]

"Upon a Little Lady" includes a variety of references to music, from the initial description of the darkened sun as Apollo and the invocation in stanza 4 of Apollo's lyre to the note that Eudora's lute lies on the pavement during the beating ("When Beautie's wrong'd, no wonder Musick dies!") to the suggestion that Eudora may be beating the Nymph with her "Harmonious Hand" because the Nymph has proved herself to have "a Diviner Wit" and Eudora is jealous. In light of the equation of music with poetry, reinforced here by the mention of wit, these references would suggest that all three women—Eudora, the Nymph, and the speaker—are poets, especially when the cupids, the Nymph, and Eudora all join in singing "chaste Aires" while one of the cupids plays his lyre. The autobiographical suggestion, of a community of women poets engaged in some kind of intense relationship with each other, is intriguing.

Music dominates the last poem in the book, "On the Soft and Gentle Motions of Eudora," a poem that is entirely successful and free of unanswerable questions. The poet addresses Thalia, presumably in her character as Muse of pastoral poetry. Thalia carries a lute, which is not one of her usual attributes but strengthens the parallel between poetry and music yet again. The poet asks Thalia to strike her lute but to do so as gently "as may sute / The silent gliding of the Howers, / Or yet the calmer growth of Flowers; / Th'ascending or the falling Dew. . . ." Only thus can the "Silken" actions of Eudora be figured forth. She is so sweet and modest

That 'tis not the Lowd though Tuneable String,
Can shew forth so soft, so Noyseless a Thing!

> O this to express from thy Hand must fall,
> Then Musicks self, something more Musical.

The poet finds her own verse "Lowd though Tuneable" and
hence inadequate to express the glories of Eudora, but she does
a brilliant job of suggesting with elegant synesthetic images the
ineffable perfections of Eudora. There is a quivering stillness in
the poem, almost a sense of suspended animation, of a vital
sweetness too precious and too subtle to be described except by
negatives and by paradoxically silent music. The contrast with
the catatonic death-in-life that the poet cries for at the end of
"The Discontent" is telling indeed. Here—if the poem is autobiographical—she has found life-in-life, she has found love.

NONE OF THIS ANALYSIS, though I hope it has demonstrated
that Anne Killigrew's poems have artistic value, has really
solved the problems raised by Dryden's ode. Indeed, it may have
created new problems. If the poems have even some of the quality that I have claimed, how can one explain Dryden's judgment,
"Art she had none . . ."? The phrase indicates a shortcoming in
her poetry, though Dryden softens the sting by going on to say,
"yet wanted none; / For nature did that want supply." So perhaps he did recognize the quality of her verse; the ode, after all,
lavishes praise upon her—but at the same time denies that she
has art. Could the great Dryden be so blindly inconsistent?
Could his focus be so radically "double"? What did he really
think of Mistress Killigrew anyway?

It is not possible to know why Dryden wrote the ode on
Anne Killigrew's death; no facts have survived about his acquaintance with her or his involvement with the publication of
her poems.[19] One can speculate, however, on the basis of what
has survived. Dryden knew her family. He was associated with
her uncle, Thomas Killigrew, and the Theatre Royal as early as
1661, but broke off that association in 1678, although he had
not fulfilled his contract for three plays a year (pp. 33, 128).
Perhaps he agreed or volunteered to write the ode to make

some amends to the family. Also, like Anne, Dryden had had to struggle for recognition. Her poems were said to have been written by "another," already well endowed with laurels; could this have been Dryden himself, the laureate? Dryden too heard commendations for "another's" work, Sir Robert Howard's play *The Indian Queen,* about half of which is probably by Dryden (pp. 35-36). Another similarity: Anne attempted a poem of epic subject matter, if not epic length, in "Alexandreis," which she "laid by" as too hard for her; Dryden too began an epic and laid it by, possibly recognizing that it was beyond his powers, as Ward suggests (pp. 116-18). Furthermore, Dryden was intimately involved with politics, producing *Absalom and Achitophel* in support of the king in 1681. Anne lived at court, in the center of the political maelstrom; perhaps like Dryden and others she parallels Charles II and David in "To the Queen," where Araunah offers his threshing floor to David. This reference would not be particularly complimentary to Charles, since David was the cause of a pestilence in this biblical story, but it would fit with Anne's general disapproval of the court's moral climate as evidenced throughout "To the Queen" and other poems. Dryden too need not have been devoted to the king's person, as Ward suggests (p. 152), despite his political support, and he did in fact comment on the court as "infectious even to the best morals" (quoted in Ward, p. 283).

In addition to these possible shared opinions, interests, and experiences, Dryden could have felt other kinds of links with the young woman. Anne was clearly modest about her gifts, as many lines in her poems show; Dryden too has been called "diffident" and "modest" by both his friend Congreve and his modern biographer (pp. 319, 182). And he knew about girls. The oldest of fourteen children, Dryden had five younger sisters before another boy was born, who was probably too much younger to be a close comrade. Ward cautions against speculation about Dryden's childhood, since no other information about it exists, but does state that "his early playmates within the home were girls" (p. 7). And later, associated with the Killigrews from the time of Anne's birth, he could very well have watched this girl grow from the cradle and go to her early grave; he could have recognized and even nurtured her gift; and, as the father only of sons, he could have mourned her loss as if she had been a daughter. His possible motives for writing the ode, then were many. There is no need to settle on one—human motivation is rarely so simple.

One more point remains to be considered, a possible solution to the problem of praise. When Dryden heaped so much praise on Mistress Killigrew in his ode, he was acutely aware of the age of this "youngest virgin-daughter of the skies" (l. 1). The dead poet who had written one hundred pages of publishable poetry was only twenty-five. Dryden's own career as a writer did not really begin until he was twenty-eight, which was rather late, as Ward notes (p. 20). He had written some exercises in verse at school. At the age of eighteen, he had published that rather embarrassing piece, "On the Death of Lord Hastings," and at nineteen, a brief congratulatory poem for his friend Hoddesdon's book. Two years later came the letter to his cousin Honor, partly in verse but not for publication. And that is all. Dryden is not known to have written anything further until "Heroic Stanzas" when he was twenty-eight, after seven years of silence. He was fifty-four when he sat down to commemorate Anne Killigrew. It is possible that he thought back over his own career as a poet and recognized that her accomplishment, at the age of twenty-five, far outstripped what his had been at that age. Perhaps this partly explains the praise.

Speculation aside, the fact remains that Dryden, however attached to Anne he may have been and however humble in the face of her superior skill, said that she had morality but no art. And art is as important as morality in poetry, according to his criteria.[20] I have only one suggestion to offer as a solution to this dilemma, though neither this point nor the rest of my analysis will solve all the problems of the ode's complex tones.

When Dryden's poet friend John Oldham died in 1683, Dryden wrote a brief poem in his memory, a mixture of praise and criticism that accurately predicted Oldham's subsequent obscurity. The praise is less lavish than that he allotted to Anne Killigrew; the criticism is essentially the same:

> O early ripe! to thy abundant store
> What could advancing age have added more?
> It might (what nature never gives the young)
> Have taught the numbers of thy native tongue.
>
> [ll. 11-14]

Then he softens the sting by adding, "But satire needs not those," a rhetorical strategy similar to that in the ode on Anne. Oldham is said to have lacked art because it is just not possible that youth could possess it. After all, *ars longa, vita brevis est.* That Dryden believed in this dictum is also apparent in a brief, almost parenthetical phrase in another funerary ode written between the poems on Oldham and Anne Killigrew, "Threnodia Augustalis," on the death of King Charles. Part of this poem is devoted to the virtues of the new king, James II, who had been in training for the position for years, "long exercis'd by fate" (p. 209, l. 430). Dryden also mentions himself obliquely: "Heroes in Heaven's peculiar mold are cast, / They and their poets are not form'd in haste. . . ." (ll. 432-33). He may possibly be indicating that he wants to stay on as poet laureate under James and thinks himself worthy of the position. Whatever the explanation, he believes that it takes time to make a poet.

Ars longa, vita brevis est. As Chaucer correctly translates the line, "The life so short, the craft so long to learn." But when the *vita* was so very *brevis,* as with Oldham (who died at thirty) and Anne Killigrew (who died at twenty-five), *ars,* ipso facto, could not have been acquired. It may be as simple as that.

Dryden's praise of Anne Killigrew's poetry is excessive. Funerary tributes, like Restoration dedications, always are. But despite the mixture of tones in the ode, it is not necessary to read it as comedy or irony or as a meaningless exercise in genre. It can and should be read as recognition of a poet whose artistry was remarkable for one so young. Three hundred years later, Anne Killigrew deserves our recognition too.

TWO

NOVEL INTO PLAY

Aphra Behn and Thomas Southerne

THOMAS SOUTHERNE WAS SURPRISED. Why should Aphra Behn, who had "a great command of the stage," confine her heroic African prince, Oroonoko, to the obscurity of a novel, when he was obviously a perfect type to star in a tragedy?[1] In the dedication to his own play about Oroonoko, he mused, "I have often wondered that she would bury her favorite hero in a novel when she might have revived him in the scene." Southerne speculated briefly about what her reasons might have been for such a peculiar decision: "She thought either that no actor could represent him, or she could not bear him represented. And I believe the last when I remember what I have heard from a friend of hers, that she always told his story more feelingly than she writ it" (p. 4). Southerne himself apparently never heard Mrs. Behn's oral version of her story, and apparently never asked her directly why she failed to put Oroonoko in a play. But he heard about the way she told it, and he had the text of her 1688 novel, with its dedication insisting that the story was true. And in 1695, six years after her death, he did the job for her and put Oroonoko on the stage. The story is much the same, but the different genre affects its import profoundly. Examining the two works side by side makes it possible to expand

Southerne's speculations about Mrs. Behn's choice of genre and to suggest some ideas about his own.

This was not the first time he had borrowed from Mrs. Behn. In 1690, he had dipped into her *Lucky Mistake* for suggestions for *Sir Anthony Love, or The Rambling Lady,* although he does not mention his source in his preface. In 1694 he consulted *The History of the Nun: or, The Fair Vow-Breaker* for *The Fatal Marriage; or, The Innocent Adultery,* this time acknowledging that he took a "hint" for the "tragical part" from Mrs. Behn. He had plenty to choose from. Fourteen novels and twenty-one plays (including three tragicomedies and one tragedy), besides poems and translations, flowed from Mrs. Behn's pen, though some were not published or performed until after her death. She made her living by writing, and is generally hailed as the first woman to have done so.[2] Her plays, which followed the taste of the town, were usually successful. Her novels broke comparatively new ground. Prose fiction had been around for a long time, of course, but the epistolary form and the relatively short tale, sometimes garnished with the trappings of heroic romance but frequently close to a recognizable reality, and immensely popular in translations from the French, were novelties as English originals. Mrs. Behn's stories are about love and courtship, marriage and money. They explore feelings, they include long passages of dialogue, they tend to conclude with a quick comic or tragic twist. Events and emotions matter—not setting, description, symbolism, style, or sometimes even grammar. They are lively productions and yet relatively simple. But *Oroonoko* is different.

First, however, a look at the other novels Southerne used and the way he used them. *The Lucky Mistake* tells of two sisters, the gloriously beautiful Atlante and the only slightly less beautiful and rather more clever Charlot. Atlante is destined for an old, lame, haughty husband, Count Vernole, who persuades her father to send Charlot to a nunnery so that Atlante's fortune (and hence his own) may be increased. But young Rinaldo, the boy next door, sees Atlante and instantly adores her. She returns his love. Both fathers disapprove, Rinaldo's quite arbitrarily and Atlante's because his honor is involved in his promise to marry her to Vernole. After various complications and discoveries and adventures, both girls are locked up in a nunnery, Rinaldo plots to free Atlante, and Vernole, thinking he is rescuing Atlante from Rinaldo, carries off the disguised Charlot. Vernole is finally convinced that Atlante will never be his. He is captivated by Charlot's clever deception and cheerful readiness to marry him rather than spend the rest of her life as a nun, so he accepts her. Honor is now satisfied, for Vernole has a daughter of the family. Atlante, nearly dead of despair and swoons, and Rinaldo, nearly dead of despair and of the wounds received in the last of various skirmishes and duels, recover on the last page and are married.[3]

Such a bald summary cannot convey what is genuinely serious about the novel. Robert Root rightly notes the *Romeo and Juliet* quality of the apparently doomed young lovers. Like that of their models, their love is mutual and true despite obstacles; there are even balconies and rope ladders. The two sisters suggest the "sense and sensibility" pairing, also a faint Shakespearean echo, that became so important for the eighteenth-century novel.[4] Although characterization is relatively slender and the resolution of the plot is a piece of comic cleverness, the issues the novel addresses are real and were important to Mrs. Behn throughout her career: the influence on marriage of the desire for money, in the forms of mere greed and of real financial necessity, and—a stronger theme in this instance—the power of parents to determine their children's lives by approving or disapproving their marriage choices. In this novel, as elsewhere, Mrs. Behn has no general answers to these questions, no solutions to the problems. She is not a social theorist. Individuals in her plays and fictions must solve the problems for themselves individually. In *The Lucky Mistake*, Charlot's trick solves the problem happily. The novel is a good read.

Southerne must have spotted the obvious staginess of the crucial "mistake" scene at the door of the nunnery. His short, action-packed scene in act 5 of *Sir Anthony Love* is set at "the backside of a nunnery,"[5] from which *both* sisters escape, first the younger, pretending to be the older, swept away by the deceived Count, as in Mrs. Behn's story, and then the older, fleeing to the arms of her true love. Their problems have been the same as in Mrs. Behn's story, though the young man in Southerne has no father to hinder his love, and the solution is the same, with honor satisfied and everyone married, if not happily, at least out from under the shadow of the nunnery. Southerne's characters differ considerably from Mrs. Behn's, however. The younger sister in his play is even more of a "mad girl" (p. 23). She is determined to avoid a nunnery, which would obviously not suit her sexual liveliness. The two girls start to plot for freedom as soon as they are onstage. The older sister, though much in love, is less romantic, more "worldly," than her counterpart in the novel.[6] It's fortunate for her that she is, for so is her young man, so much so that he beds another woman (disguised as the title character) to relieve his frustrations after a failed attempt to abduct his lady from her father's house in act 3.

The other plots in *Sir Anthony Love* have no connection with Mrs. Behn's story. "Sir Anthony" herself ties them all together, albeit loosely. Dressed as a man, she enchants the ladies, amuses the gentlemen, and attracts the attention of a homosexual Abbé. Dressed as a woman, she wins as much of the men's hearts as she wants. She duels and converses with equal skill, she revels in double entendres when she is disguised, she speaks up for women (while dressed as a man) in long discussions about marriage, reputation, authority, and wit. Cynical about marriage, at the end of the play she tricks a discarded lover into a wedding in order to arrange an immediate separate maintenance—an easy task for her quick wits. If the play, which is something of a hodgepodge, has any focus, any serious points to make comparable to Mrs. Behn's on marriage, money, and freedom of choice, it is here, in "Sir Anthony." Southerne clearly felt that she was the centerpiece. His preface to the play, which does not mention Mrs. Behn, praises Mrs. Mountfort (later Mrs. Verbruggen), the actress who created the role, giving her credit not only for good acting and good legs but also for her wit in helping to shape the lines. And "Sir Anthony" certainly dominates the stage. Even when Valentine, the young lover, is successfully abducting the older sister, "Sir Anthony" comes along to assist and keeps up a running patter of innuendo about the girl's maidenhead—when she isn't busy helping to fight off the old Count's ruffians.

But what does it all add up to? "Sir Anthony's" defenses of women are strongly feminist, but the subjects and tone of much of her repartee are indistinguishable from those of a Horner or a Dorimant. She loves Valentine but promotes his marriage to the older sister, claiming that when he is tired of his wife, as inevitably he soon will be, he will return to her as his mistress and will be even more ardent than before. She marries her former keeper, not to salvage her lost honor, but for a meal ticket. She has a hand in all the plots. She puzzles the critics of the play. Dodds, following in Lamb's footsteps, finds that she like the other characters has no moral code; sex is intellectual, passion is treated dryly, and the world of the play is cheerfully beyond morality. Root, following Kenneth Muir, finds the play a serious satire on the gallants of the period, considered both as stage conventions and as social realities.[7] Everyone agrees that somehow, for whatever reason, the play was a great success in its own time. One can find flaws, one can interpret its central point in various ways or find that it has no central point, but the evidence is clear: the audience liked it.

I suggest that the play was popular because it has something for everyone—and the seventeenth-century audience (or any audience, for that matter) did not go to the theater in search of organic unity and thematic consistency. And Thomas Southerne knew his audience. There are witty speeches and fast-paced swordplay; there are marriages and nunneries, sex and chastity, disguise, gulling, a father's defeat and a priest's embarrassment. There is also Sir Anthony Love.

Sir Anthony herself embodies something for everyone. The

more moral and sentimental ladies in the audience, provided with a chaste couple to admire, could also approve of Sir Anthony when she marries the man who ruined her and not the man she loves—though her reasons for doing so are improper. The freer spirits among the female members of the audience saw another free spirit, a potential "distressed heroine" who was not the least bit distressed but was managing very well, thank you, despite the restrictions of her world. She speaks up for women, she lives freely among the men, she indulges her sexual desires, she wields power with her wit and her sword, and she even wins financial security without the inconvenience of having a husband attached. One can only speculate about the extent to which she represented wish fulfillment for part of her audience.

As for the gentlemen, besides enjoying a good look at Mrs. Mountfort's legs, they saw a figure who combined the attractiveness and availability of a mistress with the amusing and useful camaraderie of a jolly and clever companion, a mixture not possible in real life. Better still, her cleverness is not a threat, since she exploits no one but the fool, her former keeper. She is one of the boys, and at the same time she is very much one of the girls. More wish fulfillment, perhaps. I hesitate to call her androgynous—she is too vivid in both her roles for that homogenized category. Yet it is perhaps here, in Sir Anthony Love, a woman equal if not superior to the men, rather than in the distressed tragic heroines and downtrodden comic wives usually cited by modern critics, that Southerne's brand of feminism is most clearly expressed.

He found one of his most profoundly distressed heroines in another novel by Mrs. Behn, *The History of the Nun: or, The Fair Vow-Breaker* (1689). Here Mrs. Behn tells the story of Isabella, from the age of two when she was sent to a nunnery upon the death of her mother, to her own death at the age of twenty-seven, when she was beheaded for the murder of her two husbands. The story is true, Mrs. Behn insists in her dedication, and she is particularly qualified to tell it because she herself was "once design'd an humble Votary in the House of Devotion," but doubting her own strength of mind to persist in such a life, chose instead to live in the world.[8] Except for the declaration of truth and the detailed claim in the introductory paragraphs to authority deriving from experience, Mrs. Behn does not appear as a narrator in this story beyond five brief uses of the first-person pronoun, one of which disclaims the authority needed to speak about a battle (p. 128); the other four are insignificant formulas of the "as I said before" variety. This degree of claiming to speak truth is characteristic of her fiction, though she makes no such claims in the atypical *Lucky Mistake*. In all her short novels except *Agnes de Castro*, which is based on history, she uses the first person, and in most of them strengthens that tacit claim to authenticity with an overt statement in the dedication, in the story, or in both. Only twice does she appear as an active character rather than a mere observer or reporter, however: briefly and insignificantly in *The Unfortunate Bride; or, The Blind Lady a Beauty*, at length and importantly in *Oroonoko; or, The Royal Slave*.

She begins *The History of the Nun* with a cautionary first-person comment on the seriousness of vow-breaking, setting up the story as an exemplum of that crime; she ends with Isabella's execution, before which the doomed young woman "made a Speech of half an Hour long ... a warning to the Vow-Breakers ..." (p. 142). In between, we see the baby Isabella growing up in the nunnery, given full opportunity as a girl to live in the world if she chooses but rejecting that opportunity, although her decision nearly causes the death of Villenoys, a devoted lover. He goes off to the wars to forget his sorrows when she is finally inducted into her order. Her life as a nun is exemplary until she meets and loves Henault, her friend's brother, loves him so irresistibly that she escapes from the nunnery and marries him, thus breaking her vow. Sensibly, they leave the country and try to make a living elsewhere. But Henault's attempts at farming fail, and they must live on her aunt's bounty until they obtain official pardons for their elopement

and marriage, upon which they return to Flanders. They still do
not prosper, so Henault is at last persuaded to join the army,
which will win his father's approval and support. The pregnant
Isabella swoons and miscarries when he announces his decision, but eventually he goes to war, where he meets her rejected
lover Villenoys and becomes his close friend. Henault is apparently killed in battle, Villenoys returns with the news, and after
three years of sorrow, and the loss of her aunt with the money,
Isabella agrees to marry Villenoys at last. They are entirely
happy, though they have no children, until, one night when Villenoys is away from home, Henault returns after eight years as
a slave of the Turks.

Isabella's dilemma is complex. She has committed adultery
and bigamy. Her reputation (always high among her neighbors)
will be destroyed. She no longer loves Henault. He has no
money, and Villenoys is rich. Henault will blame her for remar-
rying if he learns of it—the situation is too much for her. She
sees only one way out, and proceeds to smother Henault as he
sleeps. Villenoys returns the same night, she lies dexterously to
explain the dead stranger in the bed, and Villenoys agrees to
dispose of the body. He puts the corpse in a sack which he
slings over his shoulder. Isabella, possessed by "Thoughts all
Black and Hellish" (p. 138), thinks that she cannot live with
Villenoys if he knows her bigamous shame, so she contrives to
kill him too: she sews the sack to his coat collar so that it pulls
him off the bridge when he dumps the body, and he is drowned.
This murder is less excusable than the first, the narrator inter-
jects, "but when Fate begins to afflict, she goes through stitch
[that is, to the bitter end] with her Black Work" (p. 138). The
bodies are found, Henault's unrecognizable, and Isabella's dis-
traction is interpreted as grief. It is not long, however, before a
traveling soldier identifies the other body and Isabella is quickly
accused. She confesses equally quickly and spends her remaining days in jail, distributing her wealth to the poor (especially
the widows) as she cheerfully awaits the executioner's axe.

The story concentrates on Isabella's feelings at each stage in her history, from those of the dedicated novice to those of the tormented lover and murderess. Greatest attention is paid to her agonizing conflict when she loves for the first time and is unable to overcome her feelings; her vow is sacred but her passion is irresistible. Her feelings of torment when Henault returns and when she decides that Villenoys must die as well, though at least equally tumultuous, are handled with comparative brevity.[9] Clearly, the issue of vow-breaking is at the heart of the story's purpose, as the introductory paragraphs and conclusion also indicate.

Mrs. Behn was concerned more than once with the issue of vows and vow-breaking. In *The Lucky Mistake,* the whole plot hinges on the father's promise to provide his daughter as a wife for Count Vernole, a promise which is kept, though one daughter is substituted for the other. In *Oroonoko,* the decadence and corruption of the white colonists in Surinam are heightened by the contrast with Oroonoko, who is incapable of violating his word no matter how dire the consequences of keeping it or how many times he sees the white men violate theirs; the native Indians, who think the governor must have died when he broke his promise to visit them, share this ethos. So the golden age lives on, though only among relatively primitive people. And in her poem titled "The Golden Age," vows of love are always true and always kept. *The History of the Nun,* then, in which the vow-breaker is punished, is consistent with Mrs. Behn's continuing and conservative stance on the question.

The whole issue was a controversial one in the seventeenth century and especially in the 1680s, when Mrs. Behn was writing her novels. Susan Staves devotes a substantial chapter in her *Players' Scepters* to the subject of oaths and vows, describing the changes in attitudes that were taking place.[10] Oaths, which had been accepted as evidence in courts of law simply because they were sworn, became increasingly suspect as "an idealist universe of words" gave way to "a nominalist universe of force and passion" (p. 192). Vows, which had been thought of as real things, came to be considered mere words, largely thanks to the political and religious pressures exercised by the Revolution and the Restoration. Butler's Hudibras and Ralpho, for instance, knew perfectly well that "*Oaths* are but *words,* and *words* but *wind*" and that a little puritan casuistry could make even vow-breaking into a virtue.[11] Serving one's political ends is more important than any abstract idea of honor. Love too can take precedence over oaths and vows, as it does in Mrs. Behn's novel. As Staves notes, two tragic heroes, Jaffier in Otway's *Venice Preserved* and Titus in Lee's *Lucius Junius Brutus,* "find their devotion to their wives stronger than their desire to preserve their faith with the conspirators" (p. 241)—and they gain the audience's sympathies when they act on that devotion. The consequences of such conflicting loyalties are painful in the tragedies, but in real life, vow-breakers not only got away with it more often than not, but even gained the advantages they sought. God did not lean down from heaven and strike them dead.

But He does in *The History of the Nun.* When Isabella makes the crucial decision to break her vow and marry Henault, she engages in some interesting casuistry. She has tried everything she can think of to overcome her passion, but without success, "so, at last, she was forc'd to permit that to conquer her, she could not conquer, and submitted to her Fate, as a thing destin'd her by Heaven it self; and after all this opposition, she fancy'd it was resisting even Divine Providence, to struggle any longer with her Heart . . ." (p. 120). However much the reader may sympathize with Isabella's suffering, Mrs. Behn, by using the word "fancy'd," forbids us to acquiesce intellectually in Isabella's reasoning, which is the kind of might-makes-right logic that is so dangerous politically, the kind of acceptance of changing conditions as "providential" that validated Cromwell's rise to power—and, of course, validated the Restoration, too. The young nun goes on to argue with herself that as a human being she is necessarily imperfect, that God cannot expect perfection, and that if she resists her passion she will die—and suicide is a greater sin than vow-breaking (p. 121). Again, Mrs. Behn warns us not to agree with such logic by concluding that, "after a whole Night's Debate, Love was strongest, and gain'd the Victory" (p. 121)—not right principle or good logic, but love.

Although she saw perjurers go scot free in the 1670s and 1680s, Mrs. Behn states at the beginning of *The History of the Nun* that all vow-breaking is evil, the most evil being the breaking of vows to God, and she claims, "I am almost certain, there is not one Example to be produc'd in the World, where Perjuries of this nature have past unpunish'd . . ." (p. 98). She makes her Isabella ultimately share her own values when, having been found out and condemned to death for the two murders, she lectures the visitors to her cell on the sinfulness of vow-breaking and awaits her death "all Chearful as a Bride" (p. 142), cheerful because her approaching punishment proves that God is in His heaven and that the moral order, which gives words meaning, is real. Clearly, given the daily evidence to the contrary, Mrs. Behn is making a statement of faith rather than of fact, a conservative, even religious faith in abstract and absolute principles.

This reaction against the temper of her times could very well involve a specific political as well as moral stance.[12] The date of the novel's composition is unknown, but it was licensed on October 22, 1688, though it was not published until 1689.[13] Opposition to James II, to whom Mrs. Behn was devoted although she apparently did not share his Catholicism, had been growing before the licensing date, and he was dethroned two months later. Vows had been broken.

> Did they not swear at first to fight
> For the King's safety and his right?
> And after marched to find him out,
> And charged him home with horse and foot?
> [*Hudibras,* pt. 2, canto 2, ll. 159-62]

The revolution may have been bloodless, but it was not, for Mrs. Behn, glorious. Although the sexual passion of a French nun may seem far removed from the turmoil of England's government in 1688, the issue of broken loyalty unites them. *The*

History of the Nun tackles that issue head-on and takes a strong, idealistic stance.

A second issue with which the story deals, as do *The Lucky Mistake* and others of Mrs. Behn's fictions and plays, is that of a woman's freedom to choose a marriage partner or to choose between marriage and a nunnery. Fate chooses Isabella's husbands for her; her choices are between the nunnery and the world, between vow-keeping and vow-breaking. Whether she is genuinely free to make these choices is impossible to determine—and herein lies the novel's psychological interest and credibility despite its melodrama. As a girl, Isabella is obviously conditioned (to use a modern term) by spending her childhood in a nunnery, where she is everybody's pet. Her father insists that she be richly dressed and given the chance to know the outside world before she makes her final decision to become a nun, and she does move freely in fashionable society, but she finds nothing there to her taste. Her aunt, the Abbess, "us'd all her Arts and Stratagems to make her become a *Nun*," but Isabella's inclinations make those arts "needless" (p. 100). The aunt argues too in favor of the pleasures of the world, but Isabella defeats her arguments—which were "purposely weak" (p. 101). Her father outlines the pleasures she will lose and the severities she will incur, but when she remains resolved to become a nun, he rejoices because this has been "the wish of his Soul" (p. 142). Isabella is not forced to become a nun, as Mrs. Behn's characters so often are, and officially, in a Christian culture, one's will is free. But Mrs. Behn's ambiguities here are not contradictions or weaknesses in conception. Instead they create, without answering, the very real question: how free *is* Isabella to choose, given her history and the pressures implicit in her situation?

The same issue arises concerning her choosing to break her vows. The seriousness of her vow-breaking is not in question; her power to choose is. Fate, invoked several times in the story, causes two young men to love her passionately and makes her love Henault irresistibly and hence break her sacred vow. Fate apparently kills Henault and determines that financial need shall make Isabella marry Villenoys. We hear her internal arguments and watch her choosing in each case, but if Fate has taken sides, freedom of choice is merely an illusion. This is the stuff of tragedy.

The status of Southerne's Isabella, in *The Fatal Marriage; or, The Innocent Adultery,* is similarly ambiguous. Is she a victim of Fate, or is she tragically wrongheaded and weak in her choices? The question, however, is further complicated by the generic differences between novel and play. Mrs. Behn can tilt the interpretation of her story by authorial comment. For example, that Isabella is powerless to make real choices is suggested by the female narrator's parallel powerlessness: she laments that she "cannot alter Custom, nor shall ever be allow'd to make new Laws, or rectify old ones" concerning the power of parents over their daughters' choices in marriage and between marriage and the nunnery (p. 99). Southerne, writing a play, cannot speak in his own voice to influence our sense of his meaning. Further, Mrs. Behn can take time to trace her heroine's whole history, implying the power of her childhood "conditioning." Southerne begins near the end of the story, with the apparently widowed and certainly destitute Isabella seeking help and finding that only a second marriage will provide for her, her young son, and her other dependents. Mrs. Behn can also take time to jail Isabella and show her behavior and last speech, firmly underlining the idea that the story is an exemplum, a warning to potential vow-breakers. Southerne chooses a denouement that works better in the theater: Isabella, raving mad, though in this case guiltless of murder, stabs herself bloodily on stage, to the great satisfaction of the audience.

Performance necessarily influences meaning. What an audience perceives across the footlights may be somewhat different from what the student and critic perceive in the study. As Dryden himself pointedly observed, "there is a vast difference betwixt a publick entertainment on the Theatre, and a private reading in the Closet. . . ." Reactions to *The Fatal Marriage* are no exception. Julia A. Rich's subtle and detailed reading of the play shows us an Isabella who is "equally" a victim of forces beyond her control and of her own character and actions. The complex relationship between tragic plot and comic plot supports the idea that the pathetic heroine is, *pace* Addison and virtually all other critics, "to a large degree responsible for her own fate." Rich's argument, firmly based in the text, is persuasive. Yet what the audience saw was the innocent victim of the play's subtitle. One cannot ask that audience for a review, but Addison in *Spectator* 481 commented on the "fine Distress of a Virtuous Woman" in Southerne's play, Garrick dropped the comic plot as not only indelicate but also unnecessary, and actresses for decades relied on the play to win a sympathetic audience for benefit nights—evidence that no blame or responsibility attached to the heroine. I cannot say that only one of the two readings of the play is right. The audience saw a virtuous victim, the reader sees a more complex woman whose ambiguities are closer to those of Mrs. Behn's vow-breaker.[14]

Mrs. Behn's stated purpose in *The History of the Nun* is to supply one of many possible examples of the inevitable punishment of vow-breakers. Southerne, as a dramatist, cannot state a purpose, but one can deduce that his interest lay in exploring the motivations, the heart, the psyche, of his heroine, and in eliciting tears from his audience. The innocence and madness, the soliloquies and suicide of his Isabella are calculated to tug at the heartstrings.[15] Mrs. Behn makes some emotional appeals as well, but she is barred from the greater intensity possible to drama in performance; in fact, she even sidesteps a golden opportunity for breast-beating at the end of her story when she reports succinctly and without a quiver on Isabella's last days and execution. And her comments on Isabella's crucial but casuistical reasoning when she breaks her vow demand an intellectual rather than an emotional response. Clearly, the philosophical and psychological issues involved in the story were of central importance to Mrs. Behn. Southerne too deals with issues: a woman's powerlessness, her financial dependence, her choices, the wrongful use of parental power—Mrs. Behn's frequent topics. But in the presence of Isabella's flesh-and-blood passion on stage, the issues so nearly vanish that one is surprised to hear her father-in-law point the moral at the end when he takes upon himself the guilt for usurping "Heav'ns Prerogative," the punishing of offending children (p. 79). In this instance, these two authors working in different genres seem to have reversed the cliché that men characteristically deal in ideas and abstractions and women in emotions and relationships.

The relationship between *Oroonoko* as a novel and *Oroonoko* as a play has much in common with the relationships between the other works which I have been examining. But it is a very special case.

Critical commentary on both Mrs. Behn's and Southerne's *Oroonoko* is not lacking. From the time of Ernest Bernbaum's attack in 1913 to the present, much ink has been expended in debunking or supporting the authenticity of Mrs. Behn's Surinam material—flora and fauna, slave-trading customs, costume, language. The consensus now is that the details are accurate and that Mrs. Behn told the truth when she said she had been there, since her material goes beyond what was available to her in published sources in the seventeenth century.[16] Some recent criticism has taken new directions, studying narrative voice and the question of a feminist perspective.[17] Critics of Southerne, whose reputation seems to be on the rise, deal with his comic plot and its relationship to Oroonoko's tragedy, and with questions of heroism, idealism, and marriage. Most say something about the relationship between the play and the novel: the extent of Southerne's borrowings, the changes he made (such as making the heroine, Imoinda, white instead of black and turning the catastrophe into onstage suicide instead of dismemberment), and the consequences of these changes.[18] Southerne's critics generally seem to find the play better than the novel; critics of Mrs. Behn generally prefer the novel. Each work wins praise, and indeed each is successful in its own genre.

One approach that has not been fully explored is the generic.

There have been occasional comments, for example about the impossibility of cutting up Oroonoko onstage—"members," ears, nose, arms—and the possibility that Southerne changed Imoinda's color because he had to make plausible her great attractiveness to white male characters.[19] Or perhaps no important actress could be persuaded to appear in blackface. But Mrs. Behn herself could have made such adjustments had she chosen to put her African prince into a play. The question, and Southerne's surprise, remain: why a novel? I hope, by looking at the two works side by side, to suggest an answer to this question—an answer that, however speculative, is not the pure romancing that has marred so much Behn criticism. I will consider what novels and heroic tragedies were in the 1670s, 1680s, and early 1690s, and what they were not; I will indicate the primary focus of each work, which depends partly on genre, and hence its primary purpose—all in an attempt to answer the question: why a novel?

Mrs. Behn's novel begins with the declaration that the story is true and that she was an eyewitness to "a great Part" of the action to be "here set down."[20] She tells her story in almost straight chronology, first offering further bona fides by describing her acquaintance with Surinam and, among other things, its methods of slave trading, and then recounting Oroonoko's story of his youth in Africa as he told it to her later. This part of the story, which could be taken as background for the crisis in Surinam, has no counterpart in Southerne's play. Grandson of the king, young Oroonoko is beautiful in body and soul, a valiant warrior, and, thanks to a French tutor, adept in "Morals, Language and Science" (p. 135). When he visits the daughter of an old General who died in battle to save him, he falls in love, the beautiful Imoinda being as wonderful as he is. The aged king, however, though sexually past it, hears of the girl's charms and, after verifying with his own eyes that the report is not exaggerated, sends her the Royal Veil, a command to join his harem. She has no choice. Though contracted to Oroonoko, she comes to the king's withered arms where she languishes, still a virgin, for some time.

The novelist can take time, can give her characters time, as the dramatist cannot. Oroonoko, though in despair, slowly learns to control his feelings and is at last invited by the king to a soirée in the harem. There he sees Imoinda and reassures her with the language of his eyes that he still adores her. With the help of a self-sacrificing friend and Imoinda's duenna, he returns at night; he "soon prevail'd, and ravished in a Moment what his old Grandfather had been endeavouring for so many Months" (p. 152). But he is discovered. He escapes to the army camp, and the king has Imoinda sold into slavery. Word is brought to Oroonoko that she is dead, which almost kills him. He lies prostrate on the floor of his tent for two days while the enemy attacks. At last, however, honor triumphs, so he seeks his own death in battle. But he wins and, after a healing period of time, returns to court: ". . . Time lessens all Extremes" (p. 160).

A slave-trading Captain visits the court and gains the prince's favor with his European conversation and learning. When he is about to return to sea, he invites Oroonoko on board his ship. The prince comes, with a party of courtiers, eats and drinks merrily, and falls easily into the Captain's trap—they are all locked into chains, too fuddled with punch to resist, and the ship sails at once for South America. Oroonoko, shamed, tries to die of starvation, but the Captain persuades him that he has repented and promises to free him when they reach land. The honorable African believes him, pledges his word in return to stir up no trouble, and is unchained. He eats again. But when they arrive in Surinam, the Captain breaks his word and sells Oroonoko, separately from his followers.

This is the point, halfway through the novel, at which Southerne's play begins, and at which Mrs. Behn claims that her personal knowledge of the royal slave began. Trefry, the acting Lord Governor, buys Oroonoko, and, during the three-day voyage upriver to the plantation, learns to appreciate the intellectual and other qualities of the slave. Trefry becomes Oroonoko's friend, promising to rescue him from slavery as soon as he can. He gives the African prince the slave name of Caesar but treats him like a prince. Caesar is worshiped by fellow slaves and white men alike on the plantation—but worshiped even more passionately is Clemene, a beautiful young black girl who turns out to be Imoinda. The lovers are reunited and married. Soon Imoinda becomes pregnant. This development makes Caesar/Oroonoko even more unhappy with his chains of slavery, easy though they are, for he fears that his child will be born a slave. He tries to bargain for freedom, but without success.

Meanwhile, time is passing, as it does in life and novels. Young Aphra, who has no real counterpart in Southerne's play, grows closer to Oroonoko and Imoinda as she tells them stories (of Roman heroes for him, nuns for her) and takes one or both of them with her and her family and friends on various expeditions into the countryside to hunt for tiger cubs, visit Indians, and so forth. These pages in the novel are full of the local description that has spurred many scholars to look for, and to find, authenticity and accuracy in detail. When Imoinda's pregnancy begins to show and she weeps and sighs over their captivity and the captivity of the baby that is to be born, Oroonoko can bear it no longer. He gathers his fellow slaves about him, and, with a great speech, only part of which Mrs. Behn reports verbatim, persuades them to escape. The men are willing, but they worry about their wives and children. Oroonoko, however, expects the same level of honor and courage from the women as from the men. They agree to flee, men and women together, or to die trying. But when their pursuers catch up with them, the women and children persuade the men to seek mercy and forgiveness. Oroonoko, Imoinda, and one faithful follower stand alone. Instead of slaughtering them, the English, including Trefry, argue with them until Oroonoko, "overcome by [Trefry's] Wit and Reasons, and in Consideration of *Imoinda*," surrenders (p. 196). But promises are again broken. Trefry has been the dupe of the Lieutenant Governor. Oroonoko is seized, dragged away from

Imoinda, and cruelly whipped, after which pepper is rubbed
into his wounds and he is chained to the ground. Aphra is away
from the plantation at the time, seeking safety downriver with
the other females who feared the consequences of the slaves'
rebellious escape. She speculates that she might have been able
to prevent this treatment of Oroonoko had she been present,
and she hastens to rescue and restore him when she returns
(p. 198). Oroonoko vows vengeance on Byam, the Lieutenant
Governor, but forgives all his white friends for their part in his
humiliation.

Still a slave, and still fearing that his child will be born a slave,
Oroonoko gets permission, when he is well enough, to take
Imoinda for a walk. Out in the woods, he takes his farewell of
his beautiful wife, and with her complete accord, kills her to
preserve her honor and to prevent the slavery of his child. He
cuts her head from her body and covers her with leaves and
flowers. Overcome by grief for her death, though it was necessary for his honor as well as for hers, he lies in motionless
mourning for days until the search party finds him. Then, despite his weakness, he manages to stand. He puts his back
against a tree, cuts a piece of flesh from his throat and flings it
at his enemies, and cuts open his belly, pulling out his bowels.
Still not dead, he stabs to death an Englishman who tries to
take him, but finally he is overcome and carried to a doctor,
who sews him up again. Aphra visits him and begs him to live,
but he warns her that he will "prove very fatal to a great many"
if he does (p. 206). Unable to bear the smell of his wounds and
fearing that her own health would be undermined by melancholy, Aphra leaves the place "for some time." Then Trefry is
lured away for a day (p. 207). While they are absent, Oroonoko
is executed. He stands like a rock, smoking his pipe, as the
executioner "with an ill-favor'd Knife" cuts off his members and
throws them in the fire, then his ears and nose, then one arm
(p. 208). He goes on smoking, impassive, until at the cutting of
his other arm, he gives up the ghost. Aphra's mother and sister
watch him die, powerless to save him, "so rude and wild were

the Rabble" (p. 208). The novel ends quietly: "Thus died this great Man, worthy of a better Fate, and a more sublime Wit than mine to write his Praise: Yet, I hope, the Reputation of my Pen is considerable enough to make his glorious Name to survive to all Ages, with that of the brave, the beautiful and the constant *Imoinda*" (p. 208).

The tragic plot of Southerne's play begins with the Captain's arrival with a shipload of slaves, including the stolen prince. When Oroonoko appears for the first time, and speaks the first blank verse in the play, he expresses his contempt for the Captain for having broken his word (I.ii.195). Blanford (Trefry in the novel) buys him, impressed by his nobility. Oroonoko maintains great dignity in this scene, stating that his "nobler part" is beyond their control; they may call him Caesar if they like, but he is still himself (I.ii.254, 261). When next we see him, he tells Blanford the history of his love and claims that he can view the fair Clemene unmoved because he is ever faithful to his Imoinda. Next, Clemene appears, resisting the Lieutenant Governor's approaches as he claims, with quintessential male egotism, that she really wants him and would be displeased if he took her rejection seriously (II.ii.17-22). Oroonoko just misses seeing her at the Lieutenant Governor's house, which builds suspense neatly. When she is abducted by a party of Indians, an incident without parallel in the novel, he joins the white plantation owners in their pursuit and discovers that the famous Clemene is his own Imoinda, whom he married and impregnated in Africa before she was sold as a slave. (Just how pregnant she is when the Lieutenant Governor and everyone else swoon at her feet is something of a question; the time sequence in Africa is vague, and the weeks of the ships' journeys are not mentioned—Southerne was clearly not concerned with the biological probabilities on this point.)[21] The reunion of husband and wife is hailed by Blanford and, hypocritically, by the Lieutenant Governor, who mutters in an aside that he does not intend to lose the fair slave despite this development (II.iii.225). Mrs. Behn's Oroonoko fears the possibility that Imoinda could be exposed to the "nasty Lusts" of the slave owners if he died and left her behind him (p. 201), but the danger receives no more emphasis than this. Southerne makes a much bigger issue of the threat to his white slave's virtue from the powerful white slave owners.

In act 3, the slave rebellion gets underway, with the cowardly slave Hottman claiming to be willing to risk all for freedom; Oroonoko's friend Aboan suspects the genuineness of Hottman's courage.[22] Immediately after this encounter, Aboan is reunited with Oroonoko by the kindly Blanford and, with difficulty, persuades his royal master to join and lead the rebellion. (Mrs. Behn's Oroonoko initiated the rebellion himself.) Oroonoko feels too much bound in honor to the white men who have befriended him to turn against them and says he finds the load of slavery light, but Aboan tells him that other slaves suffer and that his child will be a slave. Apparently, Oroonoko had not thought of that. Imoinda has borne the sad knowledge with silent suffering, but Oroonoko is truly surprised when Aboan explains it to him (III.ii.149). Throughout Southerne's play, Oroonoko's idealism and heroic virtues have not been seen to include a very penetrating intelligence, whereas Mrs. Behn's hero consistently combined heroic honor with a mind both educated and naturally perceptive; her Oroonoko has been painfully aware all along of the status of his unborn son. Besides explaining the baby's status, Southerne's Aboan adds to his persuasions the danger to Imoinda's chastity, and that rouses "the lion in his den" (III.ii.206). Oroonoko, like Shakespeare's Brutus, insists, however, that their efforts to gain liberty must not be bloody (III.ii.232-33)—clearly preparing the way for the tragic ending. We wonder today, as the Restoration audience must have wondered, where idealism leaves off and stupidity begins.

With an impressive speech, Oroonoko harangues his fellow slaves, who raise questions about the difficulty of their undertaking, especially about the safety of their wives and children. While Mrs. Behn's prince demanded the same kind of honor from the women as from the men and said they deserved to die if they did not have such honor (p. 192), Southerne's prince emphasizes the helpless dependence of the women as they march to the sea (III.iv.17-28). As the plans progress, Oroonoko, after Aboan provides him with the necessary hints, discovers Hottman's cowardice but idealistically refuses to have him killed (III.iv.35-98), again inviting the tragedy.

The slaves escape, they are followed and outnumbered, the women persuade their husbands to surrender, Blanford persuades Oroonoko to surrender to save Imoinda and the baby, and the Lieutenant Governor has the prince seized and bound as soon as he gives up his sword—all very much as in the novel. Southerne recognized the stageworthiness of Mrs. Behn's scene and transferred it intact to the theater. Apparently Oroonoko is not whipped, but the wound to his honor when he is chained is sufficient to cause him to swear vengeance. Blanford and a party of women persuade the Lieutenant Governor to unchain him (as the narrator did in the novel) and to restore Imoinda to him. The Lieutenant Governor agrees. But he has Imoinda concealed in his own house. A scene of attempted rape follows, but Blanford, suspicious, has stayed behind and rescues the threatened woman. In the next scene (V.v), Aboan, wounded in body and in honor by the slave owners' instruments of torture, comes to Oroonoko to warn him that a similar fate awaits him, and begs a dagger with which he commits honorable suicide. Imoinda too arrives and, in the longest, most emotionally charged scene in the play, asks for death at Oroonoko's hand rather than the dishonor she foresees. The idea that death is the way out comes from her; Mrs. Behn's Imoinda had agreed eagerly to the idea, but her Oroonoko had initiated it. Despite the dangers and with the slave owners beating at the door, Southerne's prince cannot bring himself to kill his wife until she directs his faltering hand with her own and dies satisfied.[23] The white men enter, led by the Lieutenant Governor, Oroonoko stabs the would-be rapist and then kills himself, throwing himself by Imoinda's corpse to die—echoes of *Othello*. Blanford speaks briefly about the exalted virtue of this pagan whom God should forgive for his suicide and take to heaven, and makes some invidious comparisons with the virtues of Christians (V.v.305-11), a theme that receives a somewhat greater emphasis in the novel. Unlike Mrs. Behn's hero, Southerne's dies quickly, untortured, by his own hand, and successful in achieving his revenge. Mrs. Behn's evil Lieutenant Governor escapes unscathed.

Southerne's tragedy, like many others of the period, also includes a comic plot in which he rings the customary changes on the husband-hunting tactics of impecunious not-quite-young ladies. Charlotte and Lucy Welldon come to Surinam to find men, having failed to land husbands in London. Charlotte appears in breeches as Lucy's brother and announces her own imminent arrival, calling herself a cousin. She "marries" the wealthy Widow Lackitt after seeing Lucy securely united to the Widow's booby son, a match with financial advantages for Lucy as well as the freedom guaranteed by a stupid husband. Jack Stanmore, who wanted to marry the Widow, substitutes for Charlotte at night. The satisfied Widow rewards Charlotte with a thousand pounds. Charlotte gives the money to Jack's older brother and, back in her skirts, attracts and marries the brother while the Widow must make do with the sexual athletics of Jack. The plot has no counterpart in Mrs. Behn's novel, which is devoted entirely to the tragic story of Oroonoko. In the play, the comic part, though I have outlined it so briefly here, takes up about half the action. Despite the conventionality of the disguises and other trickery, it is a lively and engaging show. And it has significant thematic connections with the tragic plot, though almost no structural ones. Together, the two plots pose important questions about broken promises, honor and dishonor, love and marriage, and, above all, slavery—the buying and selling of human beings as laborers and of women as wives.[24]

Elsewhere, in *The History of the Nun: or, The Fair Vow-Breaker,* for example, Mrs. Behn too deals with the economic slavery of women; in *Oroonoko,* Southerne expresses a shared sense of the necessity of marrying, turning it in this instance to comic purposes. He makes his comic plot such fun, and so real in terms of the Restoration social world, that critics turn to it in relief, finding there a comforting solidity in contrast to the tragic plot's rarefied idealisms. Robert D. Hume, for one, feels that the comic characters "return Oroonoko to the real world"; "we need the comic subplot to keep our feet planted in reality," Novak and Rodes explain (p. xxxvi). But the comic plot is not universally admired. It was dropped later in the eighteenth century; even today, Jean Hagstrum finds it "ridiculous and tasteless."[25] Generally, however, it is welcomed.

In contrast to the questions of taste raised by comic realism, tragic plots and characters create other kinds of problems, particularly problems of credibility. Even in the seventeenth century, tragic idealism was sometimes felt to be rather too rarefied to be agreeable. In 1671, Mrs. Evelyn called *The Conquest of Granada* "a play so full of ideas that the most refined romance I ever read is not to compare with it; love is made so pure, and valour so nice, that one would imagine it designed for an Utopia rather than our stage." She goes on to admire that "one born in the decline of morality should be able to feign such exact virtue. . . ."[26] Pure love, nice valor, and exact virtue, characteristic of heroic tragedy, mark Southerne's Oroonoko as much as Dryden's Almanzor. Mrs. Behn's royal slave, however, is less perfect. Alongside his qualities as ideal hero—beauty of soul and body, courage, honor, and so forth—are other elements: he is a dealer in slaves, and we see him offering to buy his own freedom by selling others;[27] he deceives people more than once; he uses his friend as a pimp to arrange a meeting with Imoinda in the harem and encourages him to make love to her elderly duenna to keep her out of the way; he ravishes the willing Imoinda before they marry; when he is told she is dead, his grief is realistically lessened by time; he sulks in captivity; and the narrator never entirely trusts him. Altogether a more understandable level of human behavior than we see in the refinements of Southerne's hero.

Different levels appear in the speech of the two Oroonokos as well. Mrs. Behn's hero, who inhabits a novel, need not talk a great deal and does not. She reports his words at second hand and gives him only a dozen or so brief speeches in relatively ordinary, middle-level prose. Southerne's hero speaks elevated blank verse, in a style which Novak and Rodes find individualized in contrast to Mrs. Behn's typical novella style, and which they praise as "dignified, simple, ironic, passionate" (p. xxxvii). Passionate it most certainly is, but it is a matter of taste whether a reader finds dignity and simplicity or the egotistic rant of heroic cliché in such a line as "I am a slave no longer than I please" (II.ii.8) or "Is there a power on earth / That I can ever need forgiveness from?" (IV.ii.115-16). It would also have been a matter of the audience's taste and the skill of the actor when the play was first performed. Whether one likes it or not, it is certainly not ordinary speech.

The question of speech style returns us to the question of genre, of Mrs. Behn's choice of the novel as a vehicle for her hero. I think she made that choice because she wanted to be believed. I do not here argue that the story is true, in whole or in part. A real trip to Surinam and authentic details of its flora and fauna do not prove that Oroonoko was real. Even such historical evidence as reports of slaves smoking while stoically enduring dismemberment proves nothing about Oroonoko's reality as an individual, only that the story *could* have been true.[28] That Mrs. Behn told the story orally to her friends for years before she wrote it down increases the probability of its being true—we all have our repertoires of personal anecdotes—and also increases the probability that it acquired additional embroidery as it was retold. Again, nothing is proved. Her claim to have been an eyewitness appears in other stories as well, most notably *The Fair Jilt,* and has been dismissed as "the standard obeisance to the anti-fictional bias of the age."[29] But her statement is stronger in *Oroonoko* than elsewhere, and by her presence and her two absences the narrator plays a far more active role as character and as structural device than she does in any other story. This use of the narrator is indeed artful, yet artfulness does not preclude the possibility that the events could have happened, that she could have witnessed some and heard of others. But the point here is that, whether the story is true or not, Mrs. Behn wanted her readers to believe that it was.

The genre of the novel allows Mrs. Behn to try to create the impression of authenticity as the genre of tragedy would not. *Vraisemblance* was increasing in both French and English fiction, and readers believed much of what they read. The steamy and exclamatory *Five Love-Letters from a Nun to a Cavalier,* incredible today, was accepted as genuine. Tales of the Orient, which included Africa, though commonly full of wild improbabilities, were increasing in realism of feeling if not in realism of detail.[30] (And in *Oroonoko,* the exotic detail in Surinam *is* real, though the African part of the story is less well authenticated.) Credibility was enhanced by the fact that the border between fiction and history was fuzzy. Both genres allowed a first-person narrator, editorial comment and judgment, and the artful arrangement of events. But the border between novels and romances was clear, at least in theory. Congreve, in the preface to his novel *Incognita* (1692), describes the two forms:

> Romances are generally composed of the Constant Loves and invincible Courages Of Hero's, Heroins, Kings and Queens, Mortals of the first Rank, and so forth; where lofty Language, miraculous Contingencies and impossible Performances, elevate and surprize the Reader into a giddy Delight, which leaves him flat upon the Ground whenever he gives of[f], and vexes him to think how he has suffer'd himself to be pleased and transported, concern'd and afflicted at the several Passages which he has Read, viz. these Knights Success to their Damosels Misfortunes, and such like, when he is forced to be very well convinced that 'tis all a lye. Novels are of a more familiar nature; Come near us, and represent to us Intrigues in practice, delight us with Acci-

dents and odd Events, but not such as are wholly unusual or unpresidented, such which not being so distant from our Belief bring also the pleasure nearer us. Romances give more of Wonder, Novels more Delight.[31]

Congreve goes on to draw a parallel between romance and tragedy, and between novel and comedy. One concludes, then, that romance and tragedy are incredible, not to be believed, but that novels and comedies had a chance.

In this case, given the subject matter, it was roughly a fifty-fifty chance. Most modern critics dismiss Mrs. Behn's story as romance or as a hybrid containing a high proportion of romance. While they may believe in the flora and fauna of Surinam, they do not believe in Oroonoko. But Mrs. Manley, that prolific historical romancer, who was closer to Mrs. Behn's own time, would have judged the story to be either romance—or truth. In her preface to *The Secret History of Queen Zarah* (1705), she lumps novels and history together under "history" and contrasts that category with "romance." She also recognizes that actual history may contain characters and events as incredible as those in romance. So by her standards, *Oroonoko,* with all its exotica and improbabilities, could be either. She might not consider it a good novel, because the novel should be probable, but it stood a chance of being believed.[32]

Mrs. Behn gained some of the other advantages of history by choosing the novel genre, namely, the chance to use the techniques common to the novelist and the authentic historian: chronological storytelling in a long time span, realism of setting and other descriptive details, and the narrator's voice authenticating it all. She also took on the historian's limitations: if the story was true, she could not make changes for theatrical purposes. That is, she could not paint a black Imoinda white, whereas if an actress refused to paint herself black, a playwright might make such a change; she could not give Oroonoko a clean and stageable suicide if he had in fact been messily dismembered. Furthermore, if she wanted to be believed, she had to exercise restraint; not everyone believes with Mrs. Manley that truth can be stranger than fiction. Perhaps that is why she told her story orally "more feelingly than she writ it," indulging herself in all the truths too strange to be allowed in fiction or believed in history, truths which she played down to some extent in the writing of it.

Amid all this welter of speculation, these possibilities and probabilities, one fact is fixed: she did not write a tragedy about her tragic African prince.

Mrs. Behn had written a tragedy about an exotic African, *Abdelazar; or, The Moor's Revenge* (1677), so she knew how it was done, or at least she knew how the blood-and-thunder of popular "heroic" tragedy was done. Everyone expected such plays to be "marvellous"; no one expected them to be true.[33] Whether such plays could serve as vehicles for ideas of any seriousness and why the audiences liked them continue to be matters of debate. On one side, Hume, in his detailed and invaluable taxonomy of dramatic types in the period, finds all Restoration plays to be purely entertainment, the tragedies as incredible and as likable as grand opera (pp. 30-31, 227). On the other side, perhaps the plays do raise real questions of heroism and honor, as Mrs. Evelyn suggested; Julia Rich's argument about the central theme of Southerne's *Oroonoko* is based on the assumption that Southerne believed his medium could convey important ideas about the heroic ethos itself. And indeed the idea of heroic honor did raise questions. Audiences who had lived through the Commonwealth and were experiencing the confusion of values of the Restoration period could simultaneously admire idealized honor and laugh at it as a notion irrelevant to their world.[34] The playwright could not be sure which response a hero would evoke. Fictional figures like Mrs. Behn's Abdelazar and half-historical figures like Dryden's Almanzor, inhabiting a remote, half-unreal past, could perhaps be accepted as living by high ideals valued, and seen as valid, in their distant times and places. But Oroonoko was a man of the present time, a man who died in the early 1660s, remote and exotic in the lands of his birth and death but very much a victim of the contemporary world, a world in which heroic idealism looked suspiciously like stupidity. Placed in the context of a 1670s heroic tragedy, he might have been hooted or he might have been received ambivalently, admired and scorned, accepted only as a fiction. He could not have been taken entirely seriously; it is highly unlikely that he could have been taken as real.

In the next decade, the climate changed. By the end of the 1680s, "not a vintage period for serious drama," he could have been pitied. Drama grew more sentimental and victims were popular. "The virtuous character as victim is likely to yield pity rather than admiration," Hume argues, and Oroonoko is indeed a virtuous victim.[35] Mrs. Behn could have expected to draw tears from her audience as Southerne did had she written him into a tragedy in the 1680s. She must have wanted some other response. Indeed, she avoids some opportunities for extreme emotionalism, especially at the end of the story, as she had done in *The History of the Nun.*

Southerne does draw tears, and very successfully. Yet only one critic finds the play "realistic."[36] Others praise it for integrating the two plots thematically, for its style, and above all for its affective power. Novak and Rodes even praise it because, unlike Mrs. Behn's novel, it is free of "indecorous realism" (p. xl). The theme may have been old hat when Southerne wrote it—Dryden stated that "Love and Honour (the mistaken Topics of Tragedy) were quite worn out" in 1690—but *Oroonoko,* which is full of love and honor, was a great success and lasted (in various alterations) for 150 years.[37] Southerne created good theater when he adapted Mrs. Behn's novel. He knew audiences. But he did not create credibility.

The novel and the play coexist in the mainstream of English literature. There is no need to choose between them. But there is a need to recognize what the two authors accomplish in their two genres.

Southerne is saying to us: Gather together a party of friends and come to the theater, where I will make you laugh and I will make you cry. Perhaps I will make you think a little about slavery as an institution and about the economic slavery of women to the institution of marriage. Most certainly I will give you big speeches and high heroics to revel in. I will give you Mr. Verbruggen in blackface and a good look at Mrs. Verbruggen's legs. I don't ask you to believe my story. I ask you to participate in a community of emotion, to giggle with your friends as the lusty Widow Lackitt chases a disguised girl and to weep with your friends as I spatter the stage with pig's blood. That's entertainment!

Mrs. Behn is saying to us: Retire into your closet, alone, and shut the door. I have a story to tell and I want you to listen well. It will entertain you, yes, but above all I want you to learn to know a remarkable man who was once part of my life, a worthy man whose valuable life was thrown away stupidly and hideously in an action that I was powerless to stop. I could not stop them from whipping him, and I could not stop them from killing him. I was away when those things happened, away because as a woman I was afraid and as a woman I was sickly, as powerless as the royal slave himself—and perhaps as much of a traitor to him as the women of his own race, his fellow slaves who deserted him for their own survival and comfort. As I tell my tale, you may draw some conclusions about the institution of slavery and you may see some parallels to the tragic exile of King James II.[38] You may feel sorry for my suffering hero. But use your head as well as your heart. Think about how valuable a human being can be, and how corrupt. Think about the awful disparity between human worth and human power. I will show you that disparity in the true history of my royal slave. I will hint at it in myself, a woman powerless to save him, a woman whose only power lies in her pen. I will speak of my weakness, but the existence of my story will silently demonstrate my strength. You may see only romance or you may believe me—and I hope you do believe. In either case, you will be reading my story. And so, alone in your closet, you will not escape the fact that I have the power to make you listen.

THREE

SELECTED NIGHTINGALES

Anne Finch, Countess of Winchilsea, et al.

UNLIKE MOST WOMEN POETS of the eighteenth century, Anne Finch, Countess of Winchilsea, has not lacked recognition in the twentieth. After Myra Reynolds's major, though incomplete, edition was published in 1903, her poems appeared in collections ranging from conservative college texts in the 1930s to radical feminist anthologies in the 1970s and the 1980s. Criticism has more or less kept pace with reprinting. For the most part, critics take one of two approaches: historical, most often concerned with placing Lady Winchilsea's poems within the Metaphysical/Augustan/Romantic taxonomy, or feminist, concerned with analyzing their contents. The first is, of course, the older approach. For more than a century she was hailed as a "pre-Romantic" poet, after Wordsworth had praised the new images of nature in her "Nocturnal Reverie." Reuben Brower redirected classification criticism in 1945 in an article that called attention to Lady Winchilsea's links with the seventeenth century, especially with Marvell. Following in Brower's footsteps, Annemarie Riedenauer wrote a doctoral dissertation for the University of Vienna in 1964 in which she pasted metaphysical, neoclassical, and other labels on individual poems, passages within poems, lines, and single words. Sometimes she even concluded that certain poems were written earlier or later in Lady Winchilsea's lifetime according to the frequency of the metaphysical or neoclassical labels she could attach.[1]

Feminist criticism focuses on the contents of the poems. For example, Katharine Rogers surveys the poems with an eye to a woman's problems in adapting erotic conventions in male poetry to suit her needs. She also examines the way the poems comment on the deficiencies in women's education, on the plight of the woman poet, and on the restrictions on women's liberty. Elizabeth Hampsten devotes part of an article to similar considerations and to Lady Winchilsea's manipulation of gender-specific language. I have studied elsewhere the variety of attitudes Lady Winchilsea expresses toward the plight of women, particularly their educational disabilities, and I have examined the differences of subject matter and tone in the poems she chose to publish in her lifetime and those she kept in manuscript.[2] As always, feminist approaches vary, but such criticism, despite its variety, generally emphasizes the sex of the author and what she has to say that pertains to women.

A poem has both form and content, both a historically definable style and something to say. It exists in a tradition and it is original, it is unique. And a poet is not only male or female, but also simply human. I will try to keep all these things in mind and to avoid the confines of a single approach as I examine Lady Winchilsea's "To the Nightingale," a poem worth close study because it is good and because it shows her range of style and her original way of using a very specific tradition within a very traditional mode, the nightingale department of the pastoral. Literary nightingales have been singing steadily from their first chirps in Greek myth and idyll to yesterday's haiku. The tradition is rich, so rich that it lends itself to a wide variety of uses. I will clarify some of Lady Winchilsea's uses by comparing them to some other poets' uses, principally Crashaw's in "Musicks Duell" and Ambrose Philips's in his "Fifth Pastoral." These poems are earlier than Lady Winchilsea's, which appeared in her 1713 *Miscellany,* but I am concerned here not with specific indebtedness but only with the tradition in general. For Lady Winchilsea's highly original poem is itself part of the tradition, part of the literary mainstream. On such a subject, how could it not be?

"To the Nightingale" (pp. 267-68; and see the appendix) begins with a command to the bird to sing so that the poet can write the lyrics for its music. The poet makes some comparisons between the bird and poets in general. When the bird begins to sing, the poet or the Muse attempts twice to match it with words but fails in the attempt. With a quick sour-grapes reversal, the poet attacks the frivolity of the nightingale, who is neglecting the serious business of nest-building, and concludes with a rueful analysis of the motivation for that attack.

One can readily see how this would appeal to the Romantic Wordsworth or Coleridge: the admiration for the beauty of the bird's song; the humbling, even the humiliation, of the mere human being before the wondrous powers of nature; and, above all, what one could call the "expressive" theory of poetic creativity: "Cares do still their Thoughts molest, / And still th'unhappy Poet's Breast, / Like thine, when best he sings, is plac'd against a Thorn." (I will return to that rather curious masculine pronoun.) Alluding to the myth of Philomela, Lady Winchilsea claims a most un-Augustan source for inspiration: personal pain. Pope sometimes claimed that moral pain goaded him into writing satire, but that is not at all the same thing. This sounds more like Coleridge in "Dejection"—except that there he claims that pain kills his creativity—but he creates a poem about that very notion. Lady Winchilsea could be writing in a similarly autobiographical vein here: there were many circumstances in her life that caused her considerable pain.[3] And yet this is of course a conventional reference to the classical myth of Philomela and to the equation of singer, either bird or person, with poet. It is not necessary to choose between convention and autobiography, to label this line Augustan or Romantic. It is both.

The metaphysical label sometimes illuminates, sometimes obscures. Brower calls attention to the conceit in the middle of the poem:

> Canst thou Syllables refine,
> Melt a Sense that shall retain
> Still some Spirit of the Brain,
> Till with Sounds like these it join.

He comments on "the subtle analysis of thought, the compression effected by unexpectedly combining the concrete with the abstract."[4] One can think of comparable distillations in Donne. It is a helpful corrective to the "pre-Romantic" school of thought to be made aware of Lady Winchilsea's seventeenth-century roots. But the label can also be misleading, as when Riedenauer, considering the poem as a whole, finds in it a closeness between man and nature reminiscent of the bond among all created things that is to be found in metaphysical poetry. This is ultimately not the case in Lady Winchilsea's poem.

Crashaw provides a useful comparison. "Musicks Duell," modeled on a Latin poem by his contemporary, Strada, describes a contest between a lute player and a nightingale which the human lute player wins. The contest is a variation on the traditional belief, first described by Pliny, that nightingales competed with each other in song, sometimes dying of exhaustion in the process.[5] Crashaw's lutanist is playing to himself to cool "his owne hot cares" when the nightingale appears and sings along with him.[6] "The man perceiv'd his Rivall, and her Art" (l. 15), and the rest of the poem bears out this idea that the two are in competition and that both are artists. One might expect a contrast between nature and art, but not so. Crashaw lavishes his characteristic richness of metaphor and his knowledge of musical terms on the contest, describing a number of performances by each contestant, and, when the nightingale, worn out, tries to overmatch the lutanist one final time, he concludes:

Shee failes, and failing grieves, and grieving dyes.
She dyes; and leaves her life the Victors prise,
Falling upon his Lute; o fit to have
(That liv'd so sweetly) dead, so sweet a Grave!
[ll. 165-68]

There are no regrets to be expressed, there is no sense of disparity between man and nature, no conflict, no dualism—simply a sense of the fitness of things in a world where two artists, both the creation of the one great Artist, are acting according to their natures. There is indeed a bond between man and bird.

The atmosphere and the relationship changed considerably when Ambrose Philips got his hands on Crashaw's poem, or on the tradition in general, and wrote his "Fifth Pastoral." Philips dresses up his narrative with a singing contest among shepherds during the heat of the day, with one Cuddy telling the story of Colin Clout, who "flourish'd in *Eliza*'s reign,"[7] and his contest with a nightingale—making a contest within a contest. Cuddy reports that Colin began by playing on a pipe, which the bird easily equaled. Annoyed by his failure, he "determin'd once to try / How art, exerting, might with nature vy; / For vy could none with either in their part, / With her in nature, nor with him in art" (ll. 57-60).[8] Colin played more vigorously, but still the nightingale matched or surpassed him. Finally he picked up his harp, a rather underhanded trick, and defeated the bird. Distressed at losing the contest, she drooped, and "Down, breathless, on the guilty harp she fell" (l. 120). Colin regretted his victory, shed unavailing tears, broke the strings of his harp, and lamented in various other ways. In the end, as a gesture of atonement, he made the nightingale a little tomb set about with flowers and an osier fence. And, of course, Cuddy wins the praises of all the shepherds for telling Colin's story. The implications are vastly different from those of Crashaw's poem. Besides adding the paraphernalia of the shepherds and the second-hand narration, which emphasize the tradition of pastoral poetry, Philips has broken the mystic harmony of man and nature seen in Crashaw's poem and has substituted the dichotomy of art and nature, with art proving superior to the music of nature but tainted with guilt in the demonstration of its superiority.[9] The human world in this poem is quite separate from the world of nature; it is another order of creation altogether.

Lady Winchilsea's poem has similarities to and differences from both Crashaw's and Philips's poems. In historical terms, it has both metaphysical and Augustan elements. Like all her predecessors, she pits human being against bird. But the terms of the contest differ: words are to be matched with music, not music with music. Each artist is to perform in her own natural and characteristic medium. The most radical difference is in the outcome—Lady Winchilsea's nightingale wins. It is the only one I have found in the nightingale contest poems of the period to do so. The possibility of a victorious bird is suggested in Sylvester's translation of DuBartas, the Fifth Day of the First Week, but the outcome of the contest is not described. Lady Winchilsea's victorious bird is, it seems, original. And, again as far as I have been able to discover, hers is the only nightingale contest poem written by a woman.

The poem begins with the poet's command to the bird to sing: "Exert thy Voice, sweet Harbinger of Spring!" The command suggests human superiority. Yet the poet is attuned to the bird: this is the appropriate time for the bird to sing and the poet is prepared not only to write the words but also to heap praise on the skillful singer. Their relationship does not begin as a contest. Instead, a partnership is suggested, words to be tailored to fit the music. After all, birds and poets have much in common: both are wild creatures; both sing best when they are suffering, when the breast is placed against a thorn.

At this point, Lady Winchilsea uses a masculine pronoun for "th'unhappy Poet," which raises a number of questions and possibilities. It is probably not a typographical error: the 1713 volume, which is well printed and lists only a few obvious errors as errata, prints "he." One cannot take it as the poet trying to disguise her sex, for the 1713 title page proclaims that the poems are by "a Lady." One could pass it off as a slip of some sort; most eighteenth-century poets were men, and "poet . . . he" would almost write itself. But Lady Winchilsea was more careful of detail than that.

The picture is further complicated by the facts of nightingale life. The male nightingale, who arrives in England in the spring, several days before the female, is responsible for the famous song, while only the female builds the nest. Whether Lady Winchilsea knew these facts is debatable. She lived in the country, in Kent, where nightingales nested regularly, and might have had accurate information about their habits. But the males and females look very much alike, and some naturalists at the time believed that the females sang.[10] Besides, the story of Philomela and the whole tradition in poetry made the singing nightingale female. In Lady Winchilsea's poem, the bird is consistently "she" and is scolded for neglecting the nest-building, which is in fact the female's job.

If we had a male nightingale and a female poet in this poem, which would reverse the pronouns but fit the facts, we would see a male figure rejecting partnership in favor of a contest and defeating the female who offers words for his music. One could take the poem, then, as expressing Lady Winchilsea's sense of the woman poet's lot, her subordinate position, her inferior abilities due perhaps to her inadequate education. In other poems, such as "The Spleen" and "The Appology," she speaks disparagingly of her poetic powers; in "Mercury and the Elephant" and "The Introduction," among others, she shows, directly and indirectly, the scorn of men for female poets. The defeated female poet in "To the Nightingale," in other words, is consistent with some of Lady Winchilsea's other images of women. This reading is strengthened by the fact that "To the Nightingale" actually shows only the Muse being defeated, not overtly the poet to whom the masculine pronoun is applied, for the Muse provides the words which the nightingale "outflies." And Muses are always female.

With the bird a female, however, and the poet a male, we have a different story. The bird is always "she" in the poem and in the tradition. The poet is "he," if we forget for the moment the matter of the female Muse who supplies the words but could be dismissed as a mere convention. This allocation of the sexes contradicts the natural facts but fits the pronouns—the facts of the poem—and it would not be the first time that Lady Winchilsea had adopted a male persona.[11] This reading turns the tables on the whole nightingale tradition in which male poet defeats female bird—here, female bird defeats male poet. It would be a sweet and subtle revenge.

Disregarding the question of sex, however, there remains the inescapable fact that the nightingale is a bird and the poet is a human being. That becomes the problem. After the initial and brief assumption of human superiority when the poet commands the bird to sing, the proposed partnership and the similarities of bird and poet suggest the unity of all creation that informs Crashaw's poem. Indeed, similarity had been the basis of the various relationships between human beings and nightingales even before Crashaw. Shakespeare, in Sonnet 102, compares himself to a nightingale and claims that he has equally good sense when he, like the bird, ceases to sing so as not to bore the listener. Spenser, for whom great poets *are* nightingales, laments harmoniously with the bird at midnight. Sidney too, in various Eclogues, asks Philomela to help him express his sorrow and comments on the similar reasons for silence in the nightingale and in man. And in his poem called simply "The Nightingale," Sidney and the bird share the sorrows of love, though his are worse, he claims, because he is deprived of his lady while she just had too much of her man; there is an element of rivalry here as the poet measures his male suffering against Philomela's womanlike complaints. But even when there was overt rivalry, as in Crashaw's poem, unity and similarity continued to inform the relationship.

But unity and similarity vanish in Lady Winchilsea's poem

when the bird begins to sing and the partnership dissolves into a contest. Oneness is an illusion; difference, dualism, prevails. We have moved into Ambrose Philips's world of human separateness, but not into his world of the superiority of art to nature, for when Lady Winchilsea's poet calls on the Muse for help ("Muse, thy Promise now fulfill!"), the call is not answered. The bird "outflies" the Muse. Defeated by nature, the human poet then asserts the superiority not of art, as in Philips, but of human values, specifically the work ethic, over the simple beauty of the bird's song: "Trifler, wilt thou sing till *June?* / Till thy Bus'ness all lies waste, / And the Time of Building's past!" Here the question of the bird's and the poet's sex arises again. Although women in the eighteenth century did not build "nests," they were certainly supposed to look after the nests provided by their husbands. Even noble ladies were expected to direct the servants, to engage in "the dull mannage, of a servile house."[12] Anything that distracted them from those duties came under heavy fire, especially when the distractions took such unfeminine forms as reading and writing. The *Spectator* papers, for example, though at times advocating the education of women, kept up a steady stream of disparagement of those women whose learning interfered with their housekeeping (for example, Numbers 242, 328, 606). When Lady Winchilsea's male poet, then, chides the nightingale for neglecting her nest and wasting her time with idle song, "he" voices a common sentiment, one from which she herself had suffered. "He" deserves to be defeated by the bird.

On another level, calling the bird a "trifler" is sour grapes, and Lady Winchilsea, with her human self-consciousness, knows it, as the last six lines indicate. Here she holds the human poet up to ridicule, mocking his claim to superiority over the bird. But the human poet is not therefore simply inferior to the bird. He, or she, is different. The poet has "Speech / Unlike what thy Forests teach," something that sets human beings apart from the rest of creation.

By asserting that speech defines the human, Lady Winchilsea was taking sides in a complex debate. In her time as in ours, mankind was difficult to define. When some thinkers claimed that beasts had reason and a form of speech, possessed souls, and could even look forward to a life after death, perhaps on Mars, the traditional boundaries were clearly being threatened. Orthodox theologians rejected such ideas and clung to the immortal soul and its manifestations in reason and speech as the distinguishing characteristics, while the new scientists rejected the old ideas of analogies and resemblances between man and nature in favor of a neutral and objective approach.[13] Lady Winchilsea, then, is both scientifically up to date (and not metaphysical or Romantic) in her sense of the separateness of humanity from the rest of the creation, and theologically conservative in her assignment of speech as the distinguishing characteristic of the human. And yet the conservative definition tends to imply the superiority of the human. John Ray, Ben Jonson, and Bishop Wilkins, for example, agreed that speech was peculiar to man and beyond the capacities of inferior beasts.[14] Lady Winchilsea's poem is thus profoundly ironic when the artless music of the mere bird defeats the poet's highest and most human skill, the art of speech. She affirms differentness, but she leaves open the question of human superiority.

The idea of speech as a uniquely human attribute and, indeed, the idea of the limitations of speech recur frequently in Lady Winchilsea's poems. Most often she uses the word "syllables" to indicate human speech, implying, I think, that, though language may differentiate man from beast, it is not a simple gift of God but a human construct, capable of being analyzed into its component parts, and that, as a human construct, it has limited powers. In the nightingale poem, she asks if the Muse can "refine" her presumably rough-and-ready syllables to make them a suitable accompaniment for the bird's music. Elsewhere, in "A Letter to the Same Person" (her husband), she finds herself unable to express the fullness of her love and concludes:

But since the Thoughts of a Poetick Mind
Will never be to Syllables confin'd;
And whilst to fix what is conceiv'd, we try,
The purer Parts evaporate and dye:
You must perform what they want force to do,
And think what your ARDELIA thinks of you.

[P. 24, ll. 25-30]

Lady Winchilsea's most anthologized poem, "A Nocturnal Reverie," contains another example. She describes the sights, sounds, and fragrances of the night in which the spirit feels "a sedate Content" (p. 269, l. 39), when "silent Musings urge the Mind to seek / Something too high for Syllables to speak . . ." (ll. 41-42).[15]

This example, and less indirect lines here and in other poems, indicate not only that speech differentiates human beings from the rest of the creation, but also that the possession of an immortal soul, which speech implies, is their highest glory. Indeed, many times Lady Winchilsea speaks of heaven as the true home of the human soul. The idea appears indirectly in "A Nocturnal Reverie," when the soul grows quiet and "Joys in th'inferiour World, and thinks it like her Own" (l. 46). The emphasis is on "thinks"; the world of the soul is not the world of the nonhuman creation, though it is refreshing to pretend that it is, to rest temporarily from the burdens of humanness. The animals have no such burdens because they have no heavenly home, as Lady Winchilsea implies at the end of a short poem called "The Bird and the Arras." The bird in this poem has flown into a room in which an arras covers a wall; the arras depicts a grove of trees, and does it so well that the bird is deceived. She flies up into the tapestry trees and bumps her head on the ceiling, then tries again and dashes herself against a windowpane. Finally, someone opens the window and shoos the bird out: "some kind hand directs the certain way / Which through the casement an escape affords / And leads to ample space the only Heav'n of Birds" (p. 51, ll. 19-21). Birds belong to a lower order of creation, or at least a different order; they have no souls, no heaven beyond the sky. This essential difference underlies "To the Nightingale" as well and is part of the reason why the human poet, male or female, cannot participate in the music of the bird.[16]

The poet scolds the bird for neglecting her nest, and the poem concludes with an analysis of the sour-grapes reaction to defeat:

> Thus we Poets that have Speech,
> Unlike what thy Forests teach,
> If a fluent Vein be shown,
> That's transcendent to our own,
> Criticize, reform, or preach,
> Or censure what we cannot reach.

The song of the bird *is* superior; the poet "cannot reach" it. Must one then close the open question and conclude that nature is superior to art and that humanity is shockingly inferior to the beasts? The dualism is there, as in Philips's pastoral, and he, following the usual Augustan impulse to make judgments, judged that art and humanity are superior. The issue, as I have indicated, was complex, and the debate about it took various forms. But Lady Winchilsea's poem does not adopt the common form of a simple dichotomy between art and nature, nor does she make a simple choice between them. In another poem she does make such a choice—but that choice is part of the wit of the invitation to her husband to leave his books and come for a walk in the fields with her.[17] In "To the Nightingale" she makes no choice in the sense of a value judgment; instead, at the end of the poem, she emphasizes the separateness of the human world with its propensity to make moral judgments, to "Criticize, reform, or preach," which birds never do. And she criticizes biased, self-interested human judgments: "Or censure what we cannot reach." The poet implicates herself—or the "he" persona—in that criticism. She has been typically human in her attack on the bird. She, who had thought that the worlds of bird and poet, of animal and man, were alike, and had proposed a partnership, has been proved wrong, and proved human, by her defeat.

Other dualisms besides those of art and nature and man and beast underlie the argument of "To the Nightingale," dualisms that are part of the philosophical assumptions and critical vocabulary of the period. Passion is set over against Reason, as the poet who writes from personal pain suddenly turns practical and scolds the nightingale for delaying its nest-building. Wit and judgment, as Locke defined them, shape the argument of the poem: wit, the faculty which consists in the assemblage of ideas, makes the poet see herself as akin to the bird, while judgment, which lies in separating carefully, shows her that she belongs to a different order of being. The dualisms and the progression from partnership to contest and defeat show that the poem comprehends two opposing sensibilities without reconciling their differences, without closing all the questions. Perhaps the tragedy is that the differences between all the twos cannot be reconciled, something that Lady Winchilsea knew but that Wordsworth had to find out.

"To the Nightingale" is part of an ancient and ongoing tradition. Like all pastoral poems which celebrate nature, it is a work of high and conscious art. Like all the nightingale contest poems, it has something to say about the relationship between the contestants. And, like all good poems, it is also original and new. Lady Winchilsea has refreshed the tradition by bending it to the expression of her own complex, coherent, and unique thought.

FOUR

TOWN ECLOGUES

Lady Mary Wortley Montagu and John Gay

BEFORE SHE WENT to Constantinople and wrote the letters for which perhaps she is best known today, Lady Mary Wortley Montagu spent a year and a half in London. While her husband worked at his government job, eventually winning the post of Ambassador to the court of Turkey, Lady Mary shone in court society, continued her old friendship with Congreve and other literary men, and made the acquaintance of still others, including John Gay. She also continued writing. She had read voraciously and had written both prose and verse from the age of twelve. Some of her early writing is pastoral: in her first manuscript album she called herself "Strephon"; she wrote poems praising the country, and she imitated Virgil's tenth eclogue.[1] In London, the pastoral was to reappear in her poetry in a different form.

John Gay, today best known as the author of *The Beggar's Opera* and the *Fables,* is credited with having written the first English "town eclogue," "Araminta" (1713).[2] The genre is a curious one, part pastoral, part burlesque, sometimes imitating a classical model, sometimes not. It is clearly enough defined to be recognizable, yet loose enough to allow a variety of attitudes and forms. Adina Forsgren, in her two-volume study of Gay, describes the genre and its mixed nature in detail.[3] Gay published five such poems, following "Araminta" with "The Toilette" and three more in his collected poems of 1720. Lady Mary wrote six, published for the first time as a group in 1747, but composed during her stay in London in 1715-1716 when she first met Gay.[4] One of her eclogues is also called "The Toilette"; it is the "Friday" poem in the group of six that is arranged in a "week" like Gay's *Shepherd's Week* (1714). Clearly there are connections, although, with one exception, the relationships among the poems by the two poets are general rather than particular.

The exception is "The Toilette," in which the relationship is direct, even intimate—bewilderingly so. "The Toilette" was first published in 1716 by the unspeakable Edmund Curll, in (of course) an unauthorized edition. He suggested that Lady Mary might have written the poem, or Pope, or Gay.[5] A much revised text, authorized, appeared in Gay's *Poems on Several Occasions* in 1720. But a manuscript album of Lady Mary's includes not only Curll's version of the poem but also a statement that she wrote every line of it herself. Pope thought it was "almost wholly Gay's";[6] Walpole republished it in 1747 as Lady Mary's, whose eclogues he preferred to Gay's.[7] Robert Halsband surveys and analyzes the whole problem and concludes that Lady Mary could not seriously claim it as hers,[8] but Isobel Grundy, in the Halsband/Grundy edition of Lady Mary's work, not only includes the poem in the earliest version but also says that Gay's version of 1720 "really amounts to a different poem" (p. 182). It could be the product of some sort of collaboration, with Gay and Lady Mary working together on the first version and Gay adapting and lengthening it for his 1720 version. We can never really know. And even if one could call up their ghosts and ask just who wrote what, they might not be able to answer. When two minds, working closely together, produce a poem or a novel or other literary work, ideas and words and phrases are somehow generated by the partnership in a manner that mysteriously defies individual attribution. Perhaps that is the explanation.[9]

But no matter who wrote what, Gay clearly laid claim to the
1720 version, consisting of 106 lines, while Lady Mary laid
claim to the 1716/1747 version, consisting of 78 lines. If she did
not write all of it, she at least preferred it enough to call it her
own. These claims represent an inextricable tangle of creative
and critical activities: the generating of words and phrases and
the revisions, omissions, and additions of words and phrases.
The result of all this, as Grundy says, is indeed two quite different poems, which I shall call for convenience Lady Mary's poem
and Gay's poem. What matters, at least for my purposes here,
is not the technical question of attribution, but which poet laid
claim to which version—that is, which poet took responsibility
for which ideas and point of view. For this comparison I shall
use Lady Mary's text as printed in Grundy and Halsband, and
Gay's text as printed in Dearing and Beckwith, without considering the minutiae of variations from one edition to another of
either poem. Nor shall I look at every verbal variant between
the two basic texts; many are so slight as to be insignificant, and
besides, it would be foolish to search for significance on a mi-
croscopic level when the whole question of authorship is so
tangled. But major differences in content and organization, in
omissions and inclusions, and even, occasionally, in single
words, are worth examining in order to show how two different
sensibilities, a woman's and a man's, perceived and felt about
the same female character and the same urban scene.

Lady Mary's poem (see the appendix) opens with ten lines
describing Lydia, now thirty-five years old, deserted by the
many lovers who had once crowded the street before her door;
now she has nothing to do but look out her window or into her
mirror.[10] The body of the poem (ll. 11-68) is Lydia's lament for
her lost youth, speculation about how she shall pass the time
today, and fury at Damon, her faithless lover, who has deserted
her for his own young wife, Cloe. Lydia heaps abuse on Cloe
and on the institution of marriage until her maid appears, carrying her bandbox, and compliments Lydia fulsomely on her

appearance. Lydia then smiles and prepares to go to the play-house (ll. 69-78).

Gay's poem (see the appendix) opens with twenty-two lines describing the deserted Lydia, with much more detail about her dressing room, populated by "Shocks, monkeys and mockaws" (l. 9) who behave in a comically human fashion, and with observations about her hair and make-up. The fuller detail does not include a window as Lady Mary's poem does, however; Gay does not give us a Lydia who feels trapped. Again, the body of the poem is Lydia's lament (ll. 23-98), also more detailed but covering the same ground of regret for lost youth, distress about how to spend the time today, and jealousy of fifteen-year-old Chloe. This Chloe, however, is not Damon's wife but a rival mistress. Lydia speculates unhappily about the possible marriage and Chloe's probable behavior as a wife. She breaks down in passionate sobbing until the maid appears with bandbox and flattery. The upshot is the same—a smile and preparation for the playhouse (ll. 99-106).

Halsband notes that Lady Mary's poem is "the wittier, more paradoxical version," a beginning, in general terms, of the job of defining the differences.[11] The major difference of "fact" in the two poems, a highly significant difference, is Chloe's status as wife in Lady Mary's poem and new mistress in Gay's. Chloe, and Lydia's jealousy of her, dominate Gay's poem. His Lydia introduces Chloe's name in the tenth line of her soliloquy. After lamenting that she is no longer the "fav'rite Toast" of the beaux (l. 24), that no one writes her name on glass with his diamond any more or sends misspelled rhymes or bows to her in the playhouse or escorts her to her coach after the play is over, she concludes (in lines that Lady Mary does not use), "Ah hapless nymph! Such conquests are no more, / For *Chloe's* now what *Lydia* was before!" (ll. 31-32). Chloe has displaced Lydia; more particularly, young Chloe has displaced middle-aged Lydia. The word "For" carries considerable weight as Lydia explains to herself why she fell from power. Her age had something to do with it, but the emphasis falls on the personal, individual rivalry with her successor.

Lady Mary's Lydia does not name Cloe until she is more than halfway through her lament. Otherwise, her Lydia's opening lines are almost identical with Gay's, except for one detail: in the playhouse, the beaux used to respond to her "wand'ring Eyes" (l. 15), which may hint at some purposeful glancing about, in contrast to Gay's "restless eyes" (l. 27), clearly without purpose and perhaps bespeaking boredom and vacuity of mind. Lady Mary's Lydia lists the attentions she has lost, the same list as Gay's, but gives no explanation for her loss beyond her age. There is no one rival, there are no excuses, she is not a pseudo-pastoral "hapless nymph." While both Lydias say the "spring of Life" is "for ever lost," Lady Mary's Lydia is realistic and hardheaded enough to seek no further reasons for her loss of power over the men.

Having mourned for her lost youth, Lady Mary's Lydia then turns to the practical problem of how to get through the "hatefull Day" (l. 19). She contemplates going to church, but at "these unmodish hours" of the morning (l. 21) she would meet no one there except "ancient Matrons ... And grey religious Maids" (ll. 22-23), an appalling prospect. If she appeared among such company, she would be known to "Dispair" (l. 24), to have given up, which she is not yet ready to do. She gathers her strength; church is out of the question. She decides to dress and go shopping instead, mentioning with interest the available treasures in the fashionable stores. But shopping won't really do either, because she would have to pay for anything she acquired, even a mere fan (ll. 33-34). Lady Mary's Lydia does not dwell on the point, but beauty commanded presents[12] and fans were often a gentleman's gift to a lady; in Gay's poem, Lydia's pet monkey "gallants" her fan, that is, breaks it as a gentleman would to get her to accept a prettier one from him (l. 12 and note). Lady Mary's Lydia has no more gallants, not even a monkey. She may be short of money as well—the two conditions often went together. At any rate, shopping too is out of the question.

Gay's Lydia contemplates the same alternatives, church or shopping (ll. 43-66). She rejects church in almost identical language. She dwells on the treasures available in the shops in almost identical language, but then, instead of two lines on having to pay for her own fans, Gay gives her ten lines of sentimental reminiscence: she will not go shopping after all because the shop will remind her of Damon, who won a raffle prize there which he gave to her while at the same time losing his heart to Chloe. It was their first meeting, "th'ill-fated cause of all my smart" (l. 61), Lydia moans. The raffle prize, a piece of china, fell and shattered—"Sure omen," she concludes portentously, "that thy vows would faithless prove; / Frail was thy present, frailer is thy love" (ll. 65-66). The "omen," like the "tott'ring *China*" in *The Rape of the Lock*, is mildly mock-heroic,[13] a tone that comes and goes throughout the town eclogues of both Gay and Lady Mary. Here, its hollow inflation tends to undercut the sentimental grief of Gay's Lydia and to keep the reader from feeling very sorry for her. Lady Mary's Lydia expressed no such sentimental grief. A practical woman, she did not want to pay for her fan. On the subject of a paying gallant, she was silent, transparently silent. Her overt concern is deflected from man to money.

Unwilling or unable to go to church or to the shops, Lady Mary's Lydia turns to a burst of rhetoric to relieve her feelings: "How am I cursed! unhappy and forlorn, / My Lover's Triumph, and my Sexes Scorn!" (ll. 35-36). Here is the first mention of a more or less specific lover; nothing yet about a specific rival. She is humiliated because her lover has discarded her, and the one who chooses to break off an affair is the winner; the loser is scorned by all the rest of her own sex. Lydia goes on to list five examples of "false" behavior, compared to which Damon's "Oaths are all sincere" (ll. 37-42). The list exploits the formal rhetorical possibilities of the heroic couplet neatly: "False is the

pompous Griefe of youthfull Heirs, / False are the loose Coquettes inveigling airs, / False is the crafty Courtier's plighted
word. . . ." And so on.

Gay's Lydia uses much the same list, but before she exclaims
"How am I curst!" she compares her misery to the happiness of
her parrot and her monkey, who, although confined in cage and
fetters respectively, are happy in that they have never known
love, rivals, or the falsity of a lover's vows (ll. 67-70). But where
Lady Mary's Lydia uses two appositives to describe herself
("My Lover's Triumph, and my Sexes Scorn"), Gay's Lydia
cries that she is cursed "With perjury, with love, and rival's
scorn!" (l. 72). Gay uses some form of the word "perjury" four
times in his poem, and the idea in other terms is pervasive;
Lady Mary uses the word once (l. 67), and the idea is suggested
in only part of the poem. Even considering the difference in
length of the two poems, "perjury" clearly takes on much
greater emphasis in Gay's poem. Damon has lied to Lydia; love
itself is a curse, and she still loves; and the scorn of a single
rival (named as Chloe many lines earlier) is unbearable. Emphasizing perjury, Gay's Lydia lists the sorrows that have been
visited upon her; Lady Mary's Lydia describes herself in appositives as *a* triumph and *a* scorn. Although their sufferings are
similar, the different syntax creates subtly different effects: Gay's
Lydia is a self-pitying victim of perjury upon whom three
curses have been visited, while Lady Mary's Lydia is an object,
a "stronger" rather than a "softer" image, consistent with her
single reason for her loss of sexual power and her practical comments on shopping.

Gay's Lydia proceeds with the list of comparisons, mentioning the "loose Coquet" first (l. 73), perhaps because her Chloe
is a flirting mistress and not a wife and is very much uppermost
in her mind. The other comparisons are identical except for one
word: for Gay's Lydia, the hypocritical courtier is "cringing" (l.
75), while for Lady Mary's he is "crafty" (l. 39). Given the
problems of authorship, the point may be too small to dwell on,
but it may be indicative that Gay uses an image of weakness

and servility, while Lady Mary describes strength and purpose. It would fit.

After her rhetorical blast at Damon for his insincerity, Lady Mary's Lydia finally takes up the question of a specific rival: "For what young Flirt, Base Man! am I abus'd? / To please your Wife am I unkindly us'd?" A "young flirt," a rival mistress, naturally comes to mind first. But . . . could it be a *wife?* The intended tone of this line must be incredulity. The mores of Queen Anne's and George I's London were not those of Charles II's, in which affection and faithfulness between spouses were rare and radically unfashionable. Nevertheless, the old attitudes were not unknown. Lady Mary's own husband found Mrs. Steele "simple" for loving Mr. Steele,[14] and whether Wortley Montagu loved Lady Mary in any sense of that nearly indefinable word is a vexed question. Certainly their lengthy courtship and their marriage, in 1712, just a few years before "The Toilette," produced more pain than joy. And many of the wives Lady Mary knew made "secret complaints" of their husbands.[15] She could very well have been surprised, even incredulous, to hear of a wife more kindly treated than a mistress. Autobiography and social history aside, the whole genre of the town eclogue supports the idea of incredulity of tone in the line under discussion here. Town eclogues are generally satirical, the pastoral conventions serving as "a mode of comment on the perversion of urban values"; genuine love is not possible in this urban world.[16] Lady Mary's Lydia, very much a creature of the town, is disappointed but not surprised at being jilted; she is, however, in the perverted pastoral context, taken aback at the very possibility of marital love, or at least at the possibility that a man might prefer his own wife.

Lady Mary's Lydia goes on to describe all the things that are wrong with Damon's wife, soon to be identified as Cloe (l. 56), faults of body and mind that heighten her incredulity at Damon's preference. Her jealousy is clear, but she takes the stance of objectively analyzing Cloe's faults, strengthening the appearance of that stance by naming some of her rival's good points as well. Cloe has "Peaches bloom" in her complexion, "But does her nearer whisper breathe Perfume?" (ll. 45-46). Her "taper Shape" is attractive, "But don't you [as her husband] see her unconfin'd by Stays?" (ll. 47-48). She is attacking Damon's insensitivity, his low standards, as well as Cloe's shortcomings of bad breath and a sagging figure. Granted Cloe is young: "She doubly to fiveteen may claim pretence, / Alike we read it in her Face, and sense" (ll. 49-50). She has both the face and the stupidity of a teenager. The attack, with the pretense of objectivity and the dispassionate language, is vicious.

Gay's Lydia says much the same about her rival, given that the Chloe in this poem is not a wife. The points about complexion, breath, youthful face, and youthful sense are the same. Since Damon is not married to her, he cannot be presumed to have seen her without stays, but Lydia gives him an awful warning—"Yet if you saw her unconfin'd by stays!" (l. 36)—perhaps even more devastating than the other Lydia's remark because it leaves so much to the imagination. Gay's Lydia goes on to describe more of the unmarried Chloe's qualities: she is careless about her own reputation, and her eyes are deceptive like the fops' "perjur'd tongues" (ll. 39-42). This Lydia possesses no self-knowledge whatsoever when she censures the "young Coquet" for such behavior, for one can assume that behavior to be identical to her own twenty years earlier, since Chloe has taken her place.[17] The briefer analysis of Cloe the wife by Lady Mary's Lydia displays no such failure of self-knowledge.

The two poems have already proven themselves to be quite different works. Lady Mary's Lydia is a stronger character, clear-sighted about her altered status, unsentimental, contemptuous of Cloe and irate at "th'Inconstancy of Man" (l. 10). Gay's Lydia, surrounded by the realistic details of life that he made his trademark in *Trivia*, curses "th'inconstancy of youth" (l. 22), perhaps Damon, perhaps herself, perhaps youthfulness; she is obsessed with her rival and with the perjury of men; she is sentimental about her lost love. She is, in general, a softer character than Lady Mary's Lydia. In the final sections of the poems, the differences grow even more marked.

Having sneered at Cloe's shape and face, Lady Mary's Lydia goes on to sneer at her status as wife: "Insipid servile Thing! whom I disdain, / Her Phlegm can best support the Marriage Chain" (ll. 51-52). That the "marriage chain" was confining to women was a familiar notion.[18] Gay uses the same idea in his version of the poem, though it is expressed more briefly and less strongly: "Let servile *Chloe* wear the nuptial chain" (l. 80). These lines, and the descriptions of fashionable marriage which follow, associate both versions of "The Toilette" with a tradition of literature hostile to marriage.

In plays and novels, satires and sermons, men and women writers of the Restoration and eighteenth century looked upon marriage sometimes with favor, sometimes with hostility, sometimes in general, sometimes in particular. Fashionable upper-class marriage, like that depicted in "The Toilette," attracts a steady stream of hostile criticism, both direct and indirect. Congreve's Millamant and Mirabell in *The Way of the World,* for example, register their disapproval of loveless, extravagant marriages and, in their wonderful proviso scene, set out their own ground rules for a satisfactory and loving marriage, though still a fashionable one. Much more directly, Sarah Scott and Barbara Montagu, in their novel *A Description of Millenium Hall* (1762), condemn the criminal waste of money in fashionable marriage, the destruction of domestic virtue, and the bad example set for the lower orders. The satiric town eclogue, with its tacit juxtaposition of urban vice and rural virtue, paints an ugly picture of marriage. Both Gay and Lady Mary use these lines: "Damon is practis'd in the modish life, / Can hate, and yet be civil to a wife. / He games; he swears; he drinks; he fights; he roves ..." while his wife languishes at home among her diamonds or arranges vengeful adulteries.[19] Fashionable marriage is not the central focus of either poem, but it is an important part of the satiric context.

More generally, the institution of marriage itself, and the position of the wife in it, often come under attack in the literature of the period. In Wycherley's *The Plain Dealer,* for instance, the Widow Blackacre, though presented as a ridiculous object, tries to avoid a second marriage because it would prevent her from carrying on lawsuits in her own name. Defoe's Roxana, a more ambivalent figure, resists marriage because she would lose control of her own money and property. And Mrs. Haywood's Miss Betsy Thoughtless, also a somewhat ambivalent character, regrets her promise to marry Mr. Munden not only because it is more fun to be admired by many men than just by one, but also because she fears he will use his authority as a husband to reduce her to the status of a slave. Despite the variety of motives, one can see a persistent concern with the loss of individual autonomy. Lady Mary Chudleigh had summed it up succinctly in "To the Ladies": "Wife and servant are the same, / But only differ in the name...."[20] Wives must suffer and be still, she explains, and ladies would do better to "shun that wretched state" of marriage, despise men, and value themselves properly.

Gay's Lydia hints at this attitude toward marriage when she says, "Let servile *Chloe* wear the nuptial chain" (l. 80); this Chloe is not married, however, and this Lydia is distraught with jealousy—clearly, as Spacks says, "sour grapes" (p. 82). For Lady Mary's Lydia, the case is less clear. From the position of a mistress, albeit a discarded one, she attacks the married Cloe as phlegmatic, an "Insipid servile Thing!" She herself, she implies, is too fiery, too volatile, too vital a person to bear the restriction of marriage. She values herself and her autonomy, her freedom from the constraints and disappointments of a fashionable marriage. There may be an element of sour grapes here as well— this Lydia too is finally called "lovesick"—but she is too clearsighted a person to be dismissed so easily.

And her comments on marriage continue. She gets in a few more stabs at Cloe for being mercenary and thus able to support her husband's sullenness because she is "Powder'd with Di'monds" (l. 59). Then, nearing the climax of the poem, Lydia voices her contempt again: "Her Credulous Friendship, and her

Stupid Ease, / Have often been my Jest in happier days. . . ." (ll. 61-62). By now, the indirections, the rare "Alas" or other exclamation, the patterned rhetoric, the assumed stance of dispassionate analysis—that is, the control—have begun to slip away. We see her pain when Cloe "boasts and triumphs," but she is especially hurt at the thought that Damon "feigns" love to her, because while one could expect such hypocrisy from a husband, a lover should be sincere. Not being a wife, Lydia refuses to be treated like one:

> Am I that stupid Thing to bear Neglect
> And force a smile, not daring to Suspect?
> No perjur'd Man! a Wife may be content,
> But you shall find a Mistriss can resent---
> [ll. 65-68]

These four lines have no counterpart in Gay's poem. Lady Mary's Lydia has already implied the superiority of a mistress to a wife, or at least of herself to Cloe; here the claim to superiority is explicit. On one level, while it may be sour grapes, it is clearly self-interest, even self-aggrandizement as compensation for her feelings of humiliation. On another level, it continues the commentary on marriage, saying that a wife must play a role, must behave in an emotionally dishonest way, while a mistress, free of the marriage chain, may express her real emotions, may act out her resentment. Interestingly, it is only in this context that Lady Mary uses the word "perjur'd," so frequent in Gay's poem. She attaches it to the faithless man, but the implications slide over to the emotionally dishonest wife, who "may be content" but more probably has to "force a smile." Lady Mary Chudleigh would agree.

Does Lydia grow in stature as she claims her freedom and her emotional honesty? Or does she shrink, as she begins to lose her self-control? One's reactions are complex and contradictory, paradoxical (to use Halsband's word). Cutting across this mixture of reaction and putting an end to Lydia's soliloquy comes Lady Mary's judgmental line, "Thus Lovesick Lydia rav'd" (l. 69). It is a shock to see this complex figure reduced by a phrase to an object of satire and to have one's feelings for her thus called into question. The shock continues when the maid appears with her flattery and Lydia laps it up. The contents of the bandbox she brings are compared parenthetically to the cestus of Aphrodite, that emblem of absolute sexual power (ll. 71-72). The comparison is painfully ironic, for whatever power Lydia might have wielded in her youth, she has none now—no power to allure, no power to determine, in this urban context, the course of her own life. She is an object of satire, raving, because for a moment, as she threatens Damon, she thinks she has such power. But the satire is complex. The standards of marriage and the supreme values of youth and beauty that prevail in Lydia's world are being attacked, while Lydia is exposed both for thinking she can beat those standards and for giving in to them at the end as she accepts her maid's flattery. And the reader who has admired her clear self-assessment, her wit, her courage, and her strength, is shocked into seeing that those qualities are short-lived, useless, even ridiculous, in the world of the urban pastoral. It is a bleak and powerful satiric vision.

The reader is not shocked when Gay announces, "Thus love-sick *Lydia* rav'd" (l. 99). She has been raving all along, obsessed with Chloe's triumph from the beginning and vacillating between the topics of Chloe and of her own misery throughout her lament.[21] After her comparison of Damon's oaths to standard examples of great falseness (ll. 73-78), Gay's Lydia speaks to herself, in a manner quite foreign to Lady Mary's (who concludes by addressing the absent Damon): "Fly from perfidious man, the sex disdain . . ." (l. 79). The grapes are very sour indeed when she advises herself to scorn all males. She goes on to describe Chloe as a wife and Damon as a husband, which is speculative, since they are not married, and is hence more indicative of Lydia's fevered imagination than of her powers of observation. Many of the lines are identical with Lady Mary's, but the different situation alters the emphasis and the effect. Gay's Lydia nastily predicts that Chloe will commit adultery herself to repay the inevitable infidelities of her husband (l. 88); then again, perhaps she will be patient, "free from thought and care" (l. 91), and simply bear her condition. She may even tolerate seeing a rival "Powder'd with di'monds" (l. 91). Lady Mary's Cloe is mercenary (she gets the diamonds) but Gay's is contemptibly patient, in Lydia's speculations—or else adulterous. Her vision of the possible marriage is a jumble of extremes, not a consistent critique.

Gay's Lydia goes on to address herself yet again:

> Why are these sobs? and why these streaming eyes?
> Is love the cause? no, I the sex despise;
> I hate, I loath his base perfidious name.
> Yet if he should but feign a rival flame?
>
> [ll. 93-96]

More raving. Dissolved in tears, Lydia is entirely irrational at this point, unable to sort out hatred and love. Jealousy of a rival mistress is her final note: "To her he's faithful, 'tis to me he feigns" (l. 98). We are left with a pathetic image of mental confusion, self-pity, jealousy—an object more to be pitied than censured.

When the maid appears, she flatters Lydia in almost exactly the same words Lady Mary's maid uses, but there is no comparison to the cestus of Aphrodite. That painful irony is lacking. Yet the poem as a whole is not simple or simplistic. Spacks acutely analyzes its mixed attitudes and ambiguities, the condemnation of the world in which Lydia finds herself and the impossibility in such a world of her being other than she is. Gay's Lydia is foolish and pitiable, and Gay's sympathy for her takes away the bite of his satire; as Spacks says, "The satirist's energy disappears in . . . compassion."[22] Lady Mary's Lydia is also foolish and pitiable, but she is something more—she is, as I have demonstrated, in some senses admirable as well. This quality complicates and strengthens the satire immeasurably. The world that dictates the values and behavior of such a potentially strong character is the more strongly condemned, and we regret the loss of her potentialities. We smile when Gay's Lydia stops raving and smiles. When Lady Mary's Lydia smiles, we do not.

Gay's "characteristic note of gentleness" runs throughout his town eclogues.[23] The first, "Araminta" (1713), is hardly a satire at all. Its later subtitle, "An Elegy," seems more appropriate.[24] As in "The Toilette," a forsaken lady laments her fate; her rival has married her "perjured" lover and she dwells sadly on the course of her punctured romance. The refrain emphasizes her regret for allowing her eyes to divulge her feelings and her foolishness in not realizing "that artful Tongue could feign" (l. 108). The setting is the town—park and playhouse, dance and opera—but there is no corruption in it, only a pleasant frivolity and Araminta's charming pathos. "The *Tea-Table*" (1720) has some bite to it, though not much more than a nibble. For the most part, it is good, not-quite-clean fun. Melanthe and Doris, in "alternate chat" (l. 93), wittily assassinate the characters of Sylvia the coquette and Laura the prude. The conversation meanders along cheerfully, with sly, ironic praise the primary style in which the ladies denigrate their two friends. They are artists in slander.[25] The victims of the attack suddenly appear at the end of the poem and are not only greeted warmly but engaged for a card party that night. Gay frequently uses an ironic twist at the end of a poem to underline his satiric point.[26] Here, the twist is amusing but predictable: we are not surprised that fashionable slanderers are also fashionable hypocrites.

"The *Funeral*" ends with two twists. Sabina, in mourning for her husband who has been dead for two months, refuses to accept a love letter delivered by her maid Lucy; she swears she will be true to her husband's memory, she will wear her black veil and reject the new lover—until tomorrow—unless he "comes to day!" (l. 110). The poem is a dialogue between Sabina and Lucy, though perhaps "dialogue" is the wrong word. Lucy's role is unclear. She tells the truth about the dead husband when Sabina praises him, she reminds Sabina of her real feelings, and she praises the new lover. Sabina, however, seems not to hear any of this. The two speakers alternate in traditional fashion, but only one, Lucy, responds to the other. Spacks concludes that Lucy and Sabina are articulating the two sides of Sabina's ambiguous motives and that we can therefore see that Sabina is not all bad (p. 86). One can, on the other hand, see Sabina as entirely and transparently hypocritical and Lucy as the well-paid advocate for the new lover, attempting to smooth his path by killing Sabina's remaining tenderness, however affected it may be, for her dead husband, and by arousing her jealousy of the other ladies who admire her new lover. And her tactics are successful. Sabina does not respond to Lucy but she certainly hears her, and hears what she wants to hear. This reading makes the poem less gentle than Gay's work generally is but does not place it beyond the range of tone he characteristically uses. Finally, "The *Espousal*," subtitled "A Sober Eclogue," could be considered one of the town eclogues, especially since it too treats of hypocrisy, a frequent though not constant theme in these poems. Two Quakers, Tabitha and Caleb, discuss love and faithfulness, with Caleb repenting his former wanderings and Tabitha accepting him as reformed and promising eternal constancy. With his usual ironic twist at the end, Gay concludes this high-minded discussion with the lovers, not legally married, retiring to bed, with the proper Tabitha instigating that crucial move. Gay pokes gentle fun at various Quaker speech patterns and customs, and the poem as a whole seems to say that sex is sex no matter what kind of dress it wears. The anti-Quakerism is mild and the tone more comic than satiric.[27]

One may find that Gay's gentleness makes him a failure as a satirist, that his compassion interferes with his clarity of thought, that he is incapable of serious indictment.[28] Or one may decide that his poetry, instead of criticizing life, is a collection of charming *objets d'art*, "delicate, formalized, artificial . . . the tone perfectly caught."[29] The Gay of these opposite judgments is much the same; the attitudes, and the tastes, of the judges differ. Gentleness presents no problems, however, when dealing with the town eclogues of Lady Mary. The greater vigor of the central character and unambiguous though multipronged satire of her version of "The Toilette" are characteristic of her eclogues and of her attitudes in general, in both verse and prose.

To see Lady Mary's strength in prose, one can open her collected letters almost at random and find strong expression, no matter how complex the feeling she is discussing and no matter how often she changes her mind. She is particularly vigorous in her opinions of her own sex, opinions often far more purely condemnatory than those of Gay the gentle man. For instance, she praises her friend Philippa Mundy at the expense of most other women: "I wish Mr. M. may be sensible how happy he is in that uncommon thing (so rare that like the Phoenix its very existence is disputed), a Woman of Youth and Beauty without Coquetry. In this vile Town, the Universal follys of the fair, the ugly, in short, the whole sex that way ought to make all Husbands revere those Wives that have sense enough not to be led by the Croud, and Virtuous Courrage enough to stand the Laugh that will infailibly insult them with the name of Prudes" (1:206). She addresses Philippa again: "I confesse, contrary to the Generallity of my Sex, I am of Opinion that both good and ill Husbands are of their Wives' makeing, for as Folly is the root of all matrimonial Quarrells, that distemper commonly runs highest of the Woman's side" (1:207). Women, beware women![30] And foolish women are her target in all but one of her town eclogues.

Gay's town eclogues are discrete poems; Lady Mary's form a "week" from Monday through Saturday, like Gay's *Shepherd's Week* (1714). Written between February 1715 and July 1716, the order in which she finally arranged them is not that of composition,[31] so it must have some rationale. It can be seen as an order of increasing complexity of satiric tone and increasing intensity of theme—the theme of loss, observed caustically in others at the beginning and drawing closer and closer to home toward the end. Neither the theme nor the organization is absolutely strict or all-pervasive; it would take a very convoluted argument indeed to force every detail, indeed every poem, into the pattern. And, of course, the theme of lost love is the standard stock-in-trade of the pastoral, urban or otherwise; Gay uses it often. Nevertheless, one can see a special treatment of that theme and a degree of coherence in Lady Mary's group of poems.

"Monday: Roxana; or The Drawing-room" is the most politically dangerous of the poems[32] and the most personal argument *ad feminam*. Returning from court, oppressed by sorrows even more than her chairmen are by their "cruel load" (l. 5)— the lady is fat—Roxana laments the loss of an appointment in the Princess's household which she had expected to obtain. The satiric attack is at least two-pronged. Roxana the prude has engaged in immodest behavior, attending "filthy Plays" (l. 16) and the like, to win the favor of the Princess; the poem suggests that her prudery was hypocrisy in the first place and that her ambition, given her age (she has three grown daughters) and general unattractiveness, is foolish. The second and more dangerous prong is levelled at the Princess: if frivolous, even lewd, behavior is believed necessary to win her favor, her own standards are called into question, although Roxana hypocritically (or diplomatically) says that the Princess is miraculously virtuous in the midst of a corrupt court (l. 54). Court life in general, as well as Roxana and the Princess in particular, is satirized. Lady Mary has no sympathy for any of her objects in this poem. A personal tone gives it added bite: the young, slender, Whig Lady Mary obviously enjoyed getting her knife into the middle-aged, fat, Tory "Roxana," the Duchess of Roxburghe. Roxana's lost appointment stirred up no compassion. The verse pattern may occasionally echo Gay's "Araminta" (p. 183n), but the tone certainly does not.

"Tuesday: St. James's Coffee-house: Silliander and Patch" is the odd poem out in the Week. It is a wonderfully funny bragging match between two gentlemen, Silliander (silly plus man [Greek: *anēr, andros*]) and Patch ("a paltry fellow": Johnson). They compare notes on the favors they have won from various unnamed but noble ladies—rings, shoe buckles, snuff boxes, and opportunities to view specific areas of flesh. Patch wins. Like Gay's "The *Tea-table*" and "Monday" in his *Week,* it is a parody of the pastoral singing contests in which shepherds praise the charms of their mistresses, and as such it expresses, as do all the town eclogues, a sense of the loss of rural innocence. The gentleman to whom it was addressed and the two gentlemen disguised as Silliander and Patch may have felt some loss of dignity. But the poem has no important link to the theme of loss in the rest of the group. It stands with Lady Mary's "Monday," however, as an example of satire that is relatively simple because it is entirely unsympathetic.

The tone begins to change with "Wednesday: The Tête à Tête," the one poem other than "Friday: The Toilette" in which Lady Mary uses Gay's trick of an ironic twist at the end to create satire. For eighty-two lines, the poem could be a truly rural pastoral. Dancinda laments the loss of her heart to Strephon, describing his courtship and complaining in classic style that she dare not yield to him because he would then despise her. The loving woman's eternal dilemma is expressed in conventional terms and yet with strength and passion. Real questions and real issues are raised: dare a woman confess that she loves? how can she conceal it? is love anything more than lust? how can she prove her love without losing the man who asks her to prove it? But then "She paus'd; and fix'd her Eyes upon her Fan" (l. 83), the first hint, apart from the context of the whole group of poems, that we are not in a pasture. Strephon confirms the town setting by taking a pinch of snuff in the next line, and all the lady's passionate argument is called into question. Her image of her own virtue is unequivocally destroyed when the maid knocks at the door and warns her of her husband's approach; Strephon "cursing slips down the back Stairs" (l. 92). The poem has other endings as well. Pope wanted Lady Mary to conclude, after the maid's knock, with Dancinda blaming Strephon for wasting time: "You have but listen'd when you should have kist!" Another ending, by Lady

Mary, gives Strephon a speech in which he differentiates between lust and love, apparently successfully, because the lady allows him to "put out the Light, / And all that follow'd was Eternal Night."[33] Lady Mary's first ending has the advantage of brevity, which makes the shock sharper. But all three serve the same purpose, the undercutting of the lady's lament. Yet one cannot forget that the lament raises real issues, real not only for an innocent shepherdess but also for any woman who loves in a social context that limits her sexual freedom.

This poem has a doubleness, but it is unlike Gay's doubleness, which Spacks calls "ambiguity." Gay's town eclogues arouse mixed feelings toward his characters—scorn blended with pity, contempt blended with tolerant amusement. Lady Mary's "Wednesday" creates two separate reactions: concern for the issues raised and then contempt for the lady raising them. The two levels are sharply distinguished. The issues are obviously important ones, and, being aware of the writer's sex, the reader takes them all the more seriously: here is the voice of authority and perhaps of experience. The ironic twist shows, in a flash, that the speaker is a hypocrite and either an adulteress or fast on the way to becoming one. The condemnation is unambiguous. Although she has been speaking of serious issues, she has not emerged as an individualized character, so she is easy to condemn.[34] But the issues remain.

Concern and condemnation are not kept tidily apart in "Thursday: The Bassette Table: Smilinda, Cardelia." The satiric tone is growing more complex. The theme of loss is central: Cardelia has lost at cards and Smilinda has lost at love. The two ladies debate which loss is the greater, in pastoral singing-contest form. The terms of the two topics mix and cross: the faithless lover is a "sharper" and basset is a "passion." Both love and cards are games, as in *The Rape of the Lock,* and both are passions. The emphasis, however, falls upon the game, for Smilinda too plays cards and indeed lost her lover to her rival at the gaming table. Both the ladies are being satirized: one has trivialized love and the other inflated the importance of cards.

They even seem to be boasting about their suffering, as each tries to top the other in detailing her pain. Both passions are uncontrollable: "I know the Bite, yet to my ruin run, / And see the Folly which I cannot shun," Cardelia laments (ll. 74-75). Cardelia loses her reason when she looks on the charms of basset (ll. 86-87), while Smilinda loses her prudence in the arms of her sharper (ll. 98-99). The lady who is to judge this contest is Betty Loveit. If this were Restoration comedy, one would expect the name to indicate simply sexual eagerness, as it does in Etherege's *Man of Mode*. But this Loveit "all the pains of Love and Play does know" (l. 23), having often tried both. And at the end of the poem, impatient for her tea, she awards prizes to both the contenders. The judge in Gay's "Monday" similarly declares a draw and expresses his boredom with the songs. That conclusion is purely comic, but there are satiric complexities in Loveit's judgment in Lady Mary's poem. It implies that love and cards are equally significant, or equally trivial; that both are games; that in the world of the town eclogue, all passions are the same, though perhaps the passion for tea is strongest. If we had expected love to be more important, as Loveit's name leads us to do and as our own priorities should, we find the poem's satire leveled at us because we do not understand the town.

The same strategy is part of the complexity of "Friday: The Toilette: Lydia," complicated, as I said earlier, by the admiration we are made to feel for the emotional honesty and self-assertion of Lydia, until we find that she "raves."

"Saturday: The Small Pox: Flavia" brings the complexities to a climax. While Smilinda, the forsaken lover in "Thursday," might be modeled on Lady Mary herself, Flavia, lamenting the loss of her beauty to the ravages of smallpox, definitely is. Lady Mary, who was disfigured by the disease in 1715, said she expressed her own feelings in this poem.[35] The value of beauty is the satiric center of the poem. In the marriage market, and in fashionable society in general, beauty was a precious commodity. Money could buy a husband when beauty was lacking, but with beauty, one had a wider field to choose from and needed rather less money. But beauty is ephemeral, especially in an age of primitive medicine and dentistry, and, like other things of the flesh, has no value for the orthodox moralist. That beauty confers power, indeed wealth, on a woman is thus evidence of the corruption of the world. Also, beauty has aesthetic value, which has nothing to do with morality and on which one cannot set a price. All this, along with the fact that the author was expressing her own feelings, creates a poem of great complexity and power.

Like "The Toilette," "The Small Pox" consists almost entirely of the protagonist's speech lamenting her loss. Flavia lies on her couch. "A Glass revers'd in her right hand she bore" (l. 3); the detail is emblematic, ceremonial, like the reversed arms of the escort in a military funeral. Flavia is now *hors de combat*. It is a small detail, but it sets the mock heroic tone of the poem, a tone that comes and goes throughout both Lady Mary's and Gay's town eclogues and that dominates this poem more than any other. Perhaps Lady Mary chose the mock heroic tone because the subject is beauty and its power, as in *The Rape of the Lock*. Certainly that tone works: its elevation and importance fit her own real feelings and the value that beauty had in her world, while its ironic gap shows the littleness of the topic from the moral point of view—the insignificance of ephemeral beauty and the wrongness of those who value it. The mock heroic poet can have it both ways.

Flavia laments, "How am I chang'd!" (l. 5), regretting the loss of her complexion "That promis'd Happyness for Years to come" (l. 8). She is already an object of satire, if she believes that beauty could last. She is morally wrong to think that it could confer happiness on its possessor. And yet, in some respects and to some extent, in this world, could it not? Flavia goes on to reveal how enchanted she used to be with her own image, as Belinda worshiped hers in *The Rape of the Lock*. She dwells sadly on former evidences of her power: gifts of opera tickets, cherries, china, and much attention:

> For me, the Patriot has the House forsook,
> And left debates to catch a passing look,

> For me, the Soldier has soft verses writ,
> For me, the Beau has aim'd to be a Wit,
> For me, the Wit to Nonsense was betraid,
> The Gamester has for me his Dun delaid. . . .
>   [ll. 28-33]

Perhaps one should add this passage to the list of Pope's sources for the following lines in *An Essay on Man:*

> Ask for what end the heav'nly bodies shine,
> Earth for whose use? Pride answers, " 'Tis for mine:
> For me kind Nature wakes her genial pow'r,
> Suckles each herb, and spreads out ev'ry flow'r;
> Annual for me, the grape, the rose renew
> The juice nectareous, and the balmy dew;
> For me, the mine a thousand treasures brings;
> For me, health gushes from a thousand springs;
> Seas roll to waft me, suns to light me rise;
> My foot-stool earth, my canopy the skies."
>   [I, 131-40][36]

Both poets are attacking pride. Pope's proud man lays claim to cosmic importance, while Flavia claims power equally vast, given the scope of her world, power to make various kinds of men contradict their own essential natures. Flavia, who is Lady Mary herself, the men, and their world are all objects of satire in these lines, and yet the grief, like some degree of the power, is real.

Next, Flavia glances around the room and exclaims over her portrait, now out of date, and her toilette, now useless. "Meaner Beauties" (l. 55) may now shine but only because they have no competition from her. The pride, the former self-worship, the boasting are all obvious. And yet, so is the sadness of her loss. Doctors had promised she would be well and beautiful again, but their oaths were false. In the last two verse paragraphs, Flavia counsels herself to "bid the World Adieu" (l. 84), since "Monarchs, and Beauties" (l. 85) are unpitied, even mocked, when they are deposed. The comparison shows her awareness that, in losing her beauty, she has lost her power. She will retire to an "obscure recess" (l. 89) from the parks, operas, and parties of the world, and hide her face "in shades" (l. 94). Real pastoral landscape is to be a retreat from the urban pastoral world, a morally superior retreat in which no false friend will pretend compassion (l. 91) and "Where Gentle streams will weep at [her] distress" (l. 90). And yet, this world, pathetic fallacy and all, is of course a fiction, a literary fiction. There is no place to hide.

Each of Lady Mary's town eclogues can stand alone as a skillfully wrought, interesting poem, sometimes complex and sometimes simple in satire, sometimes topical, sometimes autobiographical. Gay's town eclogues, with their different kind of appeal, are intended as single poems, but Lady Mary has put hers together in a series in which the whole is greater than the sum of its parts. One's admiration for her artistic skill and control and for her penetrating vision of her social world grows as the series unfolds. That admiration reaches its peak when, at the end, she shows us herself, disfigured and in tears, making, as many poets have, good art out of grief.

FIVE

EDUCATIONAL *SPECTATORS*

Richard Steele, Joseph Addison, and Eliza Haywood

THE *Spectator* (1711-1712, 1714), written by Richard Steele and Joseph Addison (with a little help from their friends), and the *Female Spectator* (1744-1746), written by Eliza Haywood, have a great deal in common. Although the *Spectator* was a daily paper and the *Female Spectator* a monthly, their personae appear to be truly brother and sister, as Mrs. Haywood pretends. The introductory remarks of her first book claim that she is proceeding "in imitation of my learned Brother, of ever precious memory," while the last, Book 24, opens with a letter from a correspondent who notes that she "closely tread[s] in the steps of [her] late brother and predecessor, the SPECTATOR. . . ." Both periodicals claim to be produced by a club of friends, a fiction which soon fades in both. Both print correspondence from their admirers and critics, genuine or fabricated. Both use short stories, anecdotes, and character sketches to illustrate their precepts. Although the *Spectator* addresses a wider audience and deals in a broader range of subjects, it frequently concerns itself with "the fair sex" and proposes to "lead the Young through all the becoming Duties of Virginity, Marriage, and Widowhood."[1] The *Female Spectator*, although it occasionally claims to have gentlemen subscribers and publishes letters from some of them, essentially addresses a female readership and is concerned with those same duties. Both champion modesty, good nature, and virtue; both denigrate folly and vice. Both speak to a middle-class readership with plenty of leisure time on its hands. Both have things to say about education, broadly and narrowly defined. Indeed, both claim to *be* educational: while amusing their leisured readers, they are at the same time providing valuable lessons.

Given these many large, general similarities, it is no surprise that most historians and critics of eighteenth-century periodical literature see the two *Spectators* as original and imitator—one of many imitators—and as preachers of the same Word. George F. Whicher, Mrs. Haywood's first biographer and critic, calls the *Female Spectator* a "bold attempt to rival Addison upon his own ground," setting the tone for most subsequent criticism. George S. Marr, who thinks the *Female Spectator* has received more attention than it deserves, comments on "the accredited machinery" it continued to use.[2] Others find the *Female Spectator* "a poor continuator to Addison and his colleagues,"[3] "squarely in the tradition of the *Tatler* and the *Spectator,*"[4] continuing "in the old traditions,"[5] remarks which pertain to both genre and specific contents. A recent study by Eberhard Einhoff concentrates on the image of women and the topics of marriage and education in Defoe's *Review,* the *Spectator,* and the *Female Spectator.* He notes differences in emphasis and greater realism in the *Female Spectator,* as well as a few topics and tones not to be found in the model, but he draws no significant conclusions. David Macaree attacks those who disparage the *Female Spectator* as "merely imitative" of Addison and Steele and finds that Mrs. Haywood's periodical "has a literary interest of its own besides being a fascinating document for social history."[6] Macaree's analysis is necessarily limited, however, because he used only the collection of oddly selected snippets from the *Female Spectator* edited by the Priestleys.[7]

Two critics stand out in this small crowd, James Hodges and Helene Koon. Hodges takes the *Female Spectator* out of the periodical essay tradition and relocates it in the tradition of courtesy literature. In a massively documented article, he describes the *Female Spectator* as teaching conduct in a practical fashion and sees Mrs. Haywood as sincere in her desire to help her female readers deal with the "actual difficulties and problems" of their lives.[8] This comes much closer to the mark than the general run of comparisons with Addison and Steele. Closer still is Helene Koon. Although she begins by saying that the *Female Spectator* "follows directly in the steps of its illustrious parent, the *Spectator,*" she pays more attention to what is original in the *Female Spectator*'s content and tone than to the similarities. Like Hodges, she finds the *Female Spectator* more practical in its advice and in general a more worthy work of literature than it has usually been deemed. Most acutely, discussing the various kinds of female characters Mrs. Haywood creates in her anecdotes and short stories, Koon says that they are "intelligent creatures who, accepting the fact that they have been born into a world they cannot control, seek acceptable models for survival."[9]

Exactly. Survival is what the *Female Spectator* is all about. Cloaked in her similarities to her "brother," the Female Spectator offers her readers heartfelt advice on how to deal with a world that will inevitably cause them suffering no matter how prudent they may be, a world that they must learn to endure: if they will follow her lessons, they will minimize—not eliminate—their pain; if not, they will be destroyed. It is the world of *Spectator* morality, which Mrs. Haywood knows she and her readers cannot alter. Indeed, they will only suffer more if they try. So, with increasing seriousness and a depth of feeling entirely foreign to Addison and Steele, she instructs the fair sex in strategies for survival: social, emotional, mental, financial, and physical survival.

A comparison of some elements in the two *Spectators* will shed light in both directions. The purposes of the two papers, the characters of Mister and Madam Spectator, the various tones in which they conduct their lessons, and the emphases of their lessons, converge and diverge in revealing ways. Comparing these points, as well as the topics and literary strategies they share and do not share and their overlapping and contradictory opinions, will help to clarify what the two Spectators saw when they looked at their worlds.

Mr. Spectator's purpose, often quoted, is familiar: "... I shall endeavour to enliven Morality with Wit, and to temper Wit with Morality.... I shall be ambitious to have it said of me, that I have brought Philosophy out of Closets and Libraries, Schools and Colleges, to dwell in Clubs and Assemblies, at Tea-Tables, and in Coffee-Houses" (Number 10). Hoping to contribute to both the "Diversion" and the "Improvement" of his readers (Number 1), the Spectator often concentrates on "the female World," to whom he believes he will be particularly useful: "... I shall always endeavour to make an innocent if not an improving Entertainment, and by that Means at least divert the Minds of my female Readers from greater Trifles.... I shall endeavor to point out all those Imperfections that are the Blemishes, as well as those Virtues which are the Embellishments, of the Sex" (Number 10). He will eschew scandal and politics; he will satirize vices and follies but not individuals. As Donald F. Bond neatly sums it up, the general aim of the *Spectator* is "that of softening the rough edges of life, of raising the general standards of morality, and at the same time of providing interesting material for thought and conversation" (pp. xix-xx).

The Female Spectator too promises to eschew scandal and to "expose the vice, not the person" in her examinations of immorality (Book 1). She dips into politics in a general way in Book 9 and elsewhere takes a couple of stabs at Walpole, but it is not a major theme. She plans to be "both useful and entertaining" and to communicate her observations about human nature in such a way that her readers may learn "to regulate their own" affairs properly (Book 1). Like her brother, she will accomplish her aims by using both example and precept, example, as she repeats several times, being the stronger method of imprinting lessons on the mind, a point with which Mr. Spectator agrees. In Book 8, she restates her purpose: "To check the enormous growth of luxury, to reform the morals, and improve the manners of an age. . . ." She sounds very much like Addison and Steele.

At the end of her labors, in Book 24, Mrs. Haywood states her purpose yet again, but this time with a difference. Her tone has grown more serious—her entertaining fictions less frequent and her stern moralizing more frequent—as the *Female Spectator* has gone on. Now she abandons the calm language of the *Spectator* for a clarion call to action. She laments the mental sloth and failures in self-knowledge that characterize so many people:

> Hence it is, that good taste, good manners, and indeed all virtues are so little understood.—Hence it is, we are so often deceived by semblances and vain appearances, and mistake the shadow for the substance.
>
> To awaken the soul, and rouse it to a proper exertion of its faculty of discernment, has been the chief aim of these lucubrations; since from a too great supineness in so material a point, flow, as from their fountain-head, almost all the errors we are guilty of.

Then she quotes a letter from a correspondent, written in "so elegant and masterly a manner, as cannot . . . fail of invigorating the most indolent." It is a wake-up call.[10] And near the end of the same book, she combines the call with a threat: "those who I may be happy enough to touch so far as to make them reflect what it best becomes them to do, will easily forgive the friendly call that wakes them from a slumber might be fatal to them; and those who, resolute to persevere, despite for the present all friendly warnings, I dare answer will feel mischiefs, which will convince them which of the two, their own caprice, or the FE-MALE SPECTATOR's advice, it most behoved them to pursue." The energy of her language, with its various rhetorical flourishes, indicates a vivid sense of the serious consequences of wrong thinking and wrong doing. Her purpose, as she perceives it in retrospect, has been to provide the minds of her readers with a similar energy as they strive for survival.

Addison and Steele are cooler in tone. Of course, it is impossible to make entirely valid generalizations about the tone or almost any other element in the *Spectator*, given its variety of authors, attitudes, and ideas. Such variety is one of its chief attractions. But reading through its many issues, one gains general impressions of dominant tones and emphases, not, perhaps, statistically provable, but nevertheless valid enough to discuss. Part of the overall impression stems from the way Mr. Spectator presents himself as a character. He vanishes during Addison's Saturday sermons, during letters from correspondents, and sometimes during essays written by guest authors, but his image is a significant element throughout the *Spectator* papers as a whole, especially in the first 150 papers.[11] Mr. Spectator devotes the entire first paper to himself, beginning thus: "I have observed, that a Reader seldom peruses a Book with Pleasure 'till he knows whether the Writer of it be a black or a fair Man, of a mild or cholerick Disposition, Married or a Batchelor, with other Particulars of the like nature, that conduce very much to the right Understanding of an Author." The irony of the last clause is elegant, and, as irony generally does, places the writer in a superior position, shared perhaps by a few like-minded readers, but condescending to and slightly contemptuous of those readers to whom his teachings are addressed. He goes on to describe the particulars of his life and character, from his remarkable gravity when he was in the cradle to his life as an observant adult in London's coffeehouses. "Thus I live in the World, rather as a Spectator of Mankind, than as one of the Species. . . ." He has the authority to pronounce on human behavior because he has seen so much of it; he writes instead of speaking because he is by nature a silent man. He also has a short face, an amusingly self-deprecating touch that recurs several times. His irony is occasionally directed against himself in other ways as well, though most often in ways that fail to conceal his real pride in his own character and accomplishments. For instance, in the passage quoted earlier about his usefulness to females, he calls their occupations only "greater Trifles" than his paper, on which he hopes they "will not grudge throwing away a Quarter of an Hour in a Day," which sounds very modest. But he has been proudly touting his usefulness at length. He concludes his sentence in a tone of superiority and with clear contempt for the idle ladies he will instruct, who will not grudge "throwing away a Quarter of an Hour in a Day . . . since they may do it without any Hindrance to Business" (Number 10). Mr. Spectator's attitude to women is a complex topic,[12] and his character has more, and more debatable, facets than I can deal with here. Suffice it to say that he is a detached and ironic observer of the human condition for which he legislates.

The Female Spectator too begins her papers with autobiography, but from the outset her tone and her image are quite different from her brother's. She too understands that readers like to know something about an author, but instead of mocking them for their desire, she says that she shares it: ". . . I, for my own part, love to get as well acquainted as I can with an author, before I run the risk of losing my time in perusing his work; and as I doubt not but most people are of this way of thinking, I shall, in imitation of my learned Brother . . . give some account of what I am. . . ." (Book 1). The motive is respectable: people do not want to waste time. Her account of herself begins with her personal appearance: "I never was a beauty, and am now very far from being young. . . ." For a woman, age and beauty are significant; they determine a great deal about the life she can live. Whether a man is "black or . . . fair" does not matter, and the Spectator is quite right in his contempt for readers who think it does. Mrs. Haywood expresses no such contempt in her introduction. She claims to be sincere, she tells of the wrongheadedness of her youth, which was "a continued round of what I then called pleasure," and she describes the breadth of her experience in the world. This gives her the authority for the papers to follow and the lessons they will contain, the authority of experience. Her brother, however, was a grave and silent observer from babyhood, and he is hardly even "one of the Species" of humankind; his authority comes from observation rather than participation. The difference is significant. The Female Spectator, repeating several times throughout her essays that she is sincere, reaches out to share her wisdom with the readers around her. Mr. Spectator characteristically looks down upon his.

When the two Spectators address the topics of ridicule, raillery, and satire directly, their opinions about these modes occasionally meet but more often diverge, as one would expect, given their characters and their stances vis-à-vis their readers. Mr. Spectator devotes more than one paper largely or entirely to these topics, besides frequent comments in other contexts. Numbers 47 and 249, for example, analyze laughter, comedy, ridicule, and related modes with careful attention to distinctions and definitions. His attitude toward these modes is mixed: both good and evil result from their practice. "The Talent of turning Men into Ridicule, and exposing to Laughter those one Converses with, is the Qualification of little ungenerous Tempers," he pontificates, and goes on for two paragraphs in the same vein. But the next paragraph begins, "If the Talent of Ridicule were employed to laugh Men out of Vice and Folly, it might be of some use to the World. . . ." (Number 249), which is obviously how he sees his own propensity to use that tone. Raillery is anatomized in detail in Number 42, the false notions about it and wrong practice of it as well as the right and skillful. Irony is said to be the stock in trade of the "Snarler" (Number 438), yet irony, from the first sentence of the first paper, pervades the *Spectator.*

One could cite hundreds of instances of these modes, from blatant ridicule and simple sarcasm to mixed and complex irony. One of the funniest examples is a letter purportedly from the master of an academy that trains young ladies in "the *Exercise of the Fan*" (Number 102). Mr. Spectator introduces the letter with a pretense of ingenuousness: "I do not know whether to call the following Letter a Satyr upon Coquets, or a Representation of their several fantastical Accomplishments, or what other Title to give it. . . ." We know, whether he does or not. The letter begins: "Women are armed with Fans as Men with Swords, and sometimes do more Execution with them. . . ." The military parallel continues throughout the letter, which describes in detail the stages of the ladies' training and the subtleties of each exercise. The teacher's mind is clearly disciplined and systematic; he analyzes "The *Fluttering of the Fan*" as having these parts: "the angry Flutter, the modest Flutter, the timorous Flutter, the confused Flutter, the merry Flutter, and the amorous Flutter." If a lady really concentrates, she may become mistress of these flutters in three months. The teacher is serious; the Spectator is contemptuous. He is writing ridicule, with, of course, the motive of laughing the ladies out of their folly. The point is hardly subtle; the picture of the female world is, like all satire, unkind. And yet Addison and Steele were gentlemen, advocating polite behavior. In *Tatler* 21, Steele had defined the gentleman as one whose "good breeding is shown rather in never giving offense, than in doing obliging things. Thus, he that never shocks you, though he is seldom entertaining, is more likely to keep your favor than he who often entertains, and sometimes displeases you." Mr. Spectator had to entertain to keep his readers buying his paper, he had to displease in order to fulfill his moral mission, and yet to teach politeness and good nature he had to create a model of good breeding. It couldn't be done all at the same time. So the *Spectator* necessarily varies in its practice, both denigrating and using satire and ridicule.

Though the Female Spectator is not without irony and ridicule, she is rather more consistent in her attitudes toward and uses of these modes. Her official stance, a common one at the time, is almost identical to her brother's: "though I am no friend to what they call banter, ridicule, or irony . . . yet when it is made use of to cure the faults of those persons we have no authority to reprove, I think it highly laudable" (Book 18). She too makes some careful distinctions and definitions: "The difference between ridicule and raillery is so very small, that the one is often mistaken for the other. . . . Raillery is always personal,—ridicule ought never to be so. . . ." (Book 21). Though her theory is like her brother's, however, her practice differs.

From the first book to the last, she comments on behavior that is ridiculous and that deserves ridicule. For example, two ladies at a theater and a prude at a masquerade incurred "just punishment" when they were ridiculed for their wrong behavior, but the Female Spectator just reports on that ridicule; she does not carry it out in her own voice. When her comments are extended beyond a simple judgment and the report of deserved scorn, they generally fall into this pattern:

> . . . despising and despised, without one real friend, she [a disdainful coquette] lives a gawdy, glittering, worthless member of society, and endured by those whose example has rendered her such, on no other account, than that immense wealth, which they find means to share with her, while she imagines they are doing her an honour.
>   Unhappy woman! [Book 16]

And again: "But supposing the subject of our ridicule to be ever so just, that the errors we condemn are so obvious, that there is not the least room to doubt of them, are not we certain, alas! that such errors will infallibly draw on the guilty head a train of misfortunes, which ought rather to excite our pity than our mirth?" (Book 13). The statement of faith in ultimate justice here may be seen as naive and is certainly not consistent with the general sense of the human condition that dominates the *Female Spectator*. But the idea is useful for its moral point and as a warning, and it justifies the mixed feeling of scorn and compassion that ridiculous behavior calls forth in the Female Spectator. When the wrongdoing is more serious, she condemns outright; when it is less serious, pity blends with her mockery. Unmixed contempt, her brother's frequent attitude, is not her way of feeling.

Mrs. Haywood devotes roughly half of Book 21 to raillery and ridicule. She leans on the authority of the Abbé de Bellegarde as she advises caution in "wit"; she counsels against railing at physical defects (though the Spectator had fun with his own short face and with clubs of thin and fat men); she advises us never to make fun of religion or of our parents. All this is very proper. But *why* should one steer clear of ridicule and raillery? The Female Spectator is not content simply to call them evil; she gives reasons.

One reason emerges when she tells a story to illustrate her point about parents, a story of a preposterously thrifty father who at the last minute stopped a match between his son and a nearly perfect lady because that lady adjusted a coal in the fireplace in a manner that suggested insufficient attention to its cost. The son refrained from ridiculing his father, swore his lady to secrecy when he explained all to her, and waited in respectful and obedient celibacy until his father died and left him all his wealth. His prudence in thus honoring his father—and securing his fortune—so impressed the lady's father that he permitted the delayed wedding to take place. The moral is clear: no matter how obviously ridicule would have been justified, filial piety paid. The young man got both the money and the girl.

Equally practical are some other reasons for restraining ridicule. Because it is often assumed that "a woman, who is so fond of expatiating on the faults and follies of her neighbours, does it only with a view of drawing off any attention to her own" (Book 13), a sense of self-preservation dictates that one should control one's tongue. Reputation is in question here, and is indeed a reiterated concern. Once a lady's reputation is damaged by ridicule, it is entirely lost, Mrs. Haywood suggests. Because she "cannot suffer more than she has already done!" (Book 13), the despairing victim will then probably go on to commit more faults, further degrading her moral character. Even if things do not go this far, ridicule is dangerous. One may argue that it can be contradicted when the person ridiculed is present and hears the charges. But the person may be absent. Furthermore, even when the object of scorn is present, she may not have "sufficient spirit, or presence of mind," to answer ridicule successfully. Again, when good fame is besmirched, happiness is destroyed forever (Book 21).

If the worst should happen, if one should be damaged by ridicule, try to ignore it, the Female Spectator advises; that is to be discreet, and discretion pays. Furthermore, one's enemy will be deluded into thinking he can get away with anything and will go too far one day, and so will inevitably be punished. Thus one has one's revenge at no trouble or cost to oneself (Book 21). The appeal to self-interest, typical of the Female Spectator, is hardly subtle. Her brother, too, sometimes makes such an appeal. But the emphasis on reputation is a particularly female perception. In a society in which a woman's reputation was a major part of her stock in trade in the marriage market, the whole course of her life depended on keeping it intact. Mrs. Haywood, who had lost hers, knew its importance.[13]

Addison and Steele offer various reasons why ridicule and raillery can be evils. They speak of clumsy raillery disturbing the amenities of conversation. The object of satire will be perplexed and made to blush; the satirist will not make an agreeable figure in the world (Number 422). The small-minded satirist "cuts himself off from all manner of Improvement," and men are laughed out of virtue and good sense when a ridiculer attacks "every thing that is Solemn and Serious, Decent and Praise-worthy in Human Life" (Number 249). Some of these reasons are relatively trivial; some are more important. All are rather general and for the most part calmly stated. True, Mr. Spectator says heatedly that making a man blush is "a degree of Murder" and "an unpardonable Offence" (Number 422), which sounds serious, but the seriousness seems to depend on an incredibly exaggerated notion of male dignity. When the Female Spectator speaks so often and so strongly of the ridicule that damages reputation, she is concerned not with dignity but with survival.

Not that the Female Spectator was incapable of ridicule herself. Although she indulges in it far less than her brother, her tone is at times ironic and on a few occasions she really lets herself go. In the one book openly devoted to political matters (Book 9), which is largely a dialogue between a Hanoverian

and an English lady, the Female Spectator and her staff laugh
uncontrollably at the Hanoverian's description "of the galloping
progress of the French and Spanish armies . . . in order to reach
these kingdoms. . . ." Her scornful irony is plain:

> Bless us! what a terrible monster is this house of Bourbon! If
> these ideas of it should reach some distant countries in Great
> Britain and Ireland, it might fright the good women into fits, and
> occasion many a miscarriage, and thereby lessen the number of
> future soldiers, which would be a great prejudice to us should
> the war continue, or we continue to be engaged in it till the
> Queen of Hungary, the French king, or Spanish queen, are will-
> ing to recede from the views they at present seem to have.
>
> If any one should think I treat this matter too ludicrously, the
> Hanoverian Lady must bear the blame, who has really put me
> quite off the way of serious reasoning.
>
> But I will return to myself as soon as I can. . . .

Sarcasm is not her usual style. She has obviously enjoyed indulging in it, but she draws back, reminding us that it can be
undesirable.

Sometimes the Female Spectator uses the mask of a correspondent, as Addison and Steele do, behind which to express
her irony. In Book 19, a gentleman advising ladies to study
botany politely excuses them from anything so "old-fashioned"
as preserving and preparing herbs for useful purposes; such activity would not be inconsistent with the Female Spectator's
own view of occupations suitable for ladies, however. There is
irony too in her own voice when, after telling the story of the
adultery of Augustus and Livia and hoping it will not cause any
of her readers to follow Livia's example, she concludes: "It
would be a happy thing if there were no precedents of a much
later date than those of Augustus and Livia, to justify the frail-
ties of both sexes. Theirs, I hope, will be of no ill consequence
to this present age; and as the virtues of the old Romans are
pretty much exploded on the account of their being old-
fashioned, their vices sure will be rejected for the same, if no

other, reason." There is a touch of contempt here for the criterion of fashion among her readers. But here, and on a few other occasions, I suspect that she is having her cake and eating it too—the right-thinking reader would be amused by her irony, and the wrong-thinking reader, believing in the criterion of fashion, might accept the lesson just because of her wrong criterion. Throughout the *Female Spectator,* Mrs. Haywood appeals to any and all motives to get her lessons accepted, motives of the most elevated moral nature and of the most blatant self-interest and vanity. She may be doing so here.

A few more examples. Her satire is keen when she describes a persistent visitor as "a buzzing fluttering kind of animal" and when she lists the thirty-eight pounds' worth of cosmetics required by a gentleman in the army and calls them "the ammunition of this doughty hero" (Book 2). She invents a brief scene from a play to make fun of the taste for puppet shows ("Never did any age like this require a Juvenal"), and she turns the tables on the usual dramatic mockery of citizens with a list of even more ridiculous characters from the upper reaches of society (Book 12). When a lady correspondent accuses her of directing her satire only toward the fair sex, she produces an apparently balanced piece that castigates gentlemen who wear ridiculously long swords and ladies who wear excessively wide hoops. But the ladies come off rather the worse, for she recounts a hilarious incident of a lady so dressed, holding her skirt up out of the mud; when a flock of sheep happened along the street, she dropped her skirt in a fright, and a ram was caught under her hoop: "down fell the lady, unable to sustain the forcible efforts the ram made to obtain his liberty," and everybody hooted with laughter (Book 15). Could the sexual overtones have been unintended? Mr. Spectator too attacks outsized hoops in a lively paper (Number 127), pretending to believe that the ladies are all pregnant. He turns his wit loose in extravagant speculation about other possible implications and consequences of the fashion with mock heroic comparisons to Alexander the Great and the Pantheon or "Rotonda."[14] He has great fun with the subject.

Mrs. Haywood contents herself with a vivid narration which promises both acute embarrassment and the loss of valuable clothing if one's big hoop gets one in trouble. Less "literary," but far more practical.

The Female Spectator is teaching her readers how to survive. Sometimes satirical but more often forthright and sincere, she provides some fun and entertainment but emphasizes practical ways of getting along in the world. She appeals to a variety of motives in her various readership, hoping, it seems, to win assent to her lessons from silly coquette and modest maiden alike. Mr. Spectator is less easy to describe. More aloof and with a wider range of concern, he comes at the task of improving his readers from any number of angles. He sneers and preaches, bullies and cajoles. His purposes and practices are far more diffuse than his sister's.

The topics and modes and attitudes that the two Spectators do not share are as revealing as those they do. Mrs. Haywood has no stories of country life and country society, nor any connected series of stories, comparable to the Sir Roger de Coverley papers. She deals almost always with urban, domestic interiors. She has no literary criticism comparable to Addison's series of papers on *Paradise Lost,* though she mentions various works of literature, which she advises her readers to read for the contents more than the style. Although, like her brother, she has much to say about good taste and about the pleasures and dangers of the imagination, her emphasis is on the expression of taste in social behavior, not on the finer points of aesthetic philosophy which Mr. Spectator expounds. Behavior dominates her ideas on virtue as well; she repeatedly advises her readers to behave *as if* they were virtuous, since such behavior might succeed in making them genuinely so—and if it did not, nobody would be the wiser. Mr. Spectator reverses the procedure: cultivating virtues and extinguishing vices in the mind will produce proper behavior (for example, Number 16). Addison and Steele say they do not deal in politics, and, for the most part, they keep their promise; furthermore, they deem "Politicks and

Matter of State" highly inappropriate topics of conversation for ladies (Number 300) and party zeal bad for the complexion (Number 57). Mrs. Haywood promises that she will write about politics and, when challenged by a correspondent for failing to keep her promise, gives us the debate in Book 9 between the English and Hanoverian ladies, which nicely demonstrates that women can deal with such a topic. Mr. Spectator does not use the debate form. He does use allegory in a number of his fictions; Mrs. Haywood uses it only once, in the story of "the Topsy-Turvyan island" (Book 19). She preaches no formal sermons, dodging many questions of theology by referring them to the greater authority of a clergyman; Mr. Spectator's Saturday papers are frequently sermons. In these and other ways, she can be seen as thinking concretely and specifically, while her brother tends to think in abstractions and generalities.

The Female Spectator grows impassioned on several topics which her brother disregards or mentions only briefly, sometimes even facetiously. In Book 7, she tackles the difficult question of gratitude and ingratitude in matters of love; it is a serious problem and can create catastrophes in women's lives. Mr. Spectator deplores ingratitude to God for His blessings, but he is not concerned with ingratitude among human beings. Prejudice (Book 21), scandal (Book 13), and lying (Book 18) call forth some of Mrs. Haywood's strongest statements as she demonstrates how reputations and domestic tranquillity can be destroyed by these means. Addison and Steele mention the sad fact that prejudice is widespread and they disapprove of scandal, but they devote no serious attention to these topics. Like the Female Spectator, they oppose lies, but unlike her, they will admit the value of certain kinds of well-intentioned lies (Number 234). Always interested in definitions, they divide liars into boasters, castle builders, heedless promisers, and party men. Their qualified opposition to lying is based primarily on the principle that lies are evil, though they appreciate the imagination involved; they suggest that liars themselves may suffer in reputation, but they do not describe the damage liars can do to others. Mrs. Haywood emphasizes victims, the vulnerable; Addison and Steele emphasize the doers.

Mr. Spectator makes no mention of separation and has only one reference to divorce in an amusing letter from a correspondent who, believing that a man may get rid of his wife if she turns out not to be the person he married, claims that his wife's use of cosmetics has transformed her into somebody else (Number 41). The Female Spectator has much to say about these topics and many stories to tell. Sometimes separation is a good idea, she says, and illustrates this point with a story in which the separated couple learn that they really love each other after all and are happily reunited (Book 17). Most often, she cautions that no matter how miserable the marriage, a woman alone is in an unhappier state. She speaks of wicked—and good—stepmothers, the problems of being a stepmother, and the problems of stepchildren. She tells about the pains of a marriage in which the man and wife followed different religions (Book 16). And she frequently mentions the solitude of female life, the hours that must somehow be passed harmlessly when a lady has no genuine claims upon her time because her society does not expect her to nurse or care for her own children, engage in any kind of productive work, or do much of anything beyond being decorative. Despite tea parties and theaters and masquerades and ridottos, such a lady must inevitably be often alone, obliged somehow to fill her hours. Mr. Spectator remarks only that solitude is unnatural for women because they were made to be "the Cements of Society" (Number 158). As he perceives the world, no problem exists.[15]

In making these comparisons, I do not mean to imply that either Spectator is at fault for discussing or not discussing any particular topic, for perceiving or not perceiving the world in any particular way. I am attempting only to delineate what their perceptions were and to show where they converge and where they diverge. A host of further topics and perceptions exist to be compared—the broad and subtle variations are fascinating. The largest and most significant of these are education and marriage.

Education, and the education of women, was a topic of much concern throughout the Restoration and eighteenth century, from Bathsua Makin, Swift, Defoe, and Mary Astell to Hannah More and Catherine Macaulay. The works of Addison, Steele, and Mrs. Haywood have significant places in the mainstream of these varied writings. Both Spectators think that education, generally speaking, is a good thing. Both are aware of the importance of the earliest influence brought to bear on a child in determining his or her future intellectual and moral life, though the Female Spectator, by repeated references, makes more of this point than does her brother. Both find the acquisition and possession of knowledge useful and pleasurable, and both say that the pursuit helps to fill vacant time. In making this last point, Mr. Spectator seems to be directing his remarks primarily toward men (for example, Number 94); the Female Spectator directs hers toward women. The Female Spectator quotes "a famous French author" as her authority for the idea that "Education but polishes, not makes the diamond" (Book 16); Mr. Spectator uses the same image (Number 554) as well as another: "I consider an Human Soul without Education like Marble in the Quarry" which the "Polisher" makes beautiful (Number 215). Certain subjects of study have specific uses. "Natural Philosophy," for example, teaches us to adore the Creator of the creation we are examining (Number 393; Books 15 and 19). Affliction may be more easily borne if one is educated to expect and support it (Number 163, 312; *Female Spectator,* passim). Mr. Spectator sometimes expresses general, sweeping notions (mathematics are a purgative for the soul, as Plato says [Number 507]), sometimes highly practical notions (proverbial wisdom is good for trade [Number 509]). The Female Spectator can be equally practical: if you know something about the actual practice of gardening, you are less likely to be cheated by your gardener (Book 19). And she can be equally philosophical, as will appear later.

Besides these general similarities on education, the two Spectators have some differences—different topics of concern and different emphases and attitudes. Addison, Steele, and, in several papers, Eustace Budgell devote much attention to the formal education of boys. They argue that the less intellectual boys should not be pushed by ambitious parents into overcrowded professions when they would be happier and more successful in trade (Number 21). They argue the merits of private schools and public schools (Number 313). They deplore corporal punishment and the practice of sending dullards on the educational Grand Tour; they support dancing, Latin, geography, and a variety of other studies. The purpose of all this is clear: "The design of Learning is . . . to render a Man an agreeable Companion to himself, and teach him to support Solitude with Pleasure; or, if he is not born to an Estate, to supply that Defect, and furnish him with the Means of acquiring one. A Person . . . may be said to study for Ornament . . .[or] for Use" (Number 353).

The purpose of learning for ladies, however, is to render them agreeable companions for gentlemen. Officially, Mr. Spectator deplores the deficiencies of women's education. He publishes a letter from "a young Woman of Nineteen" who bewails her own ignorance and the nurture which was devoted exclusively to the beauty of her face and figure (Number 534). He replies to a fashionable woman's letter about her young kinswoman's naïveté with a stern statement of principle: "The general Mistake among us in the educating our Children, is, That in our Daughters we take Care of their Persons and neglect their Minds; in our Sons, we are so intent upon adorning their Minds, that we wholly neglect their Bodies. It is from this that you shall see a young Lady celebrated and admired in all the Assemblies about Town. . . . [but] in the Prime of her Years . . . out of Fashion and neglected" (Number 66). He deplores training in husband-getting. Yet paper after paper of the *Spectator* itself is devoted to teaching women to develop the virtues that men admire—chastity, modesty, humility, obedience—and to adopt behavior that will make them agreeable to men, especially to men of sense like Mr. Spectator himself. He calls women's learning "accomplishments" and "embellishments." He promises to provide a list of books suitable for the fair sex, but despite reminders from his readers to fulfill that promise, he never does. He publishes letters from distressed husbands whose wives are spending too much time studying. One wife is picking up a few scraps of Greek, with the result that "she's already too mad for *Bedlam*" (Number 278); another wife is so busy studying music, painting, and modern languages that she wastes all her husband's money and neglects her children (Number 328); a pair of nieces, who "should have been considering the proper Ingredients for a Sack-Posset," are busy turning themselves into Virtuosos (Number 242). These complaints are purportedly from Mr. Spectator's readers and their tone is not simple: the Greek scholar is learning Greek from a dangerously attractive young man, the spendthrift wife is genuinely endangering her family's welfare, and the female Virtuosos are ridiculed for the same activities for which male Virtuosos are regularly attacked. Yet the contempt for a woman's intellectual curiosity is unquestionably there.

No discussion of education for women would be complete without some mention of needlework. Mr. Spectator (in this case, Thomas Tickell) devotes one whole paper to the subject, Number 606. He begins with a letter from an elderly lady who deplores the way the "proud idle Flirts" of the younger generation waste time gadding about instead of stitching. Mr. Spectator agrees with her, without irony as far as I can tell, though it is hard to swallow such statements as "I have duly weighed this important Subject. . . ." He exclaims about the pleasures of embroidering:

> What a delightful Entertainment must it be to the Fair Sex, whom their native Modesty, and the Tenderness of Men towards them, exempts from publick Business, to pass their Hours in imitating Fruits and Flowers, and transplanting all the Beauties of Nature into their own Dress, or raising a new Creation in their Closets and Apartments. How pleasing is the Amusement of walking among the Shades and Groves planted by themselves,

in surveying Heroes slain by their Needle, or little *Cupids* which they have brought into the World without Pain!

It's hard to object to an activity which puts one on a par with God and promises painless motherhood. He goes on, this time to attack women who have the audacity to write poetry:

> This [needlework] is, methinks, the most proper way wherein a Lady can shew a fine Genius, and I cannot forbear wishing, that several Writers of that Sex had chosen to apply themselves rather to Tapestry than Rhime. Your Pastoral Poetesses may vent their Fancy in Rural Landskips, and place despairing Shepherds under silken Willows, or drown them in a Stream of Mohair. The Heroick Writers may work up Battels as successfully, and inflame them with Gold or stain them Crimson. Even those who have only a Turn to a Song or an Epigram, may put many valuable Stitches into a Purse, and crowd a thousand Graces into a Pair of Garters.

As Bond notes, this may be specific allusion to Lady Winchilsea, whose collected poems had appeared in the previous year (5:72n). She wrote in all the genres Tickell mentions and in one poem, "The Spleen," expressed her contempt for embroidery and her preference for writing. Perhaps the rising young poet did not like the competition. At any rate, he thinks embroidery is fun. Furthermore, it has other benefits. Ladies who sew will be too busy to talk scandal and politics. (He seems unaware that one can converse while stitching.) And ladies who sew will not be out spending money extravagantly. Tickell concludes his paper with the story of "Chaste *Penelope*" weaving the shroud to keep her unwanted suitors at bay.

A week later, the *Spectator* published a letter from a correspondent named Cleora, a letter which Bond believes to be genuine (5:81n). Cleora heaps sarcasm on Mr. Spectator for his views on embroidery: "The Virgins of *Great Britain* are very much obliged to you for putting them upon such tedious Drudgeries in Needlework...." She too loves birds and beasts but prefers them as they really are to silken imitations. Gilt leather makes prettier hangings than tapestry, and she intends to go out to buy some immediately "to encourage the Manufacture of my Country." The patriotic motive is sound and the other attitudes understandable and for the most part respectable. But she undermines her own case by claiming, "I hope to kill a hundred Lovers before the best Housewife in *England* can stitch out a Battel. . . ." This undermining makes me suspect the letter is not a genuine contribution. The lady's character is called in question by such a claim to flirtatious power, and that flaw casts a shadow on her rejection of embroidery. Tickell took up the subject once again briefly in Number 632, in a letter from a correspondent who thought that perhaps ladies could be allowed to write poetry when their backs were tired "with stooping to their Tapestry." What he really recommends, however, is decorating a grotto with shells, and he contributes a poem on the subject. Despite the slight concession, the attitude is fairly consistent.

The Female Spectator does not scorn needlework. Yet, like anything else, it can, she knows, be overemphasized. On this and other subjects she consistently advises a golden mean. Her reasons for limiting needlework are practical, as always: "Nor can I by any means approve of compelling young ladies of fortune to make so much use of the needle, as they did in former days, and some few continue to do:—there are enough whose necessities oblige them to live wholly by it; and it is a kind of robbery to those unhappy persons to do that ourselves which is their whole support" (Book 15). Young ladies of fortune need not do it, in fact should not do it, because young ladies without fortune can do little else. She does not appeal to patriotism, like Cleora. She appeals to her readers' compassion for women who try to earn a living. Ladies should not know too much about cookery either, just enough to supervise their employees and prevent being "imposed upon" by them. She concludes, concerning these two skills, that "to pass too much of her time in them, may acquire her the reputation of a notable house-wife, but not of a woman of fine taste, or any way qualify her for polite conversation, or for entertaining herself agreeably when alone." The implication is that a wealthier, more interesting, and generally more desirable man would choose "a woman of fine taste" rather than "a notable house-wife," that life is more pleasant if one can engage in polite conversation, and that, even with such advantages, a lady is often alone. She also implies that needlework is boring rather than fun. Only reading, *real* education, she says elsewhere, can occupy the mind. It is the key to survival.

As the Female Spectator progressed through the twenty-four books of her lucubrations, and as her tone grew more serious, her comments on education became more frequent and longer. I will trace some of these references through in the order of their composition, to show the broadening and deepening of the theme. I am primarily concerned here not with the *Female Spectator* itself as educational, but with Mrs. Haywood's ideas about education, specifically the education of women.

From the first book to the last, the Female Spectator takes note of the profound influence that early training in childhood has on one's whole life and comments frequently on the importance of self-knowledge, most often in the context of knowing one's own heart in affairs of the heart. (Mr. Spectator gives some rules for how to attain self-knowledge in Number 399.) She frequently mentions books and reading, sometimes with a caution against overdoing it and with her usual advice to seek a golden mean: "too much reading . . . is apt to dull the spirits . . ." (Book 4). Like her brother and many other authors of the period, she remarks occasionally on the fact that learning lasts longer than beauty—though she promises only "respect" to the educated lady (Book 5) rather than love, which Mr. Spectator implies will be her reward (for example, Number 10), though more often he says that modesty and other feminine virtues are the only sure winners of love (for example, Numbers 6, 395).[16] In Book 7, the Female Spectator bursts out in a paean to books:

What clods of earth should we have been but for reading!—
how ignorant of every thing but the spot we tread upon!—
Books are the channel through which all useful arts and sciences
are conveyed.—By the help of books we sit at ease, and travel
to the most distant parts; behold the customs and manners of all
the different nations in the habitable globe; may take a view of
heaven itself, and traverse all the wonders of the skies.—By
books we learn to sustain calamity with patience, and bear pros-
perity with moderation.—By books we are enabled to compare
past ages with the present; to discover what in our fore-fathers
was worthy imitation, and what should be avoided; to improve
upon their virtues, and take warning by their errors.—It is
books which dispel the gloomy melancholy our climate but too
much inclines us to, and in its room diffuses an enlivening chear-
fulness.—In fine, we are indebted to books for every thing that
can profit or delight us.

The Female Spectator's own books, of course, are intended to
perform these same valuable functions.

The first sustained discussion of education for women appears in Book 10, beginning with a letter purportedly from
"Cleora" deploring the lack of it. It may not be coincidental that
the Female Spectator chose the same name for this correspondent as Tickell did for his lady who sneered at needlework.
Cleora's letter is a spirited attack on men for denying women
education and then blaming women for being fools: "Why do
they call us silly women, and not endeavour to make us otherwise?" Her good logic continues as she compares Mahometans
and Christians: because Mahometans teach their women that
they have no souls, it makes sense to deny them education, but
Christians believe that all people have souls, and yet, illogically,
deny women the education they need to get to heaven. "There
are, undoubtedly, no sexes in souls," Cleora states, directly con-
tradicting Steele in *Tatler* 172, and less directly Addison in *Spectator* 128, where he entertained the notion of sex in souls as
probable. Cannily, Cleora argues that men should provide
women with education because it will make them "more obe-

dient daughters, more faithful wives, more tender mothers. . . ."
Elsewhere, the Female Spectator speaks of education as valuable for women for their own sakes, but here, addressing those who have the power to grant or withhold it, she makes her correspondent appeal to male self-interest: how can they "refuse us what would so much contribute to their own felicity!"
The Female Spectator herself comments on Cleora's letter at length. Her argumentative strategies vary, including promises of greater happiness for the husbands of educated women. But she also mentions the curse that Eve brought upon all women, that their husbands should rule over them, and argues that women should be taught "how to lighten this burthen"; for their own sakes women need husbands, and they also need to know how to put up with them, a problem which education can help to solve.

She refutes the argument put forth by men that women don't need education because they don't go out to work, saying that men too are often trained in skills they will never have to use. She argues against men who say that they will lose authority in their families, claiming instead that the most domineering women are usually the most ignorant. And she promises that educated women will not neglect their domestic duties.

Among the subjects she proposes for women to study are geography, history, music, dancing, poetry, fiction (in moderation), and, above all, philosophy: "But of all kind of learning the study of philosophy is certainly the most pleasant and profitable:—it corrects all the vicious humours of the mind, and inspires the noblest virtues; it enlarges our understanding;—it brings us acquainted with ourselves, and with every thing that is in nature; and the more we arrive at a proficiency in it, the more happy and the more worthy we are." As always, she gives her reasons. And the link between the study of philosophy and emotional survival will become clearer, as we shall see, when she speaks of Lucretius and of Milton.

Book 12 contains a letter from Philenia describing the ease with which French ladies learn, simply by listening to the conversation of intelligent gentlemen rather than poring over books. The *Female Spectator* contains several passages in which France is said to be superior to England for ladies. This time, she laments the impossibility of such conversation in England because it would look like too great familiarity and therefore create scandal.

Part of Book 15 is devoted to education, most notably a long letter from "Philo-Naturae," who recommends the study of plants and animals as a replacement for fashionable amusements. Even bugs and bees can be instructive and entertaining. He provides a variety of reasons why ladies should engage in such study: it is amusing, it improves one's "divine [and] moral virtues," it "affords matter for agreeable conversation," it helps to pass the time when one is bored in the country, it raises the soul to contemplate the Creator of the bugs and bees, and it will even make one famous if one discovers a new creature. This last appeal is rare in the *Female Spectator;* it is interesting to see an author famous in her own time appealing to what must have been an almost entirely repressed motivation in other women. The Female Spectator agrees with the sentiments of Philo-Naturae and promises us that she and her staff will soon visit the country, microscopes in hand.[17] She follows up his letter here with more thoughts on appropriate reading; history, travel literature, certain kinds of poetry, Bayle's Dictionary, and a list of specific authors are all recommended to produce "Pleasure innate, applause deserved, and virtue unaffected" in the lady student. The Female Spectator concludes this discussion of education with her comments on needlework, already mentioned.

Book 17 finds the Female Spectator and her staff in the country examining snails and caterpillars and paying a visit to a neighbor whose telescope affords a clear view of Venus. Clouds cover the heavens, however, before the ladies can catch a glimpse of Mars, "as if the furious planet disdained to permit our contemplation." The Female Spectator moralizes on parallels between animal life and human life and finds all of God's works wonderful. This expedition and the materials it is concerned with function in various unspoken ways in the Female

Spectator's scheme of education. She provides education herself here with much factual information about biology and astronomy and some of the current questions being debated at the time, such as the possibility of life on other planets. She also provides a lesson by showing herself learning, offering herself as an example of a woman seeking and successfully obtaining knowledge. She also silently cautions about the limits a woman could expect to meet: that Mars refused to appear for the ladies although Venus did is too neat to be a factual account of a real viewing. The same sense of limits appears in the fact that a gentleman demonstrates the telescope, which allows a view of the heavens, while the ladies themselves have only "microscopes" with which to examine the small things of the earth, the snails and caterpillars. And yet the snails are beautiful and are not, she insists, to be despised. Even the lowliest of God's works deserves respect. The analogy to lowly woman is not drawn but is inescapable.

Another letter from Philo-Naturae in Book 19 introduces the Female Spectator's final and most impassioned passages on education. This time Philo-Naturae not only waxes enthusiastic about the way Nature manifests God's goodness, but goes so far as to say that it is a religious duty to study the creation: "But the goodness of Heaven has put enough within our reach to compensate for the want of what is beyond it; and if we neglect, and think beneath our notice those things God has given us a capacity to comprehend, it is a fault, I think, equal to that of endeavouring to explore what he has thought fit to conceal from us." Like the wake-up call in Book 24, this requires us to exercise our minds. The Female Spectator finds that Philo-Naturae "can write nothing amiss" and goes on to talk of science and Christianity, flying machines, further objects for study in nature, and the joys of gardening—not just learning the theory of gardening but actually engaging in the work of it, to a limited extent. (Mr. Spectator emphasizes the pleasures of contemplation when he speaks of gardens in Number 477.) The reasons for engaging in such activities and studies are the same as before: amusement and improvement, passing the time, finding material for conversation. But this time there is one further reason.

Connected to the discussion of gardening, including grafting, is a discussion of what defines the difference between human beings and the rest of creation:

> To content ourselves with tasting the relish of more luscious fruits, which from month to month are successively presented to us;—to smell the fragrance of some flowers, and to look upon the variegated beauty of others, is beneath the dignity of a rational being. If we go no farther than this, the birds of the air, the beasts of the field, and even every creeping insect, enjoy the charms of nature in as great perfection as we do.
>
> Perhaps too, even the meanest reptile may out-rival us in this point; for, I think, it is agreed on by the learned, that the animal creation in general have a quicker and more poignant sensation than is bestowed upon us. It is in our reason, and the power of contemplating on the blessings we receive, that the chief happiness of possessing them consists.
>
> It is that, more than his outward form, which distinguishes man from the rest of sublunary beings: it is that which crowns him lord of all; and if he wilfully degrades himself, and puts himself on a level with his subjects, he is unworthy of the honour conferred upon his species, and ungrateful to the Divine Bestower. [Book 19]

She goes on, with a profusion of exclamation points and dashes (always two sure signs of intensity of feeling in the *Female Spectator*), to speak of the degradation inherent in following the pleasures of the senses at the expense of reason; even "the Mahometan" knows better. The main idea here is common enough: man is reduced to beast if he does not exercise his reason.[18] As a climax in a discussion of education, the commonplaces carry further weight. Women, less educated than men and less encouraged to be rational—indeed thought by some to be incapable of rational thinking—are at a greater risk than men of sinking to the level of the beasts, of losing their humanness. Education for women is not just a pastime. It is a passport to full humanity. Both the Female Spectator and the *Female Spectator* strive to make the reader get her passport, strive against the restrictions imposed by men and society and against the lethargies and frivolities of the ladies themselves.

In addition to education, marriage is a constant concern of the Female Spectator and a frequent concern of her brother. Despite its importance, however, I will examine it more briefly, since much of what I have noted about education and some other topics in both periodicals obviously impinges on the topic of marriage directly or indirectly. The writers' stances differ. Mr. Spectator looks at the topic with some detachment; he is himself unmarried. The Female Spectator has it always in mind as a matter of crucial concern for women, and her staff (however nonexistent) consists of women defined by their marital status: a virgin, a wife, and a widow (Book 1).

Both Spectators are seriously concerned with the choice of spouse, though this part of the topic looms much larger in the Female Spectator's lucubrations than in her brother's. Mr. Spectator believes that it is best to obey one's parents in making the choice but that parents should not force an unwanted mate upon their son or daughter. One should seek virtue and steadiness rather than money and beauty, though money is not to be disregarded. These are predictable sentiments. But Mr. Spectator has not fully thought through the issue. In Number 282, he delivers a satiric Awful Warning about a family of three young ladies who foolishly overestimated their financial worth (and personal merit), with the result that they turned down a series of eligible suitors, delaying their choice until their father remarried and left them worth far less than they had been in fact, let alone in fancy. By this time, the ladies were "on the wrong Side of Thirty," hence condemned to spinsterhood and poverty. Mr. Spectator has some sympathy for them: "I mention this Case of Ladies before any other, because it is the most irreparable: For tho' Youth is the Time less capable of Reflection, it is in that Sex the only Season in which they can advance their Fortunes."

This is a perceptive observation, but he goes on to add a letter from young Jenny Simper, who is doing her best to make her fortune in her youth, a letter which makes her look a contemptible fool: she has her eye on a baronet at church but writes to complain of the profusion of Christmas greens that keeps him from seeing her. Flirtation in church is a frequent theme in the *Spectator* and is always condemned; this flirtation has been interrupted by the clerk of the parish, we learn in Number 284, who arranged the greens on purpose to put a stop to it. There are other and more appropriate places than church in which to "advance [one's] Fortune," of course. But the juxtaposition of the perceptive sympathy about a woman's brief season, and the condemnation of the young woman who is trying to use her season, is jarring.

The topic of choice of spouse appears in nearly every book of the *Female Spectator.* James Hodges notes its dominance and conjectures that Mrs. Haywood spent more time on it than the writers of courtesy books did because she was writing a periodical journal, a genre in which the topic was common (p. 159). True. But it is also true that her emphasis on it is greater than that of her fellow journalists, and true as well that both the journalists and the courtesy book authors cited by Hodges are men. However crucial the choice of a spouse might have been for a man's domestic peace and happiness, the peace and happiness and financial security of a woman's whole life depended on that choice. It is small wonder that Mrs. Haywood said a great deal about it.

She agrees with much of what Mr. Spectator says—that children should obey parents, that parents should not force their child's choice, that money should not be the first consideration but should not be ignored. Many of her sixty-odd short stories take up one or more of these points.[19] Sometimes the parents are at fault, sometimes the child. A great many of these stories are Awful Warnings—the Female Spectator believes in education by example. She is concerned about girls being locked up too strictly, which will make them run off with the first man who offers himself, just to get away. (Mr. Spectator pays more attention to wicked fortune hunters than to their prey.) In Book 1, the Female Spectator tells about the unfortunate Seomanthe, who lived with a sour old aunt and was denied all social pleasures, with the predictable consequence that she eloped with the first man to smuggle a billet-doux to her in church; he married her, true enough, but absconded with her money and left her to live on the grudging charity of friends. Parents can also be too permissive: an ambitious mother tried to trick her daughter into bed with a royal gentleman, but the girl's virtue was firm; she fled to an elderly parson for protection, he married her to save her, and the marriage was supremely happy, which was the girl's reward for keeping her chastity (Book 1). And so it goes, with the Awful Warnings significantly outnumbering the Happy Endings, as the Female Spectator looks at girls both foolish and victimized, at parents strict, avaricious, careless, and downright immoral. In general, she is conservative: if a girl can't bear the man her parents have chosen, she may disobey to the extent of refusing to marry him, but she should not marry anybody else; parents are usually right in their choices, when they are right-thinking parents, and daughters suffer horribly for going their own way; even wrong-thinking parents—unless they are trying to sell the girl's virginity—should, for the most part, be obeyed. In the stories, foolish girls are punished, often mercilessly, with lifetimes of misery. Sometimes blame and pity mix, but conservative standards are upheld. The Female Spectator was not out to change her world or to persuade women to try to change it. She was telling her readers what the world was like and what they could expect if they even bent some of its rules.[20]

After the choice, the married life. Mr. Spectator reveres the institution and deplores the way people of fashion belittle it. He knows marriages often go seriously wrong, but he believes they can also go right: "the married State . . . is the compleatest Image of Heaven and Hell we are capable of receiving in this Life" (Number 479). He offers rules for attaining happiness in marriage: neither partner should expect too much, women should devote themselves entirely to pleasing their husbands, husbands should overlook their wives' faults, everybody should be good-natured. Women are by nature vivacious, needing the natural gravity of men to keep them from being "impertinent and fantastical" (Number 128). When birds marry, the females have the greater responsibility, but not so among human beings: ". . . as in our Species the Man and Woman are joined together for Life, and the main Burden rests upon the former, Nature has given all the little Arts of soothing and Blandishment to the Female, that she may chear and animate her Companion. . . ." (Number 128). Mr. Spectator does not estimate how many marriages go wrong, but he does know what Nature intended.

For the Female Spectator, marriage is more often hell than heaven. Her stories are full of the agony of wives, victims of avarice, neglect, adultery, fraud, rudeness, jealousy, vanity, effeminacy, and every other possible evil. If the wife has been foolish in her choice or indiscreet in her behavior, she is almost always said to deserve all she gets. Many of these fictional wives are perfect saints, enduring their suffering without complaint and with unchanging love for their husbands. One such story concerns Dorimon and Alithea, who marry early and have a son. Dorimon, who has had little other experience of women, then falls in love with Melissa, who bears him a child, which is put out to nurse at a baby farm. Alithea discovers all, rescues the baby, and brings it home to play with her own child. Dorimon happens along and, when she tells him who the baby is and that she has adopted him and loves him, he reforms. He gets rid of Melissa and rewards his uncomplaining wife with a lifetime of tender devotion. However, not all of the Patient Griselda stories have happy endings. Some of the husbands reform and some conveniently die, but a few continue in their evil ways. Mrs. Haywood is too realistic to pretend that virtue is always rewarded. But since she presents it as getting rewards more often than rebellion and disobedience do, her message is clear: the odds are in your favor if you play the perfect wife.

One Griselda solves her problem with a neat piece of deception. For a long time, she bears her husband's infidelity sweetly, and even accepts the situation when he brings his mistress home to live with them, making a friend of the competition. After long enduring, she pretends to fall ill, makes out a will extremely flattering to her husband and urging him to marry the mistress, and contrives that they read it. The husband is so impressed that he snubs his mistress, who flies into a rage and is then quite justifiably ordered out of the house. The husband's renewed tenderness revives his apparently dying wife, and they live happily ever after. This story is reported in a letter, and the Female Spectator confesses herself "extremely pleased when I hear of a woman, who failing, by an artless softness, to preserve the affection of her husband, regains it by wit and address.— Had Eudosia supinely yielded to her fate, and combated her husband's falshood and ingratitude only with her tears, she might have sunk under the burden of her wrongs. . . . but by this pretty stratagem she shewed herself a woman of spirit as well as virtue." The Female Spectator ties herself in logical knots to prove that "What she did could not be called deceit," and explains at length that Eudosia's "wit and virtue" made her deserve the reward she won. One senses that the witty and adventurous Mrs. Haywood herself approved of the trick, even if the Female Spectator felt called upon to excuse it. Nevertheless, Eudosia's strategy does fit with the Female Spectator's general sense of how things work: in another context she advises deceit similar to Eudosia's, saying, "whenever we would truly conquer, we must seem to yield" (Book 10). Yielding, real or feigned, works.

Mrs. Haywood is always concerned with what works, what is practical. Her short fictions in the *Female Spectator* are consistent in this respect with her longer novels, from the early and relatively brief *Lasselia* and *The Force of Nature* to the fully developed *History of Miss Betsy Thoughtless*. The earlier novels are more scandalous, more romantic, with murders, rapes, nunneries, and adventures galore, while the more mature novels bear a much closer resemblance to the English domestic scene, as do the stories in the *Female Spectator.* Yet the message—and the practicality—is consistent. Some young women are shown to be clever and daring, aggressive and adventurous; others are passive, obedient to parents and social standards. Of the first group, only those who learn to accommodate themselves to social standards, to curb their independence and pay at least lip-service to the powers that control their lives, come to good ends. Those who do not learn are punished. No matter how much the modern reader wishes it weren't so, and no matter how much the modern reader suspects that Mrs. Haywood also regretted the taming of her spirited girls, the message is clear and consistent: conformity pays. Mr. Spectator agrees that obedient females are preferable to independent ones, though his preference is based on considerations of virtue and morality rather than the necessities of survival.

The two Spectators often arrive at similar stands by different routes. At times, however, they take opposite positions. Jealousy, sometimes attendant upon marriage, courtship, or other affairs of the heart, is the topic upon which the Female Spectator confronts and contradicts her brother most directly. Mr. Spectator discusses jealousy in both husbands and wives at some length. Number 170 defines the passion as "that Pain which a Man feels from the Apprehension that he is not equally beloved by the Person whom he entirely loves." He explains that "an ardent Love is always a strong Ingredient in this Passion. . . . Jealousy . . . arises from an extraordinary Love. . . ." He goes on to describe the effects of this malignant disease, the kinds of men most given to suffering from it, and possible influences of climate. The next paper (Number 171) tells wives how to "live well with a jealous Husband," sensible strategies such as never whispering to anyone else and never praising qualities in other men that one's husband lacks. But when he takes up the topic of jealousy in a woman, something very odd happens. Number 178 is devoted primarily to a letter from "Celinda," who admired Number 171 on jealousy but wishes to see published "the

Pangs of it in the Heart of a Woman" to complete the picture. However, the letter describes the rudeness of a slovenly and neglectful husband who "come[s] home only to sleep off an Intemperance" and rage at his wife for being in sympathetic tears. Celinda herself says this gives her "the Anguish of a jealous Mind." The letter indeed expresses acute anguish throughout, and Mr. Spectator replies with an attack on husbands whose behavior is not "regular." But the definition of "jealousy" has shifted. One can still say that it comes from "an extraordinary Love" and shows a sense of being insufficiently beloved, but this time the spouse's insufficient love is real—painfully real—rather than imagined. Misery caused by ill treatment is not the same thing as imaginary suspicion.

The Female Spectator does not labor under any such confusions. She approaches the topic diplomatically but firmly:

> Though my late celebrated brother, and many other authors, have given the world their various opinions concerning jealousy, I fancy it will not be impertinent to add something to what has already been said on a subject, which has, and will for ever continue to create the most terrible disorders that can befal mankind; not only because whatever may serve as a preservative against it cannot be too often repeated, but also because I think, with all due deference to those who have hitherto treated on it, that they have not been so copious as might have been expected, and that the greatest part of them have done it more honour than it deserves.
>
> What I mean by doing it more honour than it deserves, is, that they speak of it only as the effect of a too ardent love and admiration of the object; whereas, though this may sometimes be the case, it is far from being always so; and, I believe, we shall find no difficulty to prove, that the origin of it may more often be deduced from the very worst instead of the noblest passion of the soul:—it may, indeed, with great propriety, be called the bane of love; but whenever it is found the off-spring, it can only be of a base and degenerate inclination, not of that pure and refined passion which is alone worthy of the name of love. [Book 10]

She goes on to claim that a sense of self-mistrust is the first cause of jealousy, a timidity and modesty, rather than mistrust of the beloved object. Then pride and restlessness of mind and other undesirable characteristics take over and perpetuate the evil. The Female Spectator grows less diplomatic, more ironic: ". . . this mischievous passion discovers rather the meanest opinions of the object than a too vehement admiration, unless suspecting a person guilty of perjury, inconstancy, and the most shocking and worst kind of deceit, can be called so." Trust, not jealousy, is part of love, she implies, and she illustrates her point with a story, an Awful Warning, in which an unloving, jealous wife is exposed and sent to the country, where she soon dies. Even if a loved husband is unfaithful, she continues, a wife should close her eyes and stifle her jealousy. Reproaching him is likely to make him treat her even worse. Forget about fairness, justice, even morality, she implies. Survival comes first. Mr. Spectator too advises blindness to one's mate's faults, but he is talking about "Blemishes and Imperfections" in a wife's "Humour" (Number 261), not about adultery, a topic he never deals with seriously. He is advising gentlemen how to be comfortable, not how to survive.

The topic of marriage is related not only to the topic of jealousy, but also to the topics of happiness and unhappiness in general, to human nature, good nature, and the immortality of the soul, with rewards for the virtuous and punishment for the vicious. Both Spectators follow up these branching topics, with the differences in emphases and attitudes that one could predict. To follow their paths would be a rewarding but extremely lengthy study. Yet one point of difference, one striking and revealing point, must be explored. Here I pick up again the topic of philosophy.

Neither Spectator views life through rose-tinted glasses. In Number 163, Addison addresses the question of happiness directly: "Enquiries after Happiness, and Rules for attaining it, are not so necessary and useful to Mankind as the Arts of Consolation, and supporting one self under Affliction. The utmost we can hope for in this World is Contentment; if we aim at any thing higher, we shall meet with nothing but Grief and Disappointments. A Man should direct all his Studies and Endeavours at making himself easie now, and happy hereafter." He goes on to offer consolation to a lady unhappy in love, advising her how to manage her sorrow and leaning heavily on the idea of future rewards. Religion is the only true consolation; he finds it clearly superior to philosophy (Number 463). Religion, "futurity," and delayed rewards are frequent themes in the *Spectator*. Mr. Spectator's pronouncements on these themes are always sound, orthodox doctrine.

The *Female Spectator* echoes such orthodoxy time and again, though she generally emphasizes getting along as well as possible on earth rather than looking toward heaven for the rewards of virtue. But once, discussing Milton and Milton's use of Plato on the subject of unhappiness, she changes her tune significantly: "Philosophy is indeed our great resource, when under the apprehension of, or really enduring ills; and when we have ravaged all that has been urged in the voluminous tracts of religious self-denial and patient suffering, thither we must come at last. . . ." (Book 20). She goes on to quote Lucretius, who, "though in many things blameable," is good on the topic of the unhappiness resulting from a restless mind. She quotes that passage, in Dryden's translation, which describes the mental restlessness resulting from a failure in self-knowledge and which concludes that one should "study nature well, and nature's laws"; she does not quote the passage, which Dryden also translated, in which Lucretius argues that one need not create imaginary fears about "futurity" because the soul is not immortal (though of course anyone could read the poem and find it). Later, however, in Book 23, in a letter from "Extratellus," she does quote it, surrounding the quotation with the correspondent's refutations of the argument and following it with her own affirmation of orthodoxy—which rather reminds me of the woman who went off to market after instructing her children to be sure not to put beans up their noses, something they would never have thought of doing if she had not cautioned them. The Female Spectator maintains the Christian stance. But again and again, in precept and example, she stresses the minimizing of pain and the rewarding of virtue in earthly life, with little if any mention of futurity even for her most agonized Griseldas. Always practical, she deals with the here and now. And in the discussion of Lucretius she suggests, ever so indirectly, that one need not add fears for futurity to one's woes, nor, for that matter, hopes for futurity to the number of one's consolations.

One further consolation of philosophy remains, a consolation directly opposite to the beliefs of Mr. Spectator, and to be found, oddly enough, in Milton. Addison deals directly with the point. When, after several introductory papers on *Paradise Lost,* he settles down to a book-by-book analysis, he devotes considerable attention to "the most exalted and most depraved" character of Satan (Number 303). Satan's rhetoric comes in for much comment as well: "His Sentiments are every way answerable to his Character." Addison quotes parts of the passage beginning "Hail Horrors, hail" and ending "Better to reign in Hell, than serve in Heaven" (1:250-63). He insists on Satan's wrongness: his "Impieties" are "big with absurdity," his words bear "only a *Semblance of Worth, not Substance,*" his interpretations are "perverse." And of course Addison is right. Satan's rhetoric is magnificent, but Milton constructs the speech so that no orthodox Christian could accept it at face value.

However, Mrs. Haywood does quote two lines of it. Her context here is a passage of lush praise of authors, in which she tacitly hands herself a few bouquets in this her final book: "If statues, medals, monuments, and other public testimonies of gratitude, be allowed to those, who by their courage, defend us in the field, or by their wisdom in the cabinet protect us; surely they must be the due of him who rectifies our manners, and purifies our mind, which alone can give us a true relish for any blessings we receive; and I know not if all the acknowledgments we could make to such a one, would be equal to the obligation."

And then she quotes Milton's Satan (lines not quoted by Addison)—with unconditional approval: "In the mind is the true seat of happiness, as the admirable Milton says, 'The mind is its own place, and in itself / Can make a heaven of hell, a hell of heaven'" (Book 24).

Mrs. Haywood had read the *Spectator* and she knew Satan was wrong. In the orthodox world of Milton and Addison, such stoicism manifested a proud independence of mind that ran counter to Christian teaching. And even if she had not read Addison, she would have seen from *Paradise Lost* itself that Satan's stoicism is invalid—he is genuinely miserable and in hell. Her reason for such heterodoxy, however, is both clear and consistent with what I have been defining as her true purpose in the *Female Spectator:* she is educating her readers in the necessity of endurance and in the strategies of endurance, and however unchristian stoicism may be, however philosophically specious its claims, it might help. It would be impractical to rule it out when one needs all the help one can get. The active, educated mind, which she has been trying to create in her readers, might be able to mitigate its inevitable sufferings by turning as a last resort to satanic self-deception. She gives the same counsel again at the end of this final book in a short story about a coquette who bears her fully deserved chastisement with heroic stoicism, thus gaining some apparent measure of happiness. And she uses the word itself in a final caution: "I am not insensible that to be of a disposition not over-anxious nor eager in the pursuit of any thing, is looked upon to savour too much of the stoic, and by some is accounted even dulness, stupidity, and sluggishness of nature. It may indeed betray a want of that vivacity which is so pleasing in conversation, and renders the person who possesses it, more taken notice of than otherwise he might be: but then if those, who argue in this manner, would give themselves the trouble to reflect how dear sometimes people pay for exerting that vivacity, . . . none would wish to exchange the solid, serious, and unmoved temper for it." Two pages later, after a few more similar words of advice and some thanks to her public, the Female Spectator comes to an end.

The Female Spectator has consistently and repeatedly urged the importance of self-knowledge, but at the end of her lucubrations she advises stoicism, which is self-deception, and does so quite overtly: "To that end [avoiding melancholy and suicide] we should never put the worst colours on things, but rather deceive ourselves with imagining them better than they are." She has also, though indirectly, held out hope for oblivion, for the death of the soul, in her references to Lucretius. The picture is not cheerful. Cloaked in Spectatorial conventions, she reveals a far deeper sense of the tragedy of the human condition—specifically, the tragedy of the female condition—than anything Addison and Steele ever expressed. They were fairly comfortable in the world they perceived, despite its shortcomings. Mrs. Haywood was not. Mr. Spectator educated his readers in morality. The Female Spectator educated hers in survival.

SIX

ARABELLA FERMOR,
1714 and 1769

Alexander Pope and Frances Moore Brooke

EVERY STUDENT OF ENGLISH LITERATURE knows the name of Alexander Pope. Not many students of English literature, even among specialists in the eighteenth century, know the name of Frances Moore Brooke—except in Canada. Mrs. Brooke, who was English, wrote poems and epistolary novels, translations, plays, two comic operas (one of which was a great success), and a periodical called *The Old Maid,* modeled on the *Spectator,* which lasted for nine months. She probably knew Richardson; she definitely knew Dr. Johnson, Fanny Burney, and others of that circle. With an actress friend, she ventured into theatrical management. She died in 1789, a respected member of London's literary establishment and destined to be hailed in the twentieth century as the first Canadian novelist, indeed the first North American novelist.[1]

Mrs. Brooke spent about five years in Canada, but even before she saw its shores she was interested in it as a colony. In her first novel, *The History of Lady Julia Mandeville* (1763), she mentions Canada as a more valuable acquisition than the sugar-producing islands, and affirms the advantages of winning the French inhabitants over to the Church of England and establishing a whale fishery. Her own sojourn in Canada, where her husband was a chaplain with the British army in Quebec City, lasted, with one or two interruptions, from 1763 to 1768, a time of comparative calm between the defeat of the French forces by General Wolfe and the first stirrings of rebellion in the American colonies to the south. Despite political infighting (in which she took considerable interest) and harsh winters, life was in general interesting and pleasant, according to the picture of it reflected in her second novel, *The History of Emily Montague* (1769).[2] About three-quarters of that novel is set in Canada: in Montreal and Sillery (near Quebec), with excursions from one city to the other and out into the countryside and, finally, a sea voyage back to England where, in the last quarter of the novel, the complications of the plot are resolved.

The History of Emily Montague is epistolary in form and obeys many of the conventions of the novel of sensibility. Ed Rivers, the first letter-writer we meet, is setting out for Canada where he can live comfortably on his military half-pay and thus leave his mother and sister Lucy in their accustomed comfort in England. He writes copious letters to Lucy and to his friend John Temple, letters full of "sensibility" reactions to the sublime in Canadian scenery, news of Canadian social life, and exhortations to Temple to give up philandering in favor of marriage. Shortly after arriving in Montreal, he meets Emily Montague, a beautiful young lady who lives with friends and who is engaged to marry Sir George Clayton, recently created a baronet. For Rivers and Emily, it is, of course, love at first sight, as one sensitive heart quivers in perfect timing with the other, although both refuse to recognize their "friendship" as love because of Emily's prior engagement to the man chosen for her by her deceased uncle. Sir George's new position fortunately causes a temporary rupture in the engagement, a break which Emily welcomes and makes permanent, but Rivers thinks he is too poor to marry her. The usual complications ensue, as the lovers try to outdo each other in selflessness and delicacy of feeling. At last, all is resolved back in England when they marry and discover shortly afterward that Emily's long-lost father (who suddenly appears) not only approves the marriage but had intended them for each other. The story is a cliché, but, spiced with a bit of jealousy about the widowed Madame Des Roches (whose Canadian acres Rivers nearly buys), decorated with descriptions of life and landscape in Canada, and dealing seriously with the important issue of freedom of choice in marriage, it has much to recommend it.

Several other epistolary voices add variety to the novel. William Fermor, who writes to the Earl of———, is a military officer stationed in Quebec City. He is an older man who reports soberly on the government, the character of the French peasantry, the climate, the politics of religion, and the language question—this last still a contentious issue in Canada.[3] Some of his paragraphs are full of general moralizing, depicting the stresses and obligations of human nature in much the same terms as Pope does in the *Essay on Man*. Although they have nothing to do with the plot, Fermor's contributions increase the novel's solidity as a document in Canada's social history and as a document in eighteenth-century intellectual history; artistically, his letters serve to vary the tone and content of the novel and occasionally to heighten the suspense, as he launches forth into a lengthy sermon or political report just when the reader had hoped for a letter untangling one of the emotional snarls in the love affair.

Both plot and themes are advanced by other correspondents. Rivers's friend John Temple occasionally answers his letters, as does his sister Lucy. Although these two writers never write to each other, being the stay-at-homes in London, they meet, fall in love, and marry, despite (or perhaps because of) Rivers's warning about Temple's amorous character. But Lucy reforms her husband and, although the relationship is less "delicate" than that of Rivers and Emily, it is still a happy one. Sir George, the man chosen for Emily by her uncle, and Mrs. Melmoth, the friend she lives with in Canada, write a few of the letters, primarily about the broken engagement. And one Captain Fitzgerald, another British military officer stationed in Quebec, attaches himself to the central group, returns with them to England, and writes to Rivers on the subject of friendship and domestic life in the country. Each of these letter-writers has a highly individual style, so individual that the reader almost never has to check the signature of a letter to tell who wrote it. And the most lively style of all, unlike anything else in the novel, is that of Emily's and Lucy's friend, William Fermor's daughter, who writes 78 of the 228 letters in the novel. Her name is Arabella.

Arabella Fermor is an artful coquette. Her presence and her letters transform *The History of Emily Montague* from a simple "sensibility" novel to a novel of "sense and sensibility," placing it in a tradition that reaches back beyond the beginnings of the novel and forward to Jane Austen. The pairing of a clever co-quette like Arabella with a milder maiden like Emily Montague was part of Shakespeare's basic stock in trade. One thinks of dazzling Beatrice and poor, conventional little Hero in *Much Ado About Nothing,* of Rosalind in her doublet and hose teasing Or-lando, watched by short, brown Celia in *As You Like It* (though Celia has more sharp-edged lines than one usually remembers). The comic tradition survived into the Restoration. One thinks of Harriet scheming to land Dorimant in Etherege's *The Man of Mode* while Emilia stands sweetly by, longing for young Bellair; one thinks of Hellena in Aphra Behn's *The Rover,* intended by her father to be a nun but dressing as a gypsy to get her man, while her sister Florinda sighs for Captain Belvile. Sentimental comedy glorified the milder maidens and pretty well knocked the clever girls out of English drama, but they reappeared, along with their softer sisters, in the novel, from Cecilia in the second part of Frances Sheridan's *Miss Sydney Bidulph* (1761), who sparkles while her sister Dolly swoons, to the better-known Marianne and Elinor Dashwood in Jane Austen's *Sense and Sensibility.* The clever girls in the novels disguise themselves and play deliberate roles less often than their predecessors in the theater, perhaps because the obvious device of stage costume is not available to their creators. But some do, and Mrs. Brooke's witty, role-playing Arabella Fermor is a delightful example of the type.

The role she plays is that of Belinda in Pope's *Rape of the Lock*. The model for Belinda was the historical Miss Arabella Fermor, who endured the famous haircut at the hands of Lord Petre, although Pope diplomatically pretended that his Belinda resembled Miss Fermor "in nothing but in Beauty."[4] Mrs. Brooke saw the name in Pope's dedicatory letter published with the poem and borrowed it for her young lady of "sense," her artful coquette who flirts and sparkles and yet ends up married, by her own choice, to Captain Fitzgerald.

The links between *The Rape of the Lock* and *The History of Emily Montague* are various and important. The verbal links, which I will describe, most particularly the constant presence of "Arabella Fermor," keep Pope's poem steadily in the reader's mind. Mrs. Brooke accomplishes two purposes with this device. First, her re-creation, in a sense her correction, of Arabella's character makes us take a second look at Pope's Belinda and rethink his purposes in presenting her as he does. Second, the presence of *The Rape* broadens the scope and significance of Mrs. Brooke's novel as a whole. Her story takes place in a comfortable middle rank of society, but the allusions to Pope's poem, and two tragic episodes tucked into the main line of her story, extend her scene and its import. Pope stepped out of Belinda's pretty world once with the devastating line, "And wretches hang that jurymen may dine"; Mrs. Brooke makes us aware of both the social heights above and the depths below her Arabella's world.

The most obvious link between *The History of Emily Montague* and *The Rape* is Arabella's name. Carl Klinck notes the name in his introduction to the New Canadian Library edition of the novel but says only that Arabella was "apparently named for the lady . . . celebrated in *The Rape of the Lock*." Elsewhere, he comments on the ongoing "search for a real life Arabella Fermor in the Quebec of the 1760's," one comparable to the model for Rivers, who had already been discovered.[5] Mrs. Brooke's Arabella could, of course, be a composite of a real-life and a literary model; I am not qualified to guess at a real-life source, but I am sure that Pope's Arabella, rather than some other one, is her literary model. Other literary Arabellas do exist, of course. For example, Charlotte Lennox's heroine in *The Female Quixote* (1752) bears that name. But that naive young lady, who sees life through the haze of romance fiction, has nothing in common with Mrs. Brooke's clear-eyed wit. And no literary Arabella (except Belinda's source) has the surname Fermor.

Mrs. Brooke clearly knew Pope's other works in detail, too, which makes the case for the Belinda/Arabella connection even stronger. Besides William Fermor, whose sentiments, noted earlier, include a direct quotation from *An Essay on Man*, Rivers echoes Pope's philosophy when he comments on the virtues of country gentlemen, in whom "self-love and social are the same" when they raise oaks for the navy, as he plans to do (pp. 370 and 342). Emily too has a quotation from Pope, describing Lucy's splendor at a ball (p. 396). Arabella has six. For example, she dubs Emily's approved suitor, Sir George, "that *white curd of asses milk*" (p. 278), the nasty description Pope concocted for the bisexual Lord Hervey. She takes a farewell walk in the evening when she is about to leave her Canadian home and quotes *Eloisa to Abelard:* "Deepen'd the murmur of the falling floods, / And breath'd a browner horror on the woods" (p. 304); Arabella escaped Eloisa's romantic tragedy but feels a "melancholy solemnity" at her departure that reminds her of Pope's convent landscape. And Arabella claims, comically, to have written pastorals at the age of seven (p. 387), a sidelong glance at the precocious Pope. Curiously, *The Rape of the Lock* itself never appears in direct quotation.[6] Arabella's name is the main link.

Although there are no quotations from *The Rape,* there are other unmistakable references to it besides Arabella's name. Madame Des Roches, the French Canadian lady who has a hopeless passion for Rivers, sends him "an elegant sword-knot" and gives Emily a cross of diamonds when she leaves Canada to return to England (p. 304). In *The Rape of the Lock,* Belinda wears "a sparkling *Cross*" (2:7), which is usually pictured in illustrations and portraits as diamond and would thus match her earrings, which are identified as diamond (3:137); the cross is so wonderfully enhanced by the beauties of Belinda's bosom that "*Jews* might kiss, and Infidels adore" that emblem of Christianity (2:8). In the novel, Emily's sentimental bosom could never inspire such blasphemy despite her beauty, though one could imagine such an effect were Arabella to wear the cross. By giving the cross to Emily rather than Arabella, perhaps Mrs. Brooke was both playing it safe and indicating something about Emily's more obvious virtue. As for the swordknot, this item of male plumage figures prominently in the list of attractions that keep Pope's Belinda in a dither: in "the moving Toyshop" of her heart, "Wigs with Wigs, with Sword-knots Sword-knots strive ..." (1:100-1). There is perhaps even a further link in that the Madame Des Roches who presents these gifts is undoubtedly a Catholic, as are all the actors in Pope's comedy.

The links, then—the name, the allusions, the quotations from Pope's other works—are strong enough to establish that the literary model for Mrs. Brooke's Arabella is Pope's Belinda. But this raises a difficulty. Arabella is a highly amusing letter writer who exercises her wit (and her wits) on everything and everyone within her ken: her gentlemen admirers, her French rivals, Emily and her suitors, the Canadian landscape and climate and social scene, and, most notably, herself. She quotes a wide range of poets besides Pope, she translates Montesquieu, she supplies her friend Emily with comfort and good advice, she sees through her father's parental strategies, she manages her own affairs of the heart (with the exception of one incident) with grace and skill. And she keeps good humor still. Why, then, is she named Arabella Fermor? For all her coquettish character, is she not the polar opposite of Pope's butterfly?

What Mrs. Brooke has done, using the possibilities for psychological intimacy offered by the epistolary novel, is to take Pope's Belinda and, while retaining the frivolous character perceived by the outside observer, turn her inside out and show us the mind, the motives, the wit, and the wisdom of the artful coquette.[7] In advancing this argument, I am not proposing a "revisionist" interpretation of *The Rape of the Lock;* Belinda, as Pope sees her and makes us see her, is enchantingly beautiful, proud, shallow, fashionable, charming, silly, splenetic—a painted china vessel that shatters when her narcissistic self-image is damaged. He sets up a mock heroine whom he then rightly admires and condemns, loves and scorns, in that curious and subtle mixture of attitudes that comes across in this most captivating of poems.[8] And yet, although he looks into her dreaming mind and later spies "An Earthly Lover lurking at her Heart" (3:144), he does not really give us the inner life of his butterfly. He shows us her pride, especially when she attacks her lover, but nothing more. He might have considered any fuller characterization inappropriate for his mock heroic genre and his satiric purpose. Or he may have believed that Miss Fermor had no inner life. John Richetti has argued that Pope's satiric point in *The Rape of the Lock* is that women have no identity except a social-sexual one; they "lack a personal self." Pope's ladies, especially his Belinda, are unable to be anything but "synthetic goddess[es]."[9] That is certainly all that Pope gives us to see. Whatever his own feelings about women may have been—he did understand much about the conditions of their lives, and he both loved and respected Martha Blount—in *The Rape of the Lock* he gives us an outside, a social butterfly observed.

Despite the almost entirely "inner" perspective of the epistolary genre, we can also see Arabella Fermor's outside, her observable behavior, through both her own eyes and the eyes of other letter writers. And that outside is Belinda. Both Belinda and Arabella are beautiful: Pope describes the power of Belinda's beauty, and Mrs. Brooke gives both Arabella herself and other letter writers comments on Arabella's beauty, which, though slightly inferior to Emily's, has even greater power because of her liveliness (see, for example, p. 318). Both are young: the historical Miss Fermor was probably twenty-two when she suffered the famous haircut,[10] and Mrs. Brooke's Arabella is twenty-two (p. 251), "far too young as well as too gay" to be any protection for Emily, Mrs. Melmoth opines (p. 99). Both girls are devoted to cards and "parties of pleasure." Both are concerned about their appearance: Belinda worships for hours at her mirror, and Arabella laments when she finds three gray hairs, which she blames on the Canadian climate (p. 119). Arabella is rather more concerned with clothes than with cosmetics, however (p. 104); indeed, she finds love to be a better cosmetic than paint (p. 170). Both girls flirt with crowds of admirers: "ev'ry Eye" is fixed on Belinda (2:6) and her eyes "shine on all alike" (2:14); Arabella must break off a letter to Lucy because "there are a dozen or two of beaux at the door" (p. 91). As for their relations with other ladies, Rivers observes that all the men are in love with Bell Fermor and all the women hate her (p. 42), though that is not quite true. Clarissa's relationship to Belinda in *The Rape* is highly controversial. One can take her presenting of the scissors to the Baron as indicating the kind of envy and hatred Rivers perceived, or one can take it as a gesture of true friendship designed to redeem the narcissistic Belinda, in which case it parallels the devotion between Emily and Arabella.

The question of good humor, or lack of it, is central to *The Rape of the Lock*. Clarissa, intended by Pope to "open more clearly the MORAL of the Poem" (p. 199n), speaks out after the haircut on the necessity of maintaining good humor (5:30-31), but Belinda frowns and sails into battle instead. Mrs. Brooke's Arabella, usually good humored, is never as severely tested as Belinda, but she can indeed be peevish; she even calls herself "as peevish as an old maid" when she is bored with the company of Sir George (p. 113). When her coquettishness drives Fitzgerald to flirt with a French lady in revenge, she is "excessively out of humor" and declares she will never forgive him (p. 182). Gentle Emily, distressed at the breach between Arabella and Fitzgerald, begs her Rivers to heal it, which he does, laying equal blame on the two lovers for the quarrel (pp. 186-87). Rivers seems to have been a better diplomat than Pope, whose poem, intended to heal a similar breach, failed to close the gap between the Fermors and the Petres; Miss Fermor and Lord Petre married others.

Another characteristic shared by the girls is considerable vigor of spirit. Belinda's is less attractive. She gives an epic shout when she wins at cards, which is not very polite. After her "fall" from grace, she sails into the battle wielding snuff and bodkin with gusto, crying "Restore the Lock!" (5:103). Clearly, Pope presents this behavior as both comic and wrong. In his mock heroic satire, wounded vanity has produced an overreaction and is therefore to be chastised. Mrs. Brooke's Arabella, because she writes letters, displays her vigor of spirit not in observable physical actions but in strongly worded opinions. Finding Emily to be rather "a poor tame household dove" for quickly forgiving Rivers when he errs, Arabella regrets that Rivers's "vanity should be so gratified" (p. 169). She herself enjoys "plaguing a fellow who really loves one" (p. 173), not out of simple malevolence but in the cause of the "free spirit of woman" (p. 182). She sounds almost like the amazonian Thalestris of *The Rape of the Lock,* who counsels Belinda not to forgive the Baron. The values that Pope endorses in his poem do not include the "free spirit of woman." Neither Thalestris nor Belinda is attractive in her independence. But Mrs. Brooke manages to make Arabella's vigorous independence attractive as well as Emily's soft-heartedness and submissiveness, thus widening the range of acceptable female behavior.

Generally, on the surface, Arabella and Belinda seem alike in character. Both girls are judged by their observers to be flirting, coquettish creatures, Belinda so judged by Pope and Arabella so judged by Mrs. Melmoth, by the "cats" in her social circle at Quebec, and even by her own father. William Fermor comments on his daughter's "volatile temper" (p. 285); Johnson defines "volatile" as "lively, fickle, changeable of mind, full of spirit," which describes Belinda truly and Arabella as others see her. On one level, Arabella is Belinda.

Not much more can be said about Belinda's character; Pope has chosen to make her superficial. Much more can be said, however, about Arabella's character. It is not transparent. Indeed, as she herself says, "I have always appeared to have fewer good qualities than I really have." Her motives for so appearing are complex. Writing to Lucy about various topics including sincerity and honesty, she claims to be so sincere and honest that she represents herself as less worthy than she really is out of "contempt for hypocrisy," which is the pose of representing oneself as more worthy than one really is (p. 252). Aware that her own thinking here is somewhat convoluted, she dubs her ideas "pindaric"—not the sort of vocabulary or mental activity or self-awareness imaginable in Belinda. It is the epistolary form that allows the good qualities of Arabella to shine through, qualities of both head and heart that do not exist in Pope's Belinda.

Arabella has a head and uses it. She reads a variety of books, and she quotes and translates French, although, diplomatically, she does not display her reading in social conversation. She calls herself "amazingly learned" and pretends playfully that this is a fault which she must "confess" (p. 251). Despite this stylistic frivolity, it is clear that she is educated. She has taken sides in the eighteenth-century debate about the nature of man and believes that "the human mind is naturally virtuous," its vices being acquired rather than innate (p. 239). She moralizes "on the vanity of human wishes and expectations" and at the same time satirizes moralists who, like Johnson, tell us that there is no happiness and that all is vanity (p. 46). She comments shrewdly on the avarice of Canadian farm settlers and reports on farming conditions in detail, admitting comically, "Shall I own the truth?"—she got all her information from "old John" (pp. 60-64). The range of her interests is wide.

She has also given much thought to the question of the

choice of a marriage partner, one of the major themes of the novel. Freedom of choice she thinks to be essential. When she first meets a group of Indian women, traveling with their children but without their husbands, she determines to "marry a savage, and turn squaw" in order to enjoy such freedom in marriage (p. 49), but when she discovers that Indian women cannot choose their own husbands, she changes her mind: "I will not be a squaw. . . . in the most essential point, they are slaves: the mothers marry their children without ever consulting their inclinations. . . ." The only "true freedom" is "the dear English privilege of chusing a husband" (p. 56). Yet not all English girls have that privilege; Sir George was chosen for Emily, and a number of forced marriages, all tragic, are mentioned in the novel. The legal rights and social pressures involved in marriage choice in the eighteenth century were complex, but Arabella has the answer: parents ought not to choose spouses for their children, but, to prevent mismatches, should control the company that their children keep (p. 130). It makes sense. "Conformity of taste and sentiment" (pp. 130-31) is important in marriage but hard to come by, Arabella observes, because men and women are educated so differently, "Every possible means [being] used, even from infancy, to soften the minds of women, and to harden those of men" (p. 198). She is happy to find conformity of taste and sentiment in Fitzgerald, which makes him so attractive that even his smallpox scars contribute to his "sensible look" (p. 87). Other letter-writers too, especially Rivers and Emily, discuss the question of choice of marriage partner, but their concern is more exclusively personal; they speak of their own frustrations, while Arabella uses her head to analyze the problem and arrive at a solution.

Intellectual alertness also leads Arabella to explore the local scenery and to scoff at the French ladies who, though living among the marvels of nature, never leave town to see them. "They seem born without the smallest portion of curiosity, or any idea of the pleasures of the imagination," Arabella claims (p. 49). She herself responds with enthusiasm to the landscape, as do the "sensibility" characters in the novel. Sensitivity to the "sublime" in scenery is part of the sensibility ethic and can cause severe cases of rapturous logorrhea. Arabella's first letter is devoted to description of landscape, pointed by an appropriate quotation from Milton (pp. 29-31). She promises "a very well painted frost piece" in the winter (p. 48) and delivers exactly that five months later (p. 148); her advance warning and her definition of the genre show that, however sensitive she is to landscape, she is sending her correspondent planned description rather than rapturous gush. Her prose does approach rapturous gush when she describes the half-frozen Montmorenci falls, "the loveliest work of creation," but she pulls herself up short and remarks, "In short, my dear, I am Montmorenci-mad," and "descends" to an account of a winter picnic (pp. 149-51). The heart feels, but the head always reasserts its control, or at least its awareness.

Arabella's feeling heart is not limited to scenery. She cares for people. Her head knows that she has such a heart and indeed disapproves of those who do not. Writing of love and friendship to Emily, once all three couples in the novel are married, Arabella criticizes her Aunt Cecily "who died at sixty-six, without ever having felt the least spark of affection for any human being," because she believed that "a prudent modest woman never loved any thing but herself" (p. 377). Here is Arabella roundly condemning the narcissism which dominates Pope's Belinda. And Arabella does love. She loves her friend Emily and sympathizes with her suffering, even when her head tells her that Emily has brought her suffering on herself by the excessive degree of her "delicacy." She is fond of Rivers and finds her pleasure in social occasions reduced when he is not there. She is moved by the sad plight of Madame Des Roches, the widow who falls in love with Rivers, and she pities Lady H——, the victim of an arranged marriage, "sacrificed at eighteen, by the avarice and ambition of her parents, to age, disease, ill-nature, and a coronet" (p. 279). When Rivers and Emily discover Miss Williams, who has sacrificed herself to care for the illegitimate child of her friend Sophia, Arabella shares the compassion her sentimental friends feel and joins in their efforts to rescue these two unfortunate souls. Earlier, her esteem for Rivers had reached a new height when the story of "a distressed family" was told in a social gathering, evoking a cold comment from Sir George but a glistening eye from Rivers, who left the room quickly and silently; a month later she learned that he had gone in order to find and relieve the distressed family (p. 106). The emotional reaction, the charity, and the silence with which the good deed was performed won Arabella's approval. Charity is, of course, one of the primary planks in the sentimentalist's platform of virtues and in many sentimental novels goes no farther than a flow of sympathetic tears. Arabella honors both the glistening eye and the hard cash with which Rivers exercises that virtue.

And finally, we know that Arabella has a heart because she gives it to Fitzgerald without reservation. In the latter part of the novel, she dwindles into a devoted wife, even willing to stay home from a masked ball to be at her husband's side when his military affairs require her emotional support. She does not love as "dyingly" as Emily (p. 144), for which she thanks her stars; she prefers Fitzgerald to all the rest of his sex but is able to "*count the hours of his absence in* [her] *existence*" (pp. 190-91). She does not languish. She plans to go on flirting after her marriage. But like that of Congreve's Millamant, who thinks she may be able to "endure" Mirabell, Arabella's love is the real thing, clearly visible beneath the verbal posturing and the flirtatiousness.

The question of flirtatiousness needs further attention, since that is Belinda's primary characteristic, as Pope presents her, surrounded by crowds of admirers and smiling on all alike. Pope shows Belinda as unable to decide among her admirers because she cannot choose between "one Man's Treat" and "another's Ball" (1:96); it is the multiplicity of her temptations and her consequent dithering, not her moral principles, that preserve her virtue. Mortals may call such behavior levity, Pope makes

Ariel explain, but "the *Sylphs* contrive it all" (1:103-4); it is devastating satire on Belinda's triviality and moral shallowness. Arabella, engaged in the same observable behavior, is another case altogether. She writes to Lucy, "I have prevented any attachment to one man, by constantly flirting with twenty: 'tis the most sovereign receipt in the world. I think too, my dear, you have maintained a sort of running fight with the little deity: our hour is not yet come" (p. 87). She knows that her hour to fall in love will come, and it does. Meanwhile, she protects her heart from passing fancies by flirting with, as she hyperbolically says, dozens, scores of gentlemen. And she does it very well. She analyzes degrees and types of coquetry (p. 381) and describes her own tactics for attracting men: "I am a very good girl to women, but naturally artful (if you will allow the expression) to the other sex; I can blush, look down, stifle a sigh, flutter my fan, and seem so agreeably confused—you have no notion, my dear, what fools men are" (p. 47). With the paradox of "naturally artful," Mrs. Brooke is emphasizing that such behavior is learned, deliberate, purposeful—conscious role-playing—not just the automatic response of a synthetic goddess. It even takes brains to behave this way. Arabella, writing about her fear of "sinking into vegetation" in marriage, plans to carry on flirting to add variety to life and to keep her mind awake (pp. 405-6). One could hardly gather from the way Pope presents Belinda that flirtation could be conceived of as an intellectual exercise— quite the contrary. But Arabella, like Millamant, wants to marry the man she loves and wants to be Arabella still, still the same autonomous individual with the same lively mind.

This awareness of her own mental processes goes beyond the question of self-preservation in marriage. Arabella has a considerable complexity of self-awareness. Belinda, whom Pope observes from the outside, has none, but Arabella's letters reveal, again and again, her acute and judgmental consciousness of self and of the contradictions of self. One of the strongest examples is an analysis of herself comparable in severity to Pope's analysis of Belinda. Arabella has been regretting Emily's planned marriage to Sir George, that "milky baronet" (p. 113), and complains about his dullness; then she turns on herself: "I am angry with Emily for concluding an advantageous match with a man she does not absolutely dislike, which all good mammas say is sufficient; and this only because it breaks in on a little circle of friends, in whose society I have been happy. O! self! self! I would have her hazard losing a fine fortune and a coach and six, that I may continue my coterie two or three months longer" (p. 114). She still regrets the marriage, but her good sense about the advantages Emily would gain and her critical awareness of her own selfishness show that she does not share Belinda's narcissism.

Again, after Rivers has mended the rift between Arabella and Fitzgerald that was caused by their flirtations with others, Arabella turns her analytical eye inward and recognizes that she was jealous of Fitzgerald's lady even though a little flirting with others does not usually alarm her; she concludes that it was her vanity as much as her love that had been wounded by his attentions to an inferior woman (p. 191). Pope shows us that Belinda's vanity is wounded by the haircut, but we are not shown that she has any self-awareness or self-judgment.

Arabella's self-awareness takes other forms besides that of moral self-judgment. She knows she is letting herself go in her description of Montmorenci falls, mentioned above, and undercuts her own raptures. (Rivers, who does tend to run on in uncontrolled raptures, is so aware of Arabella's control that he twice cuts short his own flow of words by imagining a witty rebuke from her [pp. 371, 408].) Arabella is particularly witty and frivolous in a January letter devoted to the cold weather, the New Year's visit from "a million of beaux," the clothes necessary to keep warm, and the idea that Pygmalion's statue was "some frozen Canadian gentlewoman, and a sudden warm day thawed her." Aware of her own chatter, and perhaps of the unusual exaggeration of the dozens of beaux into a million, she explains that her father has given her brandy that cold morning, which "makes a woman talk like an angel" (pp. 103-5). Again, bored with Sir George, she describes, with transparent irony, her tactics for getting rid of him: "I wish he would go; I say spontaneously every time I see him, without considering I am impolite, 'La! Sir George, when do you go to Montreal?' He reddens, and gives me a peevish answer; and I then, and not before, recollect how very impertinent the question is" (p. 117). The self-awareness behind the "spontaneous" pose is unmistakable. Irony, as in this passage about her spontaneity, is a consistent characteristic of Arabella's prose. Although Linda Shohet hesitates to say that these ironies are intentional,[11] they must be; not only is the irony all-pervasive, it is the mode necessary for the expression of an acute awareness of discrepancies, of irreconcilable contradictions, of multiple and conflicting truths—if these things are to be expressed comically. We cannot know whether Belinda is capable of comic irony; she has only a few lines to say in *The Rape of the Lock:* warlike exclamations and one longer speech lamenting the loss of such visible hairs (4:147-76). But the epistolary form gives Arabella the chance to exercise her ironic consciousness fully.

A simple instance of the ironist's double consciousness, and of Arabella's knowledge of self, appears when the news arrives that the lovelorn Madame Des Roches has refused a good offer of marriage because she wishes to be faithful to Rivers. " 'Tis a mighty foolish resolution, and yet I cannot help liking her the better for making it," Arabella concludes (p. 405), articulating somewhat indirectly her awareness of the rival claims of head and heart, of sense and sensibility, and of the unbridgeable gap between them. Less serious is Arabella's cheerful comment on a ball at Quebec at which she has been "asked to dance by only twenty-seven" young men (p. 64), an irony of understatement—or possibly overstatement. The irony is relatively simple when a letter from Mrs. Melmoth reduces Emily to tears, which Arabella describes as an "agreable effect" (p. 112). The irony is somewhat more complex when Arabella confesses to Emily that she loves Fitzgerald, whom she finds more agreeable than Emily's Rivers: "I know you will think me a shocking wretch for this depravity of taste" (p. 145). When the Canadian winter sets in, Arabella writes to Lucy in London: "The savages assure us, my dear, on the information of the beavers, that we shall have a very mild winter. . . . I take it very ill, Lucy, that the beavers have better intelligence than we have" (p. 92). And then when the winter proves to be very severe indeed, she grumps with comic irony, "I will never take a beaver's word again as long as I live. . . . I thought beavers had been people of more honor" (p. 102). The temptation to quote more is great, because Arabella is such fun, but the temptation to pinpoint and define the varieties of her ironies is slight, for the categories overlap and interpenetrate discouragingly. Suffice it to say that Arabella plays skillfully with the multiple tones of the ironic mode.

Irony underlies other strategies for comedy in Arabella's style. Clearly, she is more than a frivolous coquette, but she maintains that role wonderfully in her prose style. She decorates her sentences with squeaky little exclamations—"Let me die!", "As I am a person!"—the exact words used by the affected Melanthas and Olivias of Restoration comedy. Like them, too, she calls the gentlemen "creatures" and "absurd animals." She likes to sound careless and spontaneous: "—where was I, Lucy? I forget—" (p. 149). Only in a complex jumble of frivolity and irony does she approach the real seriousness of her feelings for Fitzgerald, the first time she writes about him: ". . . there is nothing more easy than to have him if I chuse it: 'tis only saying to some of his friends, that I think Captain Fitzgerald the most agreable fellow here, and he will immediately be astonished he did not sooner find out I was the handsomest woman. I will consider this affair seriously; one must marry, 'tis the mode; every body marries; why don't you marry, Lucy?" (p. 69). To marry because it is "the mode" is hardly to consider the matter seriously, and yet marriage was the necessary mode for young English gentlewomen of the eighteenth century and was a very serious business. There are comic pretenses in this passage as well, the pretense that she has the power to get what she wants (when we have seen other girls, and sometimes even Arabella herself, failing to do so), and the pretense that Lucy can marry if she chooses (though of course she must wait to be asked). The pretenses, the role-playing, the assumed frivolity, the complex tone, all join both to express and to protect the sensitive heart—and to amuse the reader.

Perhaps Arabella's most characteristic comic-ironic trick is her conscious hyperbole, her exaggeration of her admirers into dozens and millions, her extravagant detestation of "the whole sex" of men when only Rivers has provoked her anger (p. 160), her certainty that if Emily marries Sir George, "she will die in a week, of no distemper but his conversation" (p. 81). She praises herself hyperbolically, but we know that this is comic exaggeration, partly because of the very nature of hyperbole, partly from the wider context of her self-expression and self-judgment. Even her self-praise is comically inconsistent. When she thinks Emily is being too lenient toward the erring Rivers, Arabella exclaims, "I am sorry to find there is not one wise woman in the world but myself" (p. 163), but when she has been amusing herself with Emily and Rivers, she admits, "I love mightily to be foolish" (p. 86). She does not languish for Fitzgerald, yet she calls him "the God of my idolatry" (p. 230). She claims to have such great compassion for his horses' legs that she forbids him to risk his neck by driving to visit her in dangerous weather (p. 232). And so she goes on, oblique and direct, overstating and understating, playing at seriousness and playing at frivolity—entirely charming.

Arabella's prose style is too varied to sum up in a word, but, briefly, it can be described as analogous to the mock heroic style, that multilevel mode involving hyperbole and irony, inflation and deflation, praise and blame. Pope uses such a style to attack Belinda's pride: he makes her a goddess and at the same time shows her to be a silly debutante. Arabella is not the subject of such a style but another creator of it. Where Pope shows Belinda to be one-dimensional amid the multiple dimensions of

his style, Arabella shows herself to be multidimensional—and
one of her dimensions is Belinda.

Mrs. Brooke's Arabella—and, obviously, Mrs. Brooke—
share Pope's ironic consciousness, including his consciousness
of life as a game. When Arabella contemplates settling down in
marriage, she writes,

> What must we do, my dear, to vary our days?
>
> Cards, you will own, are an agreable relief, and the least sub-
> ject to pall of any pleasures under the sun: and really, philosoph-
> ically speaking, what is life but an intermitted pool at quadrille?
>
> I am interrupted by a divine colonel in the guards. [p. 406]

As Lorraine McMullen explains, quadrille is a later variant of
ombre, which Belinda played so well, and what counts is the
player's ability to value his or her cards accurately.[12] In *The Rape
of the Lock,* Pope's card game parallels the game of life in general
and the battle of the sexes in particular; it is one of his ironies
that Belinda wins at cards but, unless she mends her ways, will
lose at life. Arabella spells out the parallel: "what is life but an
intermitted pool at quadrille?" We can easily see her continuing
to win the game of life, equipped as she is with head and heart,
charm and good humor, and ironic self-awareness.

In Arabella Fermor, Mrs. Brooke has not only created an en-
chanting character and made us think again about Pope's portrait of Belinda. She has also forced her reader to be aware,
almost constantly, of the whole world of *The Rape of the Lock,*
with the name, the Belinda pose, and the other allusions to the
mock heroic poem present throughout. Besides enriching Arabella's character and redeeming *The History of Emily Montague*
from the tedium that usually sinks the standard novel of sensibility, her pattern of reference to Pope's poem extends the scope
and significance of the novel considerably. Mrs. Brooke has
confined her plot and characters to a middle range of society
and of experience: even though the lives of her gentlemen and

gentlewomen are lived out partly in the exotic setting of Canada, those lives are always conducted in an atmosphere of safety, comfort, and virtue. But Mrs. Brooke uses two devices to broaden that range of experience without endangering her characters: inserted episodes about other people and the connection with Pope's poem.

Two inserted episodes extend the range of *The History of Emily Montague* to the world of suffering, death, and social disgrace that Pope shows us briefly when he mentions the victims at the bottom of the heap, the wretches who hang that jurymen may dine. Mrs. Brooke's wretches are not criminals on trial but victims of another sort, victims of their own exaggerated sensibility. They suffer greater agonies, physical and emotional, than even Emily and Rivers themselves, but their agonies are not beyond the realm of possibility for our hero and heroine and therefore stand as warnings against carrying the sensibility ethic to extremes.

The first episode is the story of the hermit and his Louisa. Unable to marry in England because their parents sought more "gainful" matches, they escaped to Canada where, in a sudden storm, Louisa was drowned and her body washed ashore at her lover's feet. His sensibilities are so intense that, devoted to her memory, he is spending the rest of his days alone, waiting to die and be reunited with her. When Rivers meets him and learns his story, Rivers "cannot absolutely approve" but he does "admire" the hermit's delicacy of feeling (p. 79). There are various parallels here with the obstacles to Rivers's marriage to Emily, and when Emily sails for England, Rivers, following, finds evidence of a storm and a shipwreck which he fears might have destroyed his Emily (p. 291). Unlike the hermit, he is spared that romantic tragedy, but Mrs. Brooke makes the reader vividly aware of the vulnerability of the sensible heart, of the extremes of suffering which it invites.

The second episode is the story of Miss Williams and Sophia. Emily and Rivers, married and settled in England, discover Miss Williams looking after a young child in the village near their

country home. Living in poverty and with a questionable reputation, Miss Williams explains herself to Emily in a letter before
she will accept her charity. The child is not hers but was borne
illegitimately by her friend Sophia, the victim of a faithless
lover. Sophia's sensibility was such that she had no will apart
from her lover's, and when he deserted her, she could only give
birth and die, commending the child to Miss Williams's care
(pp. 359-67). The warning lies in Sophia's lack of an independent will. Emily is alarmingly similar. Twice, at emotional
cross-purposes with Rivers, she cleared the air between them
by declaring, "I have no will but yours" (pp. 226 and 332), a
potentially dangerous stance to take, as Sophia's story shows.
Emily is safe because Rivers is honorable. Sophia wasn't so
lucky.

Another element in Sophia's story that reflects on the main
characters in *The History of Emily Montague* is her "noble integ-
rity of soul which made it impossible for her to suspect another" (p. 365), as Miss Williams describes her. This quality is
part of her delicate sensibility and is echoed, rather surprisingly,
by Arabella's Fitzgerald, who "would rather be the dupe of a
thousand false professions of friendship, than, for fear of being
deceived, give up the pursuit" of that "generous affection" (p.
345). He despises "the cold, narrow, suspicious heart" (p.
345)—which sounds admirable indeed. But Fitzgerald is comparatively safe with his choice of trust rather than suspicion
because he is a man: he cannot be ruined and left holding the
baby. Excesses of sensibility, never good, are particularly dangerous for women—who are most prone to such excesses.

The polar opposite of the sensibility ethic is the heartless-
ness—the triviality and narcissism—of the fashionable world
that Pope depicts in *The Rape of the Lock.* We see only the fringe
of this world in *The History of Emily Montague,* but it is there.
Rivers's friend Temple belongs to it and indulges in all its lib-
ertinism until Rivers's sister Lucy marries him and redeems
him. They continue to touch upon the world of fashion, however, as we see in the account of a masked ball at which Lucy

glitters in too many diamonds (p. 396). (Emily dressed as a peasant and Arabella stayed home.) Despite the brevity of this scene, we are constantly warned of the vanity and sterility of that world of cards and coquetry by the presence, throughout the novel, of "Arabella Fermor." Mrs. Brooke agrees with Pope in disapproving of that world, though he clearly also takes pleasure in its beauties. But he recognizes its evils and attacks them in brilliant mock heroic; Mrs. Brooke keeps us conscious of Pope's attack by using the name of Arabella Fermor, who, if she did not have a good deal of intellect coupled with a reasonable amount of sensibility, would *be* Belinda. Her name and all the other links with *The Rape of the Lock* stand as warnings of an evil which Mrs. Brooke apparently found too important to confine to an inserted episode. Too much sensibility is a danger, especially to women, as the inserted episodes show. Triviality and narcissism are a danger to all humankind.

Perhaps Mrs. Brooke had yet another motive for choosing the name of her heroine. She could have wanted to give Arabella Fermor a second chance. Pope admired only her beauty, as did other poets of the time.[13] Yet even such compliments could turn left-handed, as in Thomas Parnell's poem, "On Mrs. Arabella Fermor Leaving London." Here she is gloriously beautiful and the beaux all grieve when she goes away for the summer, but "as she goes, their flames retire"; she stirs their desires only when her pretty face is in view, because that is her total being. Mrs. Brooke's Arabella has more than a pretty face. From a woman's point of view, Mrs. Brooke shows us what could have lain behind the glittering surface that Pope and others chose to depict. She shows us real character, real intelligence, in a woman playing the role of an artful coquette. As women know, it takes brains to conceal brains—and hearts—which women in various centuries often find it necessary to do. Perhaps the historical Miss Fermor was so successful at concealing hers that she deceived even the observant eye of Alexander Pope, who concluded that she didn't have any—or at least chose to give us a brainless and nearly heartless heroine in his mock heroic poem. But Mrs. Brooke chose the epistolary novel, which lets us into Arabella's brain—a lively one—and into her heart. Miss Fermor has been given a second and entirely sympathetic hearing.

SEVEN

HEROICS AND MOCK HEROICS

John Milton, Alexander Pope, and Anna Laetitia Barbauld

SATIRE, that mode for which the earlier decades of the eighteenth century are so justly famous, fell into increasing disrepute as the years went by. There had always been a few who protested against the ugliness of satire, suspicious that the satirist was ill-natured, grinding a personal axe, even unchristian. Addison and Steele's *Spectator* was uncomfortable with ridicule and irony as early as 1711, and they were far from the first. Practicing satirists routinely defended themselves against hostile opinion, attempting, like Pope in "An Epistle to Dr. Arbuthnot," to establish their credentials as disinterested moral exemplars. Toward the end of the century, Vicesimus Knox was very hostile indeed: "Ridicule . . . seems to become a weapon in the hands of the wicked, destructive of taste, feeling, morality, and religion."[1] So much for the satirist as God's scourge on earth.

Stuart Tave, in *The Amiable Humorist*, documents in detail this change in attitude, showing how good humor, good nature, and cheerfulness became the dominant desiderata, while the satirist, obviously lacking these virtues, retreated into outer darkness. Tave's analysis is accurate, but it is incomplete because he says almost nothing about women writers, who stood in a particularly problematic relationship to satire from the beginning. The very qualities that came to displace satire—good nature, good humor, and cheerfulness—had always been desirable in women; these qualities, along with submissiveness, made women pleasant creatures to have about the house. The very quality which lives at the heart of satire—the spirit of criticism—was consistently deplored when it raised its ugly head in a woman, especially when it took verbal form. As Lady Mary Chudleigh's Parson phrased the usual teaching: "Soft winning language will become you best; / Ladies ought not to rail, tho' but [that is, not even] in jest."[2] Whatever women may have thought about satire as a mode of discourse, they knew they were asking for trouble if they wrote it.

Lady Winchilsea inclined toward satire but knew the dangers. A "Poetesse" is rightly considered "a common jest" if she "Setts out Lampoons, where only spite is seen, / Not fill'd with female witt, but female Spleen," she warns, in a passage that otherwise defends women writers.[3] The passage comes from her most sustained satire, "Ardelia's Answer to Ephelia," a poem for which she apologized in the prose preface to her manuscript volume. There she expresses a general detestation for "abusive verses" and claims that "no particular person [is] meant by any of the disadvantageous Caracters" in her poem (pp. 10-11). The poem was intended only to "expose the Censorious humour, foppishnesse and coquetterie" of the fashionable world, a task which, despite her proclaimed distaste for satire, she wishes were "oftener done" (p. 11). Her attitude is mixed, moral principle in conflict with feminine good manners. Yet the satiric touch appears here and there throughout her poems and, significantly, the strongest attacks, like "Ardelia's Answer" and parts of "The Spleen," are aimed at women. No woman could be blamed for attacking foolish women, but I doubt that the reasons for this emphasis were merely prudential. Foolish women were a real threat to women of talent and intelligence, reinforcing, as they did, misogynist stereotypes. Furthermore, the stance of the satirist was necessarily that of an authority on his or her subject; the satirist had to be seen as qualified to criticize. It could be assumed that women knew about women, if about nothing else, so the mantle of the satirist could be conceded to them when they wrote about their own sex. Yet the mantle was never an entirely comfortable fit.

Other women besides Lady Winchilsea were ambivalent and often cautious practitioners of satire. Mrs. Haywood, in her role as Female Spectator, wielded the weapon of ridicule but expressed considerable uneasiness about it. Mrs. Montagu was nervous about the "bad consequences" of "Wit in women . . . [because] like a sword without a scabbard it wounds the wearer and provokes assailants." Fanny Burney managed to have it both ways when she created the ironic Mrs. Selwyn but made gentle Evelina disapprove of that lady's "masculine" manners. And Ellis Cornelia Knight, responding to Dr. Johnson's *Rasselas*, expressed a vivid sense of the mixed dangers and attractions of ridicule.[4]

Another female practitioner of satire dealt with the problems the mode created for her by adopting—twice—the mock heroic style, that style which can be taken as merely playful and so can serve as a protective cloak for the writer with something serious to say.

Anna Laetitia Barbauld knew her models for mock heroic. Something of a child prodigy who could read at the age of two, she received an unusually extensive education in the classics, in French and Italian, and in English literature from her schoolmaster father, John Aikin. Her family of teachers and clergymen, Dissenting but not puritanical, lived and worked in a vigorous intellectual climate. Josiah Wedgwood was a friend, Priestley a colleague, and Malthus a student of John Aikin's. Anna Laetitia first published her work in 1773, but long before that her poems were admired not only by her family but also by a wide circle of friends. After her marriage in 1774 to Rochemont Barbauld, she helped her husband open a school for children and, childless themselves, they soon adopted a nephew. Mrs. Barbauld began almost at once to write books for beginning readers and to teach the youngest boys in her husband's school. Her intellectual and social circle included the Bluestockings, whom she visited on trips to London. And she kept on writing: letters, essays, poems; learned parodies of Greek pastoral verse and the kind of pious clichés in rhyme that are still dear to the publishers of the smaller newspapers; literary criticism and lengthy devotional treatises; witty prose fables and Thomsonesque meditations.[5] The quantity and variety of her work are considerable, the quality and durability of interest, variable. Much is marked by an earnest religious spirit and pedagogical practicality. Much too is touched with a lively and sharp sense of satiric fun.

Her first book, *Poems* (1773), is for the most part a quite conservative collection of pastoral songs, hymns, odes to wisdom, and paeans to female friendship. She strikes a public note in "Corsica," a blank verse poem inspired by Boswell's book on Paoli and marked by lavish praise for freedom and the more rugged virtues. Comment on matters of public concern appears again in "The Groans of the Tankard" but this time disguised in light, bright, and sparkling mock heroics.

"The Groans of the Tankard" (see the appendix) uses as its setting the dining room of the school in which Mrs. Barbauld's father taught. The silver Tankard, full of water and sitting on the sideboard, observes the scene and then delivers itself of a lengthy speech, bewailing its present condition and reminiscing about its glorious past. The poem is written in heroic couplets with Miltonic touches but is mainly Popeian in tone, at times alluding directly to *The Rape of the Lock.* Betsy Rodgers calls it "light verse" (p. 61), and it's great fun. When it first appeared, the *Monthly Review* was somewhat baffled by it. Praising virtually every poem in the book, the *Monthly* could say of "The Groans of the Tankard" only that it is "a kind of burlesque; in which the Writer has succeeded much beyond what could have been expected from her chastised and regulated genius."[6]

The *Critical Review* came a bit closer to the mark. Less favorably inclined to the book as a whole, it could not "say much in commendation of The Groans of the Tankard." After doubting that the owner of such a tankard could confine himself to drinking water, the reviewer went on to grudging praise of the poet who acted "consistently enough" in praising abstemiousness, since she herself "resides among dissenters" rather than among "the sons of the church, who are supposed to indulge themselves in sacerdotal luxury."[7] From its Establishment point of view, the *Critical Review* was beginning to get the point that this playful burlesque was, under the cloak of the mock heroic, a scathing indictment of the Establishment.

To begin at the beginning, the epigraph from Horace— "Dulci digne mero!"—is a nice piece of evidence that Mrs. Barbauld not only knew her Latin poets but responded, no doubt with glee, to the ironies in Horace that readers have sometimes overlooked. She is quoting from the Odes, Book III, number 13, a poem addressed to a spring or fountain, praising it and promising it a sacrifice. The poem begins: "Fount of Bandusia, shining more bright than glass, / Worth the sweetest of wine not without garlands crowned. . . ."[8] That water should be "worth the sweetest of wine" ("Dulci digne mero") and be saluted by having wine poured into it is amusing enough. That the wine is called "mero," a substantive use of the adjective which means "pure, unmixed" (a common usage), makes the blending of wine and water even funnier. And that the phrase should head a poem in which a tankard filled with water argues for its worthiness to contain wine instead, an argument moreover that makes it the butt of the satire, is a wonderful joke.

The invocation to the Muse is couched in religious terms: "portents," "reverent," "faithful," "pious awe." The Muse is, of course, a goddess, but this much emphasis on the sacred is unusual. The ominous tone of the sacred terms prepares us for the supernatural—even Gothic—event of the speaking Tankard and for the abstemious religious atmosphere of the school dining room. If readers have not responded to the exaggeration of the piety, they soon sense that they are engaged with a mock heroic poem rather than with the genuine heroic when they are told that "hunger rages with despotic power" at noon and when they meet a pun as "the lean student quits his Hebrew roots" to dine on "English fruits." The domestic detail of this part of the poem is peculiarly a woman's perception. However learned she was, Mrs. Barbauld knew that "solid pudding and substantial pie" had a more immediate value than "airy systems." Dr. Johnson, when he praised Elizabeth Carter for knowing how to make a pudding as well as translate Epictetus, was expressing his sense of what constituted a woman's worth; Mrs. Barbauld knows that a man's or boy's stomach is more demanding than his mind, which Johnson doesn't quite admit. The meal finished, the "decent grace" is spoken and the diners look toward the Tankard—"deep, capacious, vast, of ample size." This heroic vessel is filled with "the cold beverage blue-eyed Naiads drink," plain water. The allusive, circumlocutory designation of its contents is more Miltonic than Popeian, and the echoes of *Paradise Lost* continue as the mouth of the Tankard yawns to disclose "the deep profound," a tautological phrase not found in *Paradise Lost* in that form but reminiscent of the hundreds of uses of "deep," the "vast profunditie obscure" of Chaos (7:229), "this profound" of Hell (2:980), and many other phrases. Miraculously, the Tankard begins to speak, after breaking out in a cold sweat (as metal vessels full of cold liquid do).

That an inanimate object should speak shows that Mrs. Barbauld was not unacquainted with the conventions of the Gothic novel. Besides the regulation grating of rusty hinges, rattling of chains, and moaning of wind, Gothic novels are full of supernatural noises. *The Castle of Otranto* (1764), for example, is full of creaks and groans and even boasts a talking skeleton. By adding the Gothic to the mock heroic, Mrs. Barbauld doubles the fictiveness and the funniness of her poem, a lightening which balances the real seriousness of the satire.

For real seriousness there is. The Tankard begins its lament with "How changed the scene!"—directly quoting Thomson's "Summer" from *The Seasons* (l. 784), a passage describing a sudden and violent storm of rain that blots out the sun, turning the smiling landscape to ominous gloom. For the Tankard, the school dining room is equally depressing. And water, in the form of rain or otherwise, holds no charms. Although the exact words are Thomson's, the Miltonic echoes are even more significant. In *Paradise Lost,* the newly fallen Satan faces a new scene when he opens his eyes on Hell and speaks for the first time, addressing Beelzebub: "O how fall'n! how chang'd . . . chang'd in outward lustre" (1:84, 97). The Tankard, sensing that, like Satan, it is being punished for something, asks, "for what unpardoned crimes / Have I survived to these degenerate times?" We have observed no degeneracy in the preceding passage. Instead, we have been shown lean, hard-working students eating a frugal meal, saying grace, and preparing to drink water. For the Tankard to regard this as a scene of degeneracy immediately puts it in the wrong and identifies it as the object of satiric attack. We will soon discover what the "unpardoned crimes" are. Meanwhile, like Satan, the Tankard is lamenting a fall, though Satan fell from a true state of grace and the Tankard from a false one.

The Tankard goes on to describe the contents it was proud to hold in former days. The description is Miltonic with its exotic geographical references; it is Popeian in its echoes of Belinda's dressing table; it is accurately domestic in its recipe for what could be Wassail or Lambswool or Cold Tankard. With white froth on top and a Miltonic "brown abyss" below, made from the "golden store" of Ceres, we begin with beer or ale, made from wheat or barley. Sugar, "The dulcet reed the Western islands boast," was a standard ingredient. "Banda's fragrant coast" in Indonesia produced the nutmeg that was used in most if not all versions of the drink. Other spices varied, but most commonly ginger or cinnamon or both were added to the "Spicy Nut-brown Ale" (to quote Milton); "either India's shore," both India itself and the West Indies, produced and sold both of these spices in the eighteenth century. Perhaps Mrs. Barbauld was recommending water, but she knew the right ingredients for a livelier beverage.[9]

The elevated method of presenting the recipe may be compared to Milton's description of Eve preparing dinner for Raphael and Adam:

> . . . and from each tender stalk
> Whatever Earth all-bearing Mother yeilds
> In *India* East or West, or middle shoare
> In *Pontus* or the *Punic* Coast, or where
> *Alcinous* reign'd, fruit of all kinds, in coate,
> Rough, or smooth rin'd, or bearded husk, or shell
> She gathers, Tribute large. . . .
>
> [5:337-43]

Et cetera, et cetera. The recipe may also be compared to Belinda's toilette in *The Rape of the Lock,* presided over by her maid:

> The various Off'rings of the World appear;
> From each she nicely culls with curious Toil,
> And decks the Goddess with the glitt'ring Spoil.
> This Casket *India*'s glowing Gems unlocks,
> And all *Arabia* breathes from yonder Box.
> The Tortoise here and Elephant unite,
> Transform'd to *Combs,* the speckled and the white.
>
> [1:130-36]

Et cetera. Pope transforms the Miltonic goddess who deserves the whole world's tribute into the social beauty who does not; Mrs. Barbauld continues the process of reduction by collecting the spoils of the world in the belly of the Tankard, a beauty as proud of itself as ever Belinda was.

The Tankard is proud partly because it has officiated at City banquets, dispensing nectar to alderman and mayor, "the furry tribe." The epithet, while referring to the trimming on the official robes of office, also reduces the city men to animals, a state they regularly reached by overindulgence in the contents of the Tankard, according to Ned Ward and other observers.[10] The country squire or "keen Sportsman," too, has been served by the Tankard. As it describes its patrons, the Tankard increasingly reveals its pride: the furry tribe declared its worth, but the sportsman was actually enabled by the Tankard to conquer land and sea. The Tankard has confused the power of its contents, and a spurious power at that, with its own powers, which are nil.

The next section of the poem reveals the full extent of the Tankard's hubris, although the Tankard itself seems super-ficially to be arguing simply for the proper decorum in the relationship of vessel to contents. A mere clay pot is good enough for water; fine china is suited to tea and coffee; but the Tankard, which is silver, claims "more exalted juice." The idea of a class structure and hence possibilities of disastrous misalliances between drinking vessels and their contents has a satiric edge to it, especially since it comes from a relatively egalitarian poet, a Dissenter outside the Establishment, who later supported the French and American revolutions and wrote pamphlets against the slave trade.[11] This passage echoes two in *The Rape of the Lock*. First, "China's earth" and the "grateful flavour" of the tea recall the coffee-brewing scene: "From silver Spouts the grateful Liquors glide, / While *China*'s Earth receives the smoking Tyde" (3:109-10). Second, the Tankard's account of its birth is a series of rhetorical questions, using the phrase "for this . . . ?" five times; the same phrase (four times) dominates the description of Belinda's hair-curling procedure, delivered by Thalestris:

> Was it for this you took such constant Care
> The *Bodkin, Comb,* and *Essence* to prepare;
> For this your Locks in Paper-Durance bound,
> For this with tort'ring Irons wreath'd around?
> For this with Fillets strain'd your tender Head,
> And bravely bore the double Loads of Lead?
> [4:97-102]

The agonizing creation of Belinda's curls is paralleled to the mining, smelting, and stamping of the silver Tankard in the "torturing furnace." (We are now sure the Tankard is silver because its "native bed" is Potosi, a famous Bolivian source of that metal.) Both Belinda and the Tankard suffer for vanity, and both have their vanity punished, one by haircut and one by water. The two specific and detailed echoes of *The Rape of the Lock* at this point in the poem bring in Pope's whole world of frivolous aristocrats as the next stage in the progress of the satire, following the mayor and squire. There is a comic contrast in the ephemerality of Belinda's curls and the durability of the Tankard, but the moral point parallels Pope's.

The Tankard goes on to lament the day it was doomed to serve in a Presbyterian household, "Whose slender meal is shorter than their grace." The point of view here contrasts tellingly with that in the first part of the narrative frame, where the "short repast" is also called a "sober meal" and the grace has the adjective "decent." The phenomenon is the same but the attitudes are opposite. Mrs. Barbauld is a Dissenter but the Tankard is Church of England; it has "endur'd the fiery test" (Mrs. Barbauld deplored the Test Act) and is stamped "with Britain's lofty crest." Naturally, it has nothing but contempt for the temperance of the "moping sons" of the puritans. Nostalgically, the Tankard recalls its service among Anglican clergymen, whose notorious corruption Mrs. Barbauld is satirizing here. The dean may be an echo of Pope's "Of the Use of Riches," in which, while visiting Timon's chapel, he finds, "To Rest, the Cushion, and soft *Dean* invite, / Who never mentions Hell to Ears polite" (ll. 149-50). In Mrs. Barbauld's poem, the cushions are soft while the dean is gouty, but he too looks like one not concerned with Hell. The prebend, on the other hand, is inspired, but only by the Tankard. The Dissenting satire on the shortcomings of the Anglican clergy is clear.

From alderman and mayor and squire, to Belinda, to Anglican dean and prebend, that is, from the civic governors to the aristocracy to the spiritual authorities, the satire has grown in seriousness under the comic surface of the poem. The final step of the satire is even more damning and, perhaps for that reason, more cautiously veiled. Here the Tankard reminisces about its former services to "Comus' sprightly train," those drinkers who do their reveling in "some spacious mansion, Gothic, old." One could take Comus simply as the Roman god of mirth and revelry, but Mrs. Barbauld's detailed knowledge of Milton makes a more particular association inevitable. Milton's Comus, however, worked his evil magic out in the woods and in a "stately Palace" (stage direction, l. 657), not specifically in a Gothic mansion. Those drinkers who functioned in a Gothic mansion were in some ways nastier than Comus—the "monks" of Medmenham Abbey. The literary and the real corrupters may be conflated here at the climax of the satire.

It would be rash to claim that Mrs. Barbauld's Comus is necessarily a direct reference to the Order of Saint Francis, better but wrongly known as the Hell-Fire Club. There were various organizations, strict and loose, for riotous living in the eighteenth century. And, of course, she might have been thinking only of Milton's Comus and added the phrase about Gothic mansions because the whole episode of the speaking Tankard is on the Gothic side. But the Medmenham society is a possibility. Exactly when it was founded and how widely it was known about are matters for conjecture, but it gained a sudden notoriety in 1763 (when Mrs. Barbauld was twenty years old) because Wilkes, Churchill, and Lord Sandwich, fellow "monks" but political enemies, were at each others' throats in print and public speech. Newspapers and scandal sheets made the most of the story. Whether the society practiced Satanism or not is still debated, but all kinds of blasphemous religious practices, accompanied by sexual excesses and perversions, were popularly laid at the curiously ornamented door of the society.[12]

That a great deal of drinking occurred is beyond question: the society's wine book, listing names, dates, quantities, and varieties, is still extant (pp. 77-79). The Tankard would have been kept busy. Furthermore, the architectural description—"some spacious mansion, Gothic, old"—fits Medmenham remarkably well. The twelfth-century abbey was largely ruined by the forces of Henry VIII, but a dwelling was constructed "without disturbing much of the original fabric," so it was simultaneously a Gothic heap and a spacious mansion. Sir Francis Dashwood, head of the order, improved upon this odd combination by installing stained glass windows and building "the pseudo-ruins of a tower" on a corner of the building (pp. 84-87). The practices of the society were also associated with the specially designed gardens surrounding the abbey (chapter 7) and were, at least in part, later transferred to chalk caves at West Wycombe (chapter 10); these other locations for alcoholic and venereal activities, if popularly known, could have reinforced the connection with Milton's primarily rural Comus.[13]

Leaving aside the Medmenham conjectures, Milton's Comus supplies sufficiently serious hellfire to create the climax of Mrs. Barbauld's satire. The son of Bacchus and Circe, he carries about with him not a tankard but a crystal glass full of "orient liquor" (l. 65), which, like that in his mother's cup, turns the drinker into a "brutish form" (l. 70). Milton makes it clear that those who drink from this glass are indulging "fond intemperate thirst" (l. 67), which the Tankard specializes in satisfying, as we have seen. When Comus and his rabble get the Lady into the enchanted chair and she refuses his crystal glass, Milton treats us to a description of the drink less specific than Mrs. Barbauld's recipe for spiced ale but even more sensuous: "this cordial Julep here / That flames, and dances in his crystal bounds / With spirits of balm, and fragrant Syrops mixt" (ll. 671-73). Like the Tankard, Comus sneers at "lean and sallow Abstinence" (l. 708) as he argues that the good things of nature were meant to be used. Those who "Drink the clear stream" (l. 721) do so merely in a "pet of temperance" (l. 720), he explains. But the Lady speaks up for Temperance, which causes Comus, like the Tankard, to break out in "a cold shuddering dew . . . all o're" (ll. 801-2). He is, of course, dispatched by both the Lady's virtue and her brothers' force, but it takes Sabrina, the water nymph, to release the seated Lady from her enchantment, by sprinkling her breast with "Drops from my fountain pure" (l. 911). That the Tankard should be associated with Comus in the exercise of evil intemperance to the point at which men are turned to animals or, in Mrs. Barbauld's phrase, "Thought grows giddy," brings the growing seriousness of the satire to its climax.

Not Sabrina, the beautiful water nymph, but an "ancient Sibyl" concludes Mrs. Barbauld's poem. Perhaps this is the maidservant who waits on table in the school; perhaps it is a comic and self-deprecating reference to the poet herself, less than thirty years old but "sour and stern" from the Tankard's point of view. That she is called a Sibyl, a prophetess of Apollo, adds to the mock heroic tone of the poem. "Sibyl" also means "the will of God,"[14] and it is this power which silences the scandalous Tankard and causes it to break out in another "sudden damp." The Tankard is called "the conscious vessel" at this point, and various senses of "conscious" fit its state: "having guilty knowledge," "self-conscious," as well as "having internal perception or consciousness" (see the *Oxford English Dictionary*). The Tankard shuts up—literally—leaving only low murmurs, perhaps echoes, to "creep along the ground." And, in the final allusion to *The Rape of the Lock,* recalling Belinda's repeater watch (1:18), the air continues to vibrate with the "silver sound." We are back on the level of beautiful artifacts and petty vanities, leaving behind us grave corruptions of state, church, and spirit. But we have seen them. For all its fun, the poem has as much to say about real evil as does its model, *The Rape of the Lock*—perhaps even more.

Mrs. Barbauld dealt with serious matters in the playful "The Groans of the Tankard." The mock heroic mode can be merely playful or it can cloak concern with serious matters. Mrs. Barbauld was in a particularly vulnerable position as a woman and a Dissenter, so she wrapped her indictment of the Establishment in Popeian comedy and in the trivia of domesticity allowable in a woman. One could even see the pride of the Tankard as another cloak, pride being a conventional and acceptable target of satire. To some extent, that theme masks her more controversial concerns. Except for the slightly grumpy comments in the *Critical Review,* she seems to have gotten away with it.

When she turned to prose, Mrs. Barbauld donned other cloaks, especially the allegorical. She was always fond of witty indirection and sometimes used it for purposes other than self-protection. Her writing for children and young people is full of allegories, riddles, bits of mock heroic—playful circumlocutions of all sorts—as well as heavy piety. Sometimes her prose pieces for grownups are nearly as purely playful as some of her children's pieces. "Zephyrus and Flora," for example, is a bright bagatelle in which a prudish lady writes a letter of warning to Flora's mother, cautioning her about the liberties that a young man, the breeze, is taking with the girl.[15] The allegory here has no serious point to conceal. The tone is similarly comic in "Letter of John Bull" (1792), but this time the allegory conceals an attack on the growing jingoism of England and the prevalence of loyalty oaths as the Establishment reacted against the French Revolution. "Dialogue in the Shades," on the surface a debate about ancient heroes, has an underlying antiwar theme. That theme is closer to the surface in "The Curé on the Banks of the Rhone" (1791), in which a clergyman describes true religion to a murderous revolutionary committee, which pays no attention to him. This piece is essentially tragic rather than comic satire, however, in the manner of Mark Twain's "War Prayer." But the satire is veiled: the whole story is presented as a letter from a friend and the final sentence is all that makes the satiric point.

In only one essay does the satiric vein dominate without some cloak such as fable or allegory. In the "Letter on Watering-places," a male persona, carefully established as a virtuous but not puritanical character, satirizes the behavior of ladies at a fashionable seaside resort, criticizing their extravagance, hypochondria, snobbery, and other standard follies. Like Lady Winchilsea, Mrs. Barbauld spoke openly when she attacked silly women. She has made her speaker here a man, perhaps to give the criticism added authority, but there can be no doubt that she shared the speaker's values, as her temperate and strenuously useful life indicates. On such a subject, she had no need of a cloak.

The single overt satire among her poems is "The Rights of Woman," undated but obviously an attack on Mary Wollstonecraft's "Vindication of the Rights of Woman" (1792).[16] The poem begins, apparently supporting Mary Wollstonecraft, with a clarion call to "injured Woman" to arise and assert her rights. The tone soon grows questionable, however, as woman is urged to make man "kiss the golden sceptre of [her] reign," and to "Make treacherous Man [her] subject, not [her] friend." Soon woman becomes the "courted idol of mankind" on a "proud eminence," which has uncomfortable overtones of Satan on his "bad eminence" in *Paradise Lost* (2:6). But woman cannot stay on that eminence, the poem declares, because Nature will make her coldness and pride soften until "separate rights are lost in mutual love." The inevitability of love, and its destruction of maiden pride and scorn, is also the theme of Mrs. Barbauld's "Song III," which is mildly comic. Here, in "The Rights of Woman," she uses the same idea in the service of her satire, as she modulates from ironic agreement with Wollstonecraft through exaggerated claims for female sovereignty to the conclusion that Nature will simply cancel out such wrong thinking.[17] There was no need to soften or conceal an attack on that hyena in petticoats, already established as the proper object for public scorn.

But when Mrs. Barbauld cast her satiric eye on men, indeed on the whole male sex, she donned again the cloak of mock heroic. In "Washing-Day," using rolling Miltonic periods, she stuck a pin in the balloon of masculine pride and simultaneously glorified the endless drudgery of women.

Parodies of Milton's blank verse had long been popular, and the mode was flexible enough to serve a variety of purposes. John Philips's "The Splendid Shilling" (1701), for instance, has no particular point but offers a delightful compendium of Miltonic stylistic grandeurs applied to such low topics as the narrator's worn-out galligaskins. Philips turned again to Miltonics in "Cyder" (1708) and this time the style, coupled with imitation of Virgil's *Georgics,* dignifies the humble business of making cider and places it in a context of queens, heroes, and patriotism in general. Lady Winchilsea adopted the Miltonic mode in "Fanscomb Barn" (1713), but here a satiric point lurks below the surface of the imitation. Most of the poem is a long speech delivered by Strolepedon, a wandering beggar, to his wife, Budgeta. They have begged a drink and are slightly tiddly. Strolepedon regales Budgeta with a description of Fanscomb (which she can see perfectly well for herself at the time), a description decorated with classical allusions and couched in elevated Miltonic periods. As soon as his spiel makes reference to Morpheus, however, she falls asleep. Strolepedon comes across as a domineering, pompous, conceited ass, lording it over his wife. The satire also glances at *Paradise Lost* and Milton's own volubility, especially in Book VIII, where Eve, after putting up with Raphael's lengthy descriptions of the war in heaven and the creation for two and a half books, silently slips away to tend the garden. Eve has more stamina than Budgeta, but even she wilts at last. Milton is both model for and object of Lady Winchilsea's satire.

The same can be said of Mrs. Barbauld's "Washing-Day" (see the appendix), though the main focus of the satire lies elsewhere. The poem begins with an invocation to the "domestic Muse." The narrator, looking back on her childhood, traces the progress of the evil day from the arrival of the "red-armed washers," with speculations on the weather, through the dinner hour (pity the guest, if one should come on this day!), to her banishment from her usual company and her reception by the parlor fire, where the grandmother entertains her and the other little ones. As the poem ends, the children blow soap bubbles while they listen to the sounds of rinsing and starching and ironing.

Washing day was indeed a major event in seventeenth- and eighteenth-century households. Pepys records it regularly in the earlier volumes of his diary, often introducing the day's entry with a label, "washing day,"[18] something he always did for the "Lords day" and occasionally for his own birthday and the anniversary of Charles I's death. Other days are not labeled. Clearly, washing day was important to him. He notes on November 19, 1660, for example, that his wife stayed up until 2:00 A.M. so that she could wake "the wench" to start the washing on the twentieth—the day, he notes grimly, when he came home from the playhouse and alehouse only to find "the house in a washing pickle." On November 19, 1661, he found his wife alone in a small room with a gentleman caller, which roused his jealousy until he realized that it was washing day and there was no other room sufficiently warm and dry to sit in. On March 1, 1663, he skipped the usual family prayers at night because tomorrow was washing day, a day which he prudently spent away from home, but he still found the "house foul" on his return. On March 25, 1663, washing day was worse than usual because Susan, the maid, was sick, "or would be thought so," Pepys comments suspiciously. And so it went.

Despite some improvements in plumbing and other domestic conveniences, the day was still dire in Mrs. Barbauld's time. Its importance gives a doubleness to the mock heroic treatment it gets in her poem. Clearly, the events of such a day are not true epic matter: no pagan or Christian heroes wage war with Troy or Satan. The domestic is, by definition, less significant—so much so that one feels even Milton struggling to maintain his elevation of tone when Eve prepares a fruit salad for Adam and Raphael; bathetically, she has "No fear lest Dinner coole" (5:396) when their protracted conversation makes them late. And yet washing day loomed as large on the domestic front as the siege of Troy or Heaven on the international or cosmic. It was a day when nothing else could be done, when the women of the family and their helpers reigned supreme and the husbands and fathers lurked in the shrubbery or went to the office, unwanted and unattended to.

Women had power on washing day. Here the sex of the author makes an important difference to the handling of the mock heroic. When Pope belittled Belinda for having hysterics over the haircut, one sees, for all the complexity of tone in that poem, the expected mock heroic gap between the littleness of the occasion, from the author's point of view, and the largeness of the language. In "Washing-Day," however, the largeness of the language is both appropriate to the largeness of the events, from the woman's domestic point of view, and comically, mock heroically, inappropriate, because the domestic is considered necessarily trivial. Unless the house is in a pickle! Perhaps Mrs. Barbauld chose Milton rather than Pope as her model for this poem because, on one level, she wanted the grandeur of blank verse paragraphs (rather than the chime of couplets) to support the *real* importance of the occasion, to dignify the drudgery of women.

And yet, as in Lady Winchilsea's "Fanscomb Barn," Milton himself receives a light satiric lash in the poem. The Muses have discarded their tragic buskins and "Language of gods" for "slipshod measure loosely prattling on," a most uncomplimentary description of Miltonic blank verse and perhaps also a bit of self-deprecation here. But Mrs. Barbauld practices that versification with skill. She combines regularity and metrical freedom as Milton does; she sometimes uses a short line, the kind of dramatic breaking of the pattern which Milton used in *Lycidas* and *Samson Agonistes* though not in *Paradise Lost*. After the invocation, the poem is divided into three long verse paragraphs, the first devoted to the washerwomen, the second to the sufferings of unwanted menfolk and children, and the third to the musings of the child. Each paragraph has the true Miltonic sweep, as the thought moves logically but unconfined within the paragraph's general topic.

Mrs. Barbauld imitates Milton's language as well as his versification and paragraphing. She does not use epic similes, perhaps because her poem is relatively short, but she does use an occasional Latinism or archaism ("impervious," "welkin") and a few exotic names (Erebus, Guatimozin).[19] She adopts the Miltonic trick of substituting one part of speech for another: "abrupt" for "abruptly," "indiscreet" as a noun. She uses apposition, "grandmother, eldest of forms," echoing Milton's "Night, eldest of things" (*PL* 2: 962), and she leaves out the occasional "the." She also imitates that most Miltonic of devices, the inversion of natural word order. The device was controversial and was felt to be undesirable in excess. Both Addison and Johnson objected to overuse of it, which may be why it is dear to the hearts of imitators.[20] Lady Winchilsea used it in "Fanscomb Barn"; Philips used it even more in "The Splendid Shilling." Mrs. Barbauld makes regular use of it: "From the wet kitchen scared and reeking hearth" is a fairly long mix-up, while "snug recess impervious" is simpler. The figure lends itself to another Miltonic device, that of repetition: "Or tart or pudding:—pudding he nor tart / That day shall eat . . ."; or, without inversion, "Cast at the lowering sky, if sky should lower." Milton's own repetitions are less formulaic than those of his imitators, but the formulaic repetitions certainly *feel* Miltonic, contributing to the heaviness and spurious dignity of the mock heroic style.

Mrs. Barbauld also imitates Milton, to some extent, in that she uses learned literary allusions. She begins her poem with an epigraph from *As You Like It,* lines from Jaques's speech on the seven ages of man, slightly misquoted (*AYL,* II.vi.139-66). The same speech lies behind Mrs. Barbauld's line early in the poem, "By little whimpering boy, with rueful face"; Shakespeare's schoolboy is "whining" (he never used the word "whimpering") and his face is "shining" rather than "rueful," but his unwilling creeping would make one think of rueful feelings. The allusion is plain. Perhaps too Mrs. Barbauld was remembering *The Winter's Tale* when she mentioned "pleasant curds and cream" as a subject for the domestic Muse; in that play, Camillo dubs the lovely Perdita "the queen of curds and cream" (IV.iv.161). Homer's "rosy-fingered dawn" gets an ironic twist when Mrs. Barbauld's dawn produces a "gray streak" accompanied by "red-armed washers." She also alludes to Swift's mock heroic "A Description of a City Shower" when, amid speculations about rain, the unwanted master of the family cannot have his coat dusted; in the "Shower," Swift devotes several lines to the problems created by a mixture of dust and rain in the needy poet's "Sole Coat." The allusions to the "Shower" continue with the word "welkin" in the same paragraph and with the "impatient hand" that "Twitched" the apron off the shrubs "when showers impend"; Swift begins with a scene in which "Rain depends" (which means "impends") and describes "Brisk *Susan* [who] whips her Linen from the Rope."

What does it all add up to—the Miltonic versification and style, the learned references to Shakespeare and others, the application of the heroic mode to the domestic crisis that was washing day? The reference near the end of the poem to "Mongolfier" (properly Montgolfier) is, I think, the clue. In June 1783, the brothers Montgolfier caused to rise from the ground in France a linen globe filled with hot smoky air from a fire made of chopped straw. Excitement was considerable, and a number of other balloon experiments were carried out in the same year, including one in which enthusiasm among the spectators ran so high that a violent downpour of rain drenched them all but did not dampen their interest. Among these experiments was another by the Montgolfiers before the king and queen, using a sheep, a cock, and a duck as the first passengers in a cage hung under the balloon. Silk was the material used in some balloons and human beings soon became the cargo. Smoky air was sometimes replaced by hydrogen. Aeronautics was born.[21]

In "Washing-Day," Mrs. Barbauld looks back to her childhood when she blew "and sent aloft" soap bubbles, "little dreaming then" that the "silken ball" of Montgolfier would "Ride buoyant through the clouds." But it did, and the mature poet adds the sardonic comment, "so near approach / The sports of children and the toils of men."

She had made the same point in an earlier poem, "Written on a Marble":

> The world's something bigger,
> But just of this figure
> And speckled with mountains and seas;

> Your heroes are overgrown schoolboys
> Who scuffle for empires and toys,
> And kick the poor ball as they please.
> Now Caesar, now Pompey, gives law;
>   And Pharsalia's plain,
>   Though heaped with the slain,
>   Was only a game at *taw.*

In its witty brevity and its belittling of heroes, this poem is something like Lady Winchilsea's "Song Upon a Punch Bowl," in which Alexander the Great gets drunk and cries not for another world to conquer but for another bowl of punch. It is also consistent with several of Mrs. Barbauld's prose writings that, directly or indirectly, oppose war. The masculine world of glory and conquest did not win this woman's admiration.

Male pride has been the central focus of "Washing-Day" throughout, from the epigraph on the sixth age of man when the voice turns to "childish treble" to the nuisances that menfolk make of themselves when women are engaged in the serious business of washing. The man "Who call'st thyself perchance the master" is dispossessed on washing day. Even more pointedly, his greatest exploits, imaged in the Montgolfier balloon, are reduced to the level of children's games. Not that Mrs. Barbauld was hostile to balloonists as such—indeed, in her letters she shows great interest in the whole business of ballooning.[22] But the assumption that what men do is important and what women do is not, is turned upside down. The women's washing is heroic; the men's exploits are child's play.

Such a reversal of values was dangerous. In "Written on a Marble," the idea could be dismissed as a brief joke or taken as serious criticism of war, but in "Washing-Day," with the explicit comparison between men's and women's deeds, the poet was taking a risk. She minimized that risk by using the mock heroic mode, which lends itself so well to the domestic and which could always be dismissed as merely playful. She also misquoted Shakespeare in her epigraph. She prints the lines thus: ". . . and their voice, / Turning again towards childish treble, pipes / And whistles in its sound." Shakespeare had written "his big, manly voice."²³ "Their voice," however ungrammatical, blunts the sting. So does the second ending of the poem. After the lines comparing men to children, Mrs. Barbauld continues: "Earth, air, and sky, and ocean hath its bubbles, / And verse is one of them—this most of all." This final ending masks the announcement of the satiric point, which loses what would have been the place of most emphasis, the last line. The sting is further lessened by the claim that the poem is a mere bubble. The self-deprecating quality of the lines is enhanced by the poet-as-child blowing soap bubbles a few lines earlier and continuing to exhibit childishness, as she implies, by writing poetry. The self-deprecation becomes even stronger when one thinks of the usual reference to self at the ends of other poems: Pope's claim that "this Lock" will inscribe Belinda's name among the stars; Shakespeare's conclusion to Sonnet 18, "So long lives this, and this gives life to thee"; and all the other statements that the poet can confer immortality on his subject. Mrs. Barbauld says instead that her verse is a bubble, that most ephemeral of creations. Very few women writers make the claim that they can immortalize their subjects. Anne Killigrew does in "A Pastoral Dialogue"; Lady Winchilsea does in "Melinda on an Insippid Beauty." These are, however, rare instances of women making the claim that was routine for men.

And yet Mrs. Barbauld is not simply wallowing in self-deprecation in her final lines. For she has said "And verse is" a bubble, not just her own verse. And she has equated the most thrilling inventions of men with the sports of children, however much she has blunted the sting. Wearing her cloak, she got away with it.

Mrs. Barbauld was not only a writer of literature but also a literary critic, especially a critic of fiction, including satiric fiction. She edited a fifty-volume collection, *The British Novelists* (1810), which includes several texts that are satiric in whole or in part, among them books by women. In her prefaces to these books and her essay introducing the whole collection, she com-

ments favorably on satire, without making any particular distinction between novels by men and by women. She relishes the
mock heroic humor in Fielding and the satire in Fanny Burney:
in *Evelina,* she finds that Miss Burney is "Equally happy in seiz-
ing the ridiculous, and in entering into the finer feelings," and
she dubs the satirical Mrs. Selwyn "a wit and an oddity." She is
glad that Cervantes' "immortal satire" drove romances out of
fashion, and she delights in the best imitation of Cervantes,
Charlotte Lennox's *The Female Quixote,* which she calls "an
agreeable and ingenious satire." Indeed, the only thing wrong
with *The Female Quixote* is that it is not satiric enough: the heavy
sermon at the end which "recovers" the heroine is an error; that
recovery should have been brought about by more satire, "the
sense of ridicule . . . [or] some absurd mistake."[24] Clearly, Mrs.
Barbauld felt no distaste for the satiric mode and had no reser-
vations about a woman's right to practice it.

And yet there is a hint, a slight suggestion, that women writers run particular risks. In her discussion of *Evelina,* Mrs. Barbauld comments on Fanny Burney's youth when that novel first
appeared, and she generalizes, in nostalgic tones, about the joys
of first authorship and the pleasures of success when a young
writer is still "happily ignorant of all the chills and mortifications . . . , the ridicule and censure which fasten on vulnerable
parts."[25] The passage does not mention an author's sex nor does
it specify satire as a "vulnerable part," but Mrs. Barbauld has
chosen a preface to a woman's novel, a novel which contains an
important element of satire, in which to lament the dangers of
authorship. She could have had women satirists in mind.

She had herself experienced "chills and mortifications" when
she had dared to speak out in critical tones on matters of public
concern. Her early poem on Corsica, a public topic, had not
been controversial or critical, and it escaped attack. But her
prose pamphlet on the Corporation and Test Acts, published in
1790, was highly critical, even sarcastic in its ridicule of those
parliamentarians who upheld the Acts. Although published

anonymously, it earned her the titles "that virago Barbauld" and "Deborah" from Horace Walpole. When the Reverend Keate, attacking the same pamphlet, learned that it was written by a woman, he expressed shock and surprise that "'in soft bosoms dwells such mighty rage.'"[26] Other controversial works met with varying receptions. Mrs. Barbauld suffered the strongest attack when she published "Eighteen Hundred and Eleven," a narrative poem in which she imagines a visitor from the New World exploring the ruins of an England reduced to a primitive state by its immorality and decadence and its involvement with a long continental war. Although the poem glorifies the literature and philosophy of England, it was perceived as unpatriotic and the poet came under heavy fire.

Interestingly, in its comments on "Eighteen Hundred and Eleven," the *Quarterly Review* attacked Mrs. Barbauld for becoming a satirist. Yet the poem contains none of the satirical techniques she had used elsewhere, no mock heroics, no irony, no ridicule, sarcasm, allegory, or fable, not even any witty clevernesses of language. It is sober, serious, elegiac in tone, prophesying doom. It is satire, of course, in that it expresses critical disapproval, and clearly the reviewer was reacting to the ideas in the poem. But he chose to criticize its mode, to abuse the woman for being a satirist, indeed, as he seems to think, for becoming a satirist for the first time:

> Our old acquaintance Mrs. Barbauld turned satirist! The last thing we should have expected, and, now that we have seen her satire, the last thing we could have desired. . . . we think she has wandered from the course in which she was respectable and useful, and miserably mistaken both her powers and her duty, in exchanging the birchen for the satiric rod, and abandoning the "ovilia" of the nursery, to wage war on the "reluctantes dracones," statesmen and warriors, whose misdoings have aroused her indignant muse. . . . We had hoped, indeed, that the empire might have been saved without the intervention of a lady-author. . . . an irresistible impulse of public duty—a confident

sense of commanding talents—have induced her to dash down her shagreen spectacles and her knitting needles and to sally forth. . . .

The hostility is obvious—the woman has left her proper sphere and trespassed on the affairs of men, specifically on the male preserve of satire. Indeed, the reviewer goes on to "take the liberty of warning her to desist from satire, which indeed is satire on herself alone. . . ." Mrs. Barbauld was so crushed by this and other reactions to her poem that she published no more during her lifetime.[27]

As the eighteenth century drew to a close, satire grew steadily less acceptable and the satirist became an increasingly unattractive figure. But a female satirist, who had always been unattractive unless she was criticizing other women, was now entirely beyond the pale. Yet long before she was attacked for "Eighteen Hundred and Eleven," Mrs. Barbauld had shown that she belongs to the mainstream of English literature when she so skillfully used that most central of satiric forms, the mock heroic. It's ironic.

EIGHT

CHOICES OF LIFE

Samuel Johnson and Ellis Cornelia Knight

THE ORIENTAL TALE is not every reader's favorite genre. Some find its emotional, geographical, and supernatural extravagances tedious, while others find them stylistically fascinating or psychologically revealing. Some are amused by what Martha Pike Conant labels "the imaginative group," while others, less sympathetic to the whole of the varied genre, are amused only by the "satiric group," which, when not engaged in social criticism, spoofs the oriental tale itself. Few critics have turned their attention to the oriental tale for any detailed consideration. At times, the Gothic umbrella is extended to cover Beckford's *Vathek,* for example; indeed, Beckford's admirers publish regularly. And "horror-romanticism" sometimes overlaps the oriental.[1] But little has been done to develop or refine Conant's rather simple taxonomy of the genre or to approach it in other ways.

Criticism is not lacking, however, on Johnson's *Rasselas,* which Conant classifies as belonging partly to the "moralistic" but primarily to the "philosophic" groups (pp. 97, 118-24). More recent approaches dub *Rasselas* tragedy, comedy, absurdist—what you will.[2] The problems posed by its inconclusive conclusion in particular continue to produce lively critical debate. The complexities, perhaps even inconsistencies, of John-

197

son's thought are such that the critical debate promises to be as inconclusive as *Rasselas* itself.

Yet *Rasselas* has a conclusion, a little-known sequel published in 1790 entitled *Dinarbas; A Tale: Being A Continuation of* RASSE-LAS, *Prince of Abissinia,* written by Ellis Cornelia Knight. Conant classifies *Dinarbas* with the "moralistic group" and states dismissively that it "is obviously inferior to its predecessor; its value is not literary but historical . . ." (p. 104). The bicentenary celebration of the publication of *Rasselas* drew attention once again to the sequel, and C. J. Rawson, after a lengthy plot summary, concluded that *Dinarbas* managed to "answer" Johnson not systematically but by "glib and perfunctory implication," that it sometimes contains "a not un-Johnsonian irony," and that it is "an agreeable enough book" with "a certain amiable neatness of its own." A similar mixture of scorn and condescending praise characterizes the brief discussion of *Dinarbas* in Barbara Luttrell's biography of Cornelia Knight: it is "a failure both in degree and in concept" as a sequel to *Rasselas,* but the story "has its own merits." Except for a few such comments and an occasional footnote, Miss Knight's sequel rests in obscurity.[3]

But that obscurity is not deserved. *Dinarbas* is an entertaining "oriental" yarn, as its critics admit, with more action and a more satisfactory conclusion than *Rasselas* contains. It was intended by its author not as a refutation of Johnson's gloomy view of life, as its critics have assumed, but, like the book you hold in your hand, dear reader, as a counterbalance, a completion of the picture. Miss Knight puts it this way: "It is indeed much to be regretted that the same pencil which so forcibly painted the evils attendant on humanity, had not delineated the fairer prospect. That such a prospect exists, will scarcely be denied; and if the narrative of DINARBAS, however defective, shall be found to afford any consolation or relief to the wretched traveller, terrified and disheartened at the rugged paths of life, this reflection will compensate the want of genius and literary fame of its author. . . ."[4] The *ut pictura poesis* image implies a variety of views of the human condition, perhaps even a whole gallery of paintings, in which one hangs beside another, supplementing rather than denying or canceling each other. The image of "the rugged paths of life," as traditionally Augustan as the painting image, indicates a vivid if conventional sense of the reality of evil, and yet "consolation or relief" is available—and is to be provided by Miss Knight's tale. Johnson himself did not exclude consolation and relief from *Rasselas*. With wonderful comic irony, for example, he allows that Rasselas derived "some solace" for the miseries of his boredom in the Happy Valley "from consciousness of the delicacy with which he felt, and the eloquence with which he bewailed them."[5] And apparently Johnson had plans to provide more solid consolations for his hero. In his *Life of Johnson*, Sir John Hawkins reported that "Johnson had meditated a second part [of *Rasselas*] in which he meant to marry his hero, and place him in a state of permanent felicity."[6] Miss Knight quotes Hawkins and says straightforwardly, "This passage suggested the idea of the continuation now offered . . ." (p. vii). Clearly, her plan was not to deny the validity of Johnson's vision but to extend his vision—to deny only that he had told the whole story of Rasselas and depicted the entirety of the human condition. She gives us both a re-vision and a further vision.

To begin with the plot. *Dinarbas* picks up exactly where *Rasselas* leaves off: the flooding of the Nile in chapter 49 of *Rasselas* drives the travelers indoors, where they discuss their projects for choosing happy lives and conclude only that they will return to Abyssinia; chapter 1 of *Dinarbas* begins, "The inundation having subsided, the prince and princess with their companions left Cairo, and proceeded on the way to Abissinia . . ." (p. 1). When they arrive at the border, however, they are stopped by a party of armed men who conduct them to a fortress, as unidentified strangers are not permitted to enter the country (and Rasselas, though admitting his nationality, conceals his name and rank). Amalphis, the governor of the fortress, welcomes them courteously, and our travelers send messengers to the court to request permission to enter Abyssinia. The messengers are slow, and much happens before they return. Rasselas finds himself interested in Amalphis's daughter, Zilia, and, to take his mind off her, joins Amalphis's son, Dinarbas, in a military expedition, which cements their growing friendship. Dinarbas too falls in love, with Nekayah, and suffers from her haughtiness. The two young men notice each other's gloom and decide on another military expedition as a cure, but the war comes to them instead; "a large body of Egyptians and Arabs" arrives to besiege the fortress (p. 32). Meanwhile, love grows in all four bosoms, complicated by the concealed identity of the royal brother and sister, their superior rank, and a brief spell of jealousy when Dinarbas seeks out Pekuah's conversation to distract him from his feelings for Nekayah.

The Arabs and Egyptians attack and lose the battle but manage to capture Rasselas and kill Dinarbas before they flee. The narrative follows Rasselas at this point, as he finds former acquaintances among the Egyptians and observes the behavior of a party of shepherds. When the prisoners are divided, the Arabs take Rasselas and imprison him in a remote tower in total solitude except for two slaves who bring him food and water. The narrator leaves him struggling for resignation in his tower and returns to the fortress, where, after much mourning and a splendid funeral oration, Dinarbas is about to be buried when Nekayah discovers that he is still alive. Properly cared for, he regains his health and strength with remarkable speed. As soon as he can, he pays a call on Nekayah, having heard that she wept over him and rescued him from a premature grave. The princess reveals her identity and swears Dinarbas to secrecy; he agrees that he is too humble in rank to aspire to her hand and promises that he will love in silence forever. When his health is fully restored, he sets out to find Rasselas, shortly before the messengers arrive with letters from the emperor of Abyssinia.

All is not well in Abyssinia. The emperor's eldest son has been killed in battle, the second and third sons are plotting to take over the kingdom, and the emperor demands that Rasselas, the fourth son, come to his aid. Nekayah is in a quandary. What to do in her brother's absence? The narrator now shifts back to Rasselas, who is at long last rescued by a party of Turks and returns to the fortress where he learns the news, asks for Zilia's hand in marriage, and dashes away to assist his father, still concealing his true identity from the inhabitants of the fortress. In Gonthar, the capital city, Rasselas reorganizes hs father's army and confronts his two older brothers at the conference table. Negotiations break down, Rasselas defeats his brothers in battle, one escapes and one is captured, the emperor is reestablished on the throne, and Rasselas retires to the Happy Valley with his captive brother. Nekayah, Imlac, and the astronomer soon join him there. The captive brother dies amid lengthy speeches of repentance, but the escaped brother, Menas, returns to the emperor, worms his way into favor, and gradually takes over the government, sending the emperor into retirement in the Happy Valley. His mind poisoned by Menas, the emperor imprisons Rasselas, Nekayah, Imlac, and the astronomer— separately—but Dinarbas appears, scales the walls in the best romantic fashion, tells Rasselas the story of his adventures, and, with much difficulty, convinces the emperor of Rasselas's innocence and of the perfidy of Menas. Dinarbas has the backing of the sultan he visited in his travels, and indeed calls upon the sultan's forces to help the emperor regain his throne, during which operation Menas is killed. The emperor soon dies of various infirmities, physical and moral, and Rasselas ascends the throne. He is, of course, a model ruler, marries Zilia (though she offers to release him from his engagement when she learns who he is), sanctions the marriage of Nekayah and Dinarbas (whose heroism has won him the right to the hand of the princess), and destroys the gates of the Happy Valley, setting all its inmates free. And they all live happily ever after.

Clearly, *Dinarbas* is a much busier book than *Rasselas,* with battles, treachery, politics, love affairs, and other adventures too numerous to mention, of which the minimal plot summary here gives only a suggestion. And yet, like Johnson's characters, Miss Knight's people find time to sit down and discuss, at length, their encounters, their observations, and their ideas on a wide variety of subjects. She follows, though with different proportions, Johnson's pattern of alternating philosophic discourse with plot action. The style of the discourse, too, is a fair imitation of Johnson's: contemplating a return to the Happy Valley, Rasselas says, "'wandering has often given a momentary desire of settled residence; but activity is natural to man, and he who has once tasted the joys of liberty and action, will no more be contented with perpetual rest and seclusion, than he, who may have wished for sleep in a moment of lassitude, would desire to remain inactive on his couch, after the light of the sun has awakened him from oblivion and repose'" (pp. 3-4)—Johnsonian in sentiment as well as in its balanced clauses and partly Latinate vocabulary. Miss Knight's periods do not roll quite as sonorously as Johnson's, especially when the narrative is hastening along, but the flavor is there. And among the "not un-Johnsonian" ironies is the observation that Nekayah, who believes she has conquered her feelings for Dinarbas, yet finds herself bored and weary when he is gone, and, "Unwilling to suppose her victory incomplete . . . attributed her anxiety and restlessness to the uncertainty of her fate, to the situation of her brother, to a thousand causes, none of which had occurred to her a few days before" (p. 124).

Many of Miss Knight's sentiments as well as her style echo Johnson's. For example, Nekayah, wrestling with the question of the disparity between her rank and Dinarbas's, explains that she considers such matters mere prejudice but "'a prejudice established by the universal custom of ages [which] consequently ought to be respected'" (p. 99); Johnson's respect for rank, subordination, and established custom appears over and over again in his talk.[7] They agree that public education produces better results than private because the boys are fruitfully stimulated by "emulation"—they even use the same word.[8] Miss Knight describes the importance of first impressions in the education of children, impressions "'given by women'" and "'difficult to efface'" (p. 296), to which Johnson bears witness when he tells Boswell of learning about heaven and hell as a little child in bed with his mother.[9] Johnson and Miss Knight have much in common.

Yet it is not only the similarities—of pattern, style, and sentiment—or the different affirmation about the attainability of happiness that makes *Dinarbas* so interesting to read. It is also a different mode of handling character and the consequences—or purposes—of that different mode that are intriguing. Johnson's main characters are observers of life and mouthpieces for different points of view. Sometimes they are objects of satire: the procrastinating Rasselas of chapter 4, the enthusiastic Imlac raving about poetry in chapter 10, and the insensitive Pekuah laughing at the astronomer's madness in chapter 43, to cite only a few instances. Johnson chastises them with his ironies and sometimes allows them to chastise each other; Imlac especially is used for that purpose. But more often they observe, report, and discuss. They are not involved in the life they see; they do not form relationships with the people they encounter. This is not to say that Johnson is at fault in his method of handling character. He is writing not a novel but a tragi-comic-absurdist-satiric apologue, a philosophical oriental tale, a whatever-you-call-it, designed to stimulate thought, not to imitate life. Miss Knight, on the other hand, for all her similarities to Johnson, is imitating something like life as she perceives it. Her characters are not only observers and mouthpieces, though they have those functions; they are not only objects of satire, although their naive and wrongheaded views are chastised; they are also, to some extent, novelistic characters who interact with other people, form relationships, suffer and rejoice, learn and grow and change. When these more developed characters repeat the encounters they had in Johnson's narrative or meet similar, parallel circumstances, or when they engage in discussion of the same or similar ideas, the different angle of vision that Miss Knight expresses is very interesting indeed.

Two repeated encounters reveal much of that vision: the encounters with the "young men of spirit and gaiety" in Cairo and with the shepherds.

Johnson's Rasselas, in chapter 17, joined a society of young men whom he believed to be happy, but he soon found that he was ashamed of a course of life in which "their mirth was without images; their laughter without motive; their pleasures . . . gross and sensual . . . ; their conduct at once wild and mean" (p. 80). Although he disapproved of their way of life, he found the young men frank and courteous, so he exerted himself to reform them before he left their company. His solemn speech about their follies produced only blank stares followed by derisive laughter. Embarrassed, Rasselas decamped.

In *Dinarbas,* when Rasselas is captured by the combined forces of Arabs and Egyptians, he recognizes among his Egyptian captors several of the young men he had known in Cairo (p. 49). "They received him with joy, for they had equally forgotten the abrupt manner in which he had quitted their society, and the good admonitions he had left with them" (p. 49). Rasselas is cold to them, remembering his humiliation, but finding as the days go by that he must have some company, he begins to associate with them again. This time, he is more observant, and more discriminating in his observations: "He began to discern, in the midst of frantic gaiety and remorseless dissipation, sparks of honour, sincerity and good-nature . . . : he pitied and esteemed the possessors of these virtues; and, having found by experience that severe rebuke and the air of superior prudence produced an effect contrary to his wishes, he took gentler and more successful means" (p. 51). "By applauding their ardour," Rasselas teaches the young Egyptians to distinguish true virtues from specious ones, including "courage from temerity" and "friendship from blind affection." He discovers that most of the young men are reclaimable and that friendly kindness and praise sugarcoat his message better than his former severity. Gradually, the young men reform, "Even those who before had seemed incorrigible" (p. 53), which inspires Rasselas to conduct some rueful self-examination. He asks himself why he had not tried the positive approach when he first met these young men. "He, who would wish to reform his fellow creatures, must study attentively the human heart: he must treat with tenderness the man whom weakness, not perverseness, has caused to deviate from the path of virtue: he must fortify by degrees his returning energy, nor dazzle at once the eyes of error with all the splendor of severe truth. . . . henceforward let me avoid the pride of reproof and the frown of disapprobation: let me endeavour to instruct by example, and persuade by kindness!" (pp. 53–54).

Miss Knight's Rasselas is very different from Johnson's in this incident: he reacts to and interacts with the young men as individuals, not as an undistinguished mass; with great practicality, he uses a method of reform when he finds that it works; still holding fast to Johnsonian moral principles, he works on the hearts of the young men in order to establish those principles in their heads. Most important, he advises himself, after he has thought over the matter, to avoid "'the pride of reproof'" in any further such instruction he may engage in. He has learned from his experience. And "he acquired the right of censuring their faults" by joining in the innocent pleasures and praising the occasional virtues of his students (p. 52). Johnson's Rasselas simply assumed the right to censure. Here, and many times throughout *Dinarbas,* Miss Knight herself censures what she perceives as pride in Johnson's characters, the pride of the observer-mouthpiece who forms no relationships with his or her objects of observation. But Johnson, by humiliating Rasselas at the end of the encounter with the young Egyptians, had censured not his pride but his naïveté in thinking a mere sermon could reform the young men.

It is also significant that when Miss Knight's Rasselas successfully reforms the young Egyptians, he is a prisoner of war. From a position of powerlessness, desperate for human company, he learns to use mercy and kindness, ingratiating himself with the young sinners and playing on their feelings to win them to the side of righteousness. Miss Knight has not made her Rasselas effeminate nor compromised his virtue, but as a woman she understood the power of indirect, even devious tactics in the hands of the powerless.

In the next chapter of *Dinarbas* and in chapter 19 of *Rasselas,* the prince encounters a party of shepherds. Johnson's primary intention in his encounter is to debunk edenic pastoral fiction. Imlac proposes that the travelers spend a day among the shepherds, mentioning that their life has been "'often celebrated for its innocence and quiet'" (p. 85). Rasselas and his company "induced the shepherds, by small presents and familiar questions, to tell their opinion of their own state." The shepherds turn out to be "rude and ignorant," inarticulate, with hearts "cankered with discontent"; "they considered themselves as condemned to labour for the luxury of the rich, and looked up with stupid malevolence toward those that were placed above them" (p. 85). The travelers are disgusted, but the pastoral dream dies hard: Nekayah still hopes for a happy life among the flowers and the lambs. Here, as often in *Rasselas,* experience has no effect on established notions—which is one of Johnson's satiric points.

Miss Knight reaffirms the pastoral dream in *Dinarbas.* Rasselas, still a prisoner, notices as he marches along with his captors that "great cordiality subsisted between the soldiers and the inhabitants of the country" (p. 55). The shepherds supply not only milk and "fruits of the earth" to the soldiers but also "useful instructions . . . for the remainder of the march." They even provide amusement with their "pastoral sports" (p. 55). Astonished at this hospitality, Rasselas describes his previous unhappy experience to an old shepherd and expresses his pleasure in finding that at least some shepherds retain the pastoral virtues as described by the poets. The old shepherd sets him straight, explaining that Rasselas's earlier acquaintances are even more hospitable and virtuous than his new ones and that they had reasons for appearing so unattractive when Rasselas and his party first visited them. Although he diplomatically eschews the word "pride," that is what the old shepherd is talking about. He explains that the shepherds are accustomed to looking upon the upper classes as tyrants, as people who visit them only to take the fruits of their labors or to amuse themselves with "'sentiments of ridicule'" (p. 58). Johnson gives very little detail in his handling of the encounter with the shepherds, but the "small presents and familiar questions" his travelers bestow on the shepherds could very easily be interpreted as manifestations of pride. Miss Knight's old shepherd advises Rasselas that if he wants to know the shepherds and what their life is like, he must divest himself of "'superiority'" and "'live like them'"— he must not hand out small presents and ask impertinent questions. The old shepherd then explains why the shepherds get along so well with the soldiers: the soldiers are not rich, they live lives of even greater hardship than the shepherds do, and they make it possible for the shepherds to possess their fields in tranquillity (p. 59). "'Our obligations are reciprocal,'" he concludes, so naturally they are hospitable when the soldiers pass through their lands. Mutual need creates mutual respect, whereas idle curiosity created only "stupid malevolence."

The old shepherd has further thoughts on the effect of a pastoral life on character and behavior, thoughts which support the edenic vision that Johnson set out to debunk. He explains that the party of shepherds Rasselas encountered before, in Johnson's book, are even more hospitable than the present lot because they live in more beautiful surroundings, and "'these images of the power and goodness of the Deity must expand their hearts'" (p. 57). The old shepherd admits that "'the poetical descriptions of pastoral life'" may be embellished, but insists that they are "'not wholly fabulous'" (p. 58), and adds that shepherds are more restive under the yoke of slavery than the other subjects of despotic rule because they see the freedom of other creatures "'under the ample canopy of heaven'" and therefore feel only the oppression by, not any benefits from, their masters (pp. 59-60). The shepherds are so much the children of nature that they cannot disguise their feelings or even "'conceive the necessity of feigning'" (p. 60).

Clearly, Miss Knight has a more romantic attitude toward the pastoral than Johnson. Her sentiments are almost Wordsworthian, in this instance, with a touch of the "noble savage" notion. Perhaps her sex had some influence on this attitude. Perhaps her youth (she was thirty-two when *Dinarbas* was published) and perhaps the approaching nineteenth century had further influence. Whatever the cause, she opposes Johnson's ideas on the pastoral. She does not set out to refute them—such ideas are matters of conviction and are not really subject to systematic, logical refutation. Nor does she set out to prove that he gave a false picture of shepherds' character and behavior in *Rasselas*. Instead, she *explains* that behavior; she comes at the encounter from a different angle of vision, an angle that stresses mutuality and relationship rather than clinical, prideful observation and judgment. Rasselas, the humble prisoner of war and a woman's creation, learns to see differently from Rasselas, the traveling prince, Johnson's creation.

Both Johnson and Miss Knight take up the question of a father's grief for a child's death in incidents less precisely parallel than those of the young Egyptians and the shepherds but nonetheless related. Again, the angle of vision differs. In chapter 18 of *Rasselas,* "the prince finds a wise and happy man," as Johnson's ironic chapter title has it (p. 82). The man is a stoic, lecturing like an angel on the subject of control of the passions. Rasselas admires him and seeks him out, only to find him utterly unstrung by the death of his daughter and impervious to his own arguments as repeated by his admirer. Johnson's satiric point here, besides exposing again the naïveté of Rasselas, is the wrongness of the stoic denial of feeling, indeed the impossibility that rational precept can control grief. The gulf between theory and experience is profound. It is a simple, black-and-white case, without subtleties, all the stronger as a satiric point for being so.

Miss Knight, as she often does, develops the question rather more fully and rather differently. When Dinarbas is wounded, Nekayah approaches his father, Amalphis, and is astonished to find him apparently tranquilly at work, "seated on a sofa writing" (p. 77). He informs her that Dinarbas is dead, "'fallen nobly in the exercise of his duty'" (p. 77). Nekayah is further shocked at Amalphis's lack of sensibility and accuses him of having lost "'the feelings of nature'" under the influence of "'philosophy, courage, or resignation'" (p. 78). Amalphis sets her straight, explaining that "'neither philosophy nor reason could reconcile me to the death of my son: they who would cure grief by declamation, or stifle sentiment by reason, know little of the heart of man'" (p. 78)—a direct response to Johnson's stoic and concurrence with Johnson in his condemnation of the stoic's pretensions to control.

Amalphis continues, describing the depth of his sorrow and the end of all his worldly happiness; life now leaves him only duty. "'Grief does not always shew itself by tears and exclamation,'" he continues (another glance at Johnson's stoic); "'if there is any power in philosophy, it consists in preventing us from giving exterior proofs of our affliction, but it cannot cure the wound inflicted on the heart'" (pp. 78-79). All that saves him is "'resignation to the will of Heaven'" (p. 79). Amalphis is quite Christian in his manner of managing his grief; Johnson's own Christianity is more equivocal, and he has almost entirely excluded Christianity, at least the specific doctrines of Christianity, from his oriental tale, even though Abyssinia was a Christian country.

Something more than Christianity may also be at work here. Nekayah, in an outburst that mixes condemnation of herself for misjudging Amalphis and for acting so proudly toward Dinarbas, praises Amalphis's "'true philosophy'": "'He is miserable, yet he will support his own character, and do his duty to others . . . '" (p. 80). The repression of one's own feelings to carry out one's duties to others is often demanded of men and women, especially often of women. Nekayah, princess though she is, recognizes this as "true philosophy." And it was a philosophy that Cornelia Knight had to practice for most of her life. Living in genteel poverty with her mother on the Continent, she danced attendance on that eccentric and demanding lady, who finally died at seventy-two in 1799 when Cornelia herself was forty-one. By that time, any hopes she may have had for love and marriage were gone. Her self-repression went on, as she trailed in the wake of Nelson and the Hamiltons, and as she submitted to the routine of the court (which nearly killed Fanny Burney) as companion to Princess Charlotte. Only in her last years, financially independent and enjoying again the society of the Continent, was she free to act and feel as she chose.[10] It is impossible to gauge how much her "true philosophy" cost her, for it extended even to her diaries, in which she never mentioned her several books and set down little if anything of her heart.[11] Perhaps she didn't know how. Or perhaps her sense of duty—the duty to appear cheerful—extended, like Elizabeth Carter's, even to private forms of communication.[12] However that may be, she gives to Nekayah the recognition that repression of feeling is a virtue.

The idea appears more than once in *Dinarbas*. The priest who delivers the funeral oration over the supposed corpse of Dinarbas commends the young warrior most particularly for being superior to the enticements of fancy; "'his greatest conquests were over his own passions: he subdued them, or like vanquished enemies made them subservient to his great designs, and directed them with despotic sway in the cause of virtue and honour'" (p. 87). The sentiment is common, but the military and political imagery here gives it uncommon force.[13] The idea appears yet again in a discussion of the choice of life—or rather of people who cannot choose their ways of life. Johnson entertained the idea of inability to choose quite briefly when Imlac responds to Rasselas's naive assumption that wise men choose the mode of life they think most likely to make them happy. "'Very few,' said the poet, 'live by choice. Every man is placed in his present condition by causes which acted without his foresight, and with which he did not always willingly co-operate ... '" (p. 80). Rasselas comments that he has an advantage in that his birth enables him to choose for himself. Johnson does not make of this yet another example of Rasselas's naïveté; indeed, Rasselas, merely the fourth son of an emperor, proceeds to go about the business of choosing with great freedom. But when Miss Knight kills off Rasselas's three older brothers, he is no longer free to choose—he must ascend the emperor's throne, which he finds to be a considerable burden. She has added a Johnsonian irony to the prince's sanguineness about his own freedom.

Miss Knight develops still further the question of lack of free choice which Johnson introduces and dismisses in a few lines. When our travelers first reenter Abyssinia and encounter Amalphis in the border fortress, they explain to him that they have been surveying various stations of life to determine which is most productive of happiness. He is "'amazed'" that anyone should imagine "'that happiness depended on any particular station in life'" (p. 14). He develops at length the idea of the rarity of being free to choose: the lower classes are too poor and "'the great are still more irresistibly restrained by the prejudice of custom'" (pp. 14-15). Those who can choose are "'too often guided by their passions.'" Most people, therefore, are compelled by one power or another into some state of life in which they must do their duty "'with firmness and resignation.'" One can be "'virtuous and respectable'" in any profession or state of life if one acts as one's state requires (p. 15). Amalphis waxes eloquent on the subject, describing the priest who longs for the active life of a soldier and the soldier (perhaps himself) who longs for the life of "'literary ease and philosophical disquisition'" (p. 16). The greatest hero, possessed of the greatest merit, is he who wishes to be engaged in a different profession "'and employs the energy that Heaven has given him to conquer his repugnance, and to be more active in his functions'" (p. 16). "'To suffer with patience'" is a manifestation of courage as much as acting with glory (p. 17). Patience and duty are

Johnsonian values as well, but that true heroism consists in re-
pressing, even perverting, one's deepest inclinations is the
stance of a woman whose sex limited her "station" and her
freedom to choose more drastically than those of a man were
limited. Being apparently without rebelliousness, she made a
supreme virtue of necessity. She even put the statement of this
virtue into the mouth of a male character in her book, where it
gains in authority and is seen to apply to men as well as to
women.

In these incidents of the stoic repression of grief and of heroism in an uncongenial station, as frequently throughout *Dinarbas,* Miss Knight, like Johnson, shows her royal travelers to be
naive and wrongheaded. Johnson corrects or rebukes his travelers in several ways: by authorial irony, as when Rasselas finds
that the weeping stoic is impervious to "polished periods and
studied sentences" (p. 84); by Imlac's pronouncements, as
when he informs Rasselas that few men live by choice; by the
explanations they receive from the subjects of their observation,
as when the old man enlightens not only Nekayah but even
Imlac on the gloominess of great age (p. 143); by the observations of one traveler who is better informed than another, as
when Nekayah tells Rasselas how wretched people would be if
they had "'to adjust by reason, every morning, all the minute
detail of a domestic day'" (p. 106). And, on one memorable
occasion, Rasselas "corrects" Imlac's "enthusiastic fit" by inter-
rupting his flow of verbiage on the subject of poets (p. 64).

Miss Knight's Rasselas similarly stems the tide of Dinarbas's
enthusiasm when he is reporting rapturously on the scenic and
historical glories of Greece, which he visited while searching
for the captive prince (p. 220). But such rebukes of one major
character by another are far more common in *Dinarbas* than in
Rasselas, as are rebukes or corrections by the subjects of observation. Both Amalphis and the priest Elphenor set the travelers
straight at greater length and more vigorously than the subjects
of observation in *Rasselas,* and many times, with equal vigor,
the travelers correct each other. For instance, Nekayah tries to

dissuade Rasselas from going on a military expedition with Dinarbas on the grounds that the sons of emperors ought not to risk their lives when they have slaves to do it for them. Rasselas blushes at his sister's error and explains the natural obligation of a son to defend his father (pp. 20-22). Again, Nekayah complains that Zilia, Dinarbas's sister, does not treat her with proper respect, and Rasselas answers that since Nekayah is concealing her rank, she cannot expect the deference due to a princess (p. 27); Rasselas then goes on to describe the pleasure he takes in his growing friendship for Dinarbas. In both these instances, as frequently throughout *Dinarbas*, pride is castigated and what might be taken as an egalitarian tone is introduced.

Yet Miss Knight was no more a democrat than Johnson,[14] and her characters generally preserve the decorum of rank. The real issue here is relationship, the importance of familial and friendly connections between people, as in Miss Knight's versions of the encounters with the young Egyptians and the shepherds. Her travelers are not simply observers. They live novelistic emotional lives in their relationships with the subjects of their observation and with each other, relationships that involve far more conflict, far more interaction of all kinds than Johnson bestows on his characters. And, both analytically and implicitly, Miss Knight demonstrates again and again the great value she sets on such interaction, on human fellow-feeling.

Miss Knight's novelistic treatment of character includes giving her travelers the ability to learn from their experiences. A good part of Johnson's satiric point is that his characters do *not* learn. In the "conclusion in which nothing is concluded," they are still dreaming of being ideal administrators in ideal convents, colleges, and kingdoms. Paradoxically, however, they are aware that they can never attain their dreams. So have they learned, or haven't they? Johnson won't tell. But Miss Knight does.

In *Dinarbas*, Rasselas learns from his experience as a solitary prisoner of the Arabs. Johnson's Pekuah is also held prisoner by Arabs for a time in an incident which tantalizes the reader with the possibility of "oriental" excitement—romance in the desert! seduction! perhaps even rape!—but, ironically, she undergoes only boredom and lessons in astronomy. The two incidents are not parallel, in that Rasselas is alone and Pekuah is surrounded by deferential Arabs and mindless harem ladies. She serves as Johnson's mouthpiece, when she is returned to her friends, on the subjects of female mindlessness and Arabian avarice. Although she claims that she never knew the power of gold before, she discovers the benefits of promising the Arab a generous ransom (p. 127). Yet she learns little other than astronomy from the whole experience—nothing of personal significance, nothing that alters her character. Johnson's characters are fixed.

Captivity has very real effects on Rasselas. He expects the Arab to return in a month and spends that much time fretting restlessly and staring out of his tower window, unable to think or sleep (pp. 63–65). When the slaves who feed him tell him that "a month," as defined by their master, may mean several, Rasselas is "overwhelmed with affliction" (p. 66). For a fortnight he torments himself with memories of Zilia, with fears that his friends will forget him, and with odious comparisons of his present state with his former state in the Happy Valley (pp. 66-69). At last, however, the landscape beyond his window claims his attention with "an awful tempest, exhibiting the most noble contrast of light and darkness" (p. 69). This breakthrough is followed by an evening in which he takes pleasure in clear moonlight, which inspires him to compose and memorize a poem to Zilia (pp. 69-70). Other poems follow, and the mental activity (like Pekuah's astronomy lessons) enables him to gain a victory over himself. "He felt applause in his own mind for this new-acquired patience" (p. 71), and Miss Knight, unlike Johnson, does not puncture his self-satisfaction. Johnson's Rasselas, when he is moody, depressed, and then procrastinating in the Happy Valley, is regularly the subject of authorial mockery for his adolescent ups and downs and self-congratulations. Miss Knight leaves her Rasselas in unquestioned possession of valid self-applause.

Newly strengthened, Rasselas philosophizes about his fate. His solitude offers him goods which are the obverse of its evils. Deprived of "'the reciprocal communications of friendship,'" he is "'equally saved'" from the hatred, envy, and mortifications so common in society; "'incapacitated from doing good,'" he is "'at least prevented from committing ill'" (p. 72), rather like Gray's isolated rural folk in the *Elegy,* "Forbad to wade through slaughter to a throne." Rasselas further reflects that although he is now useless, he has done his best. The others can do without him, and his absence will prove a positive benefit to Zilia, whom he would not be permitted to marry—he is spared the guilt of either disobeying his father or causing her any unhappiness (p. 73). These reflections sound rather like Imlac himself, consoling Nekayah when she blames herself for leaving Pekuah outside the pyramid to be captured by Arabs: she too acted as best she could and is without guilt (p. 117). Miss Knight's Rasselas then recalls his encounter with the hermit in Johnson's chapter 21, observing that the hermit's retirement, unlike his, was voluntary and hence unsatisfactory. "'Perhaps, while the mind has a power of wandering, it can never sink into repose: perhaps, while choice is allowed us, inconstancy will attend our desires'" (p. 74). He concludes, sounding much like Amalphis on the subject of true heroism (pp. 14–17), that "Resignation should be the favourite study of the wise, and the principal virtue of the brave'" (p. 74). He has learned, perhaps from Amalphis and most certainly from experience, that he does not have the power and the freedom to determine the course of his own life. Is this the voice of Miss Knight, the dutiful daughter, the repressed spinster? Or is this the voice of the eighteenth century, the voice that urges us to stay in our assigned places and not dare to rattle the Chain of Being? Perhaps both.

Rasselas takes further consolation in the observation that man is not alone in the universe, that the sun and stars show that God is his friend. He concludes with a meditation on his own littleness and submission to the "'Divine Leader,'" who will make the choice of life for him (pp. 74–76). And indeed, from this point on, *Dinarbas* is not concerned with "choice of life" as *Rasselas* is throughout. Events take control, and when Rasselas is rescued, he hurries off to fight for his father and eventually to succeed to the throne. Near the end of the tale, in a conversation "on various matters," Rasselas recalls the three daydreams in Johnson's final chapter and speculates how miserable they would all have been if heaven had granted their wishes (p. 305). Pekuah, caught up in the diversified life of the court, and Nekayah, about to be married to Dinarbas, agree that now they would not choose the monastic lives they had envisioned. Rasselas, too, though now he has the kingdom he dreamed of, finds it a burden he could not support without the consolations of his marriage to Zilia, which he had not included in his earlier dream. The conversation wanders on and concludes with some thoughts on the topic of ridicule, a dangerous weapon, according to the princess, because of the pain it can inflict and the enemies it can create. "'And yet,'" Imlac adds, "'if we were deprived of ridicule ... we should lose much of the power of wit, and much of the influence of general opinion— two invisible monarchs, who govern with sufficient justice, and who, if they do not prevent crimes, at least may reform errors'" (p. 311). This pronouncement sounds like a final tribute to Johnson the satirist from the nonsatirical Miss Knight.[15]

For *Dinarbas* does not satirize *Rasselas*. There is no ridicule, only the presentation of further views, additional experiences, different angles of vision. Some of the additions and differences come through in parallel incidents, while some appear in observations and discussions which arise without any real connections with the action of the two books.

Among the miscellaneous topics that arise is "greatness." In chapter 24 of *Rasselas*, "the prince examines the happiness of high stations." While it is hard to believe that only a supreme monarch can be happy, though logically his subordinates cannot be, Rasselas finds this to be indeed the case. And even supremacy is no guarantee. The Bassa of Cairo is not happy, nor is even the Sultan, for both are summarily deposed or murdered (pp. 93-94). In chapter 27, Rasselas constructs a solid argument proving that happiness cannot exist in high public stations. His bleak view stems largely from the inevitable insecurity of such stations.[16] Miss Knight does not tackle the question of insecurity at the top of the heap. Through Dinarbas's account of his travels in search of Rasselas, she acknowledges, like Johnson, that those whose "'greatness is only comparative,'" especially those who have recently risen, will find it difficult to maintain their high position. If they are ambitious to rise still higher, the difficulty will increase. They will not necessarily be miserable, as Johnson implies; they will, however, not be comfortable. Real comfort and ease can exist only at the top. The man born to greatness "'can have neither the motives of jealousy, nor of emulation'"; he cannot be humiliated, so he is naturally courteous. The great are not fastidious and insolent, as we unjustly assume, but are instead very nice people (p. 197). The angle of vision differs. Miss Knight is in general more cheerful. And, though both are staunch monarchists, their concerns differ: Johnson sees the ultimate effects of fortune on lofty position, while Miss Knight looks inward to the probable character of the ruler.[17]

On the topic of education, Johnson's Imlac recommends the study of history because we benefit from knowing the vicissitudes of "'the progress of the human mind'" (p. 109). Miss Knight's Imlac, too, recommends the study of history, and, when Rasselas suggests that only the history of one's own country would be relevant, Imlac insists that no single land can provide all the examples of the "'various circumstances of life'" that would be useful (p. 286). A practical man, her Imlac even urges the study of foreign languages to make sure that the history one is reading has not been misrepresented by faulty translations (pp. 287-88). He also comments on the usefulness of studying poetry, not only because it teaches moral and religious truth, as he had said in the much-discussed chapter 10 of *Rasselas,* but also because "'it teaches the knowledge of the heart, and develops the powers of the imagination'" (p. 288). Both

Imlacs agree that morality is "'the most essential'" end of all learning, but only Miss Knight's Imlac favors cultivating the imagination, the faculty that Johnson found so dangerous. And so it goes, as Miss Knight canvasses again many of the incidental topics Johnson raises in *Rasselas,* not always agreeing with her model, sometimes simply adding further thoughts on his topics, and sometimes coming to those topics from a different angle of vision.

Some of her points are quite foreign to Johnson's thinking, like her approval of cultivating the imagination. She also adds "sensibility" to reason and imagination as the forces energizing human behavior (p. 5). She is troubled about superstition and "'indolent fanaticism'" in religion (pp. 117-22), possibly a reaction to experiences while living in the Catholic countries of France and Italy. She sees pride as a common failing of priests (p. 113). She has thoughts on "the inconveniences of foreign aid" (p. 232) and on the management of warfare and the treatment of one's allies (pp. 232-38). Her Rasselas deals with problems of military and civil government (pp. 260ff.). Her Zilia is concerned with art and charity, the proper province of an empress, and tends to favor the orphans and widows of military men as she distributes her largesse (pp. 331-32).[18] Disparity of rank as an obstacle to marriage and the desirability of a young woman's freedom to choose her own husband, standard topics in the novel of sensibility but topics of no interest to Johnson, play a part in shaping Miss Knight's narrative.

Finally, one curious chapter entitled "Simplicity" (pp. 312-19), though possibly inspired by the attack on the fatuous deist in chapter 22 of *Rasselas,* lumps together thoughts on the supreme importance of good breeding, on the awkwardness of "singularity" in dress and behavior, on the evils of commerce and conspicuous consumption, and on faith in God as the sole source of perfect justice. The curious mixture of topics here tempts me to read this chapter more than any other as "concealed autobiography," for Miss Knight tried so hard to be well-bred despite her eccentric mother's embarrassing singularities and her own awkward height, tried so hard to shine in society despite the poverty, tried so hard to win the recognition which she thought her due for her literary and artistic accomplishments.[19] Perhaps, recognizing that the *Rasselas* format allowed the introduction of just about any topic and made it easy to put its topics in the mouths of various characters of both sexes, Miss Knight felt sufficiently free and sufficiently protected to express herself here on some of the most painful concerns of her own life.

Incidental and autobiographical topics aside, the idea of happiness is central to *Dinarbas,* as it was to *Rasselas.* Indeed, the oriental tale lends itself readily to such a theme, as adventures amid luxurious and exotic settings, with the occasional intervention of supernatural powers, suggest thrills and enchanted idylls unknown to the everyday world. Johnson's own oriental *Ramblers* and *Idlers* consistently focus on happiness: the search for it, the relation of money and marriage and learning to it, the location of it between extremes or in a future state.[20] His heroes in these essays may think they have happiness within their grasp or may be lectured on where it is to be found, but they are not, ultimately, happy men. Whether *Rasselas* preaches the doctrine that happiness is unattainable is much debated. Critics point to the bits of pleasure it offers, as when Rasselas enjoys seeking a way out of the Happy Valley, and to the final "choice of eternity."[21] One can also point to the last line of the related *The Vanity of Human Wishes,* in which the soul "makes the Happiness she does not find." But clearly, Miss Knight took Johnson's tale as a grim one, "paint[ing] the evils attendant on humanity" (p. viii) in such dark colors that she felt another "prospect" needed to be delineated. She was not alone in this interpretation. Sir John Hawkins, in his *Life of Dr. Samuel Johnson,* found *Rasselas* "of little benefit to the reader," indeed a positive danger, because it appears to "repress all hope" (p. 371). He reminds young readers that as Johnson wrote the book he "saw through the medium of adversity," and goes on to instruct them that true happiness can only be otherworldly. He mentions the projected second part and explains that Johnson had discovered, before getting around to writing it, that there is no bright side to life, "that in this state of our existence all our enjoyments are fugacious, and permanent felicity unattainable" (pp. 372-73).

"Permanent" is the key word here. Miss Knight does not claim that permanent happiness is possible, nor does she deny the existence of the many miseries of life. "'Much is to be suffered in our journey through life,'" her Rasselas concludes, and calls yet again upon resignation and submission to God's will as necessary "'to support us through the painful trial'" (p. 335). His final pronouncement on the topic deserves full quotation:

> Youth will vanish, health will decay, beauty fade, and strength sink into imbecility; but if we have enjoyed their advantages, let us not say there is no good, because the good in this world is not permanent; none but the guilty are excluded from at least temporary happiness; and if he whose imagination is lively, and whose heart glows with sensibility, is more subject than others to poignant grief and maddening disappointment, surely he will confess that he has moments of ecstacy and consolatory reflection that repay him for all his sufferings. [pp.335-36]

Miss Knight does not say with Solon (and with Johnson, as she reads him), "Until he is dead, do not yet call a man happy." She defines happiness—earthly happiness—as necessarily relative, not absolute; as fragmented, not whole; as inhering in relationships, not as abstract; and as transient, limited, perhaps even rare—but never as nonexistent. It is real.

Miss Knight's biographer, Barbara Luttrell, misses the point when she claims that "Cornelia," after quoting Hawkins on Johnson's intention to place Rasselas "'in a state of permanent felicity,'" "ignor[es] the remainder of the passage," the statement that Johnson had discovered that "'all our enjoyments are fugacious and permanent felicity unattainable.' . . . Contradiction is not refutation; Cornelia mistook one for the other, unaware that she was failing to meet Johnson on his own terms"

(p. 85). On the contrary, both Cornelia and Johnson reject the notion that permanent and absolute happiness is attainable. Elphenor, the priest in *Dinarbas,* says flatly that "'all happiness in this world is transitory'" (p. 278). This is hardly "contradiction." But Cornelia also looks at the topic from another angle, just as she looks at many incidents and ideas in *Rasselas* from another angle. And she affirms resoundingly the reality of "fugacious" happiness. She is romantic enough to pair off her characters with highly suitable mates and to allow them to affirm that their marriages contain both "sympathy" and "reason" (p. 328), qualities that Nekayah's earlier researches had shown did not coexist (pp. 104-7). But Miss Knight counterbalances even this ideal picture with frequent references to the mixed condition of human life. So she does not, on the whole, set out to "refute" Johnson. She gives us instead a complex and stimulating mixture of agreement, qualification, reconsideration, refinement, extension, questioning, and re-vision of his ideas, all wrapped up in a jolly good read.

WOMEN'S WRITING: DERIVATIVE OR MAINSTREAM?

To say that a piece of writing is derivative or that it is part of the mainstream of literature is to say much the same thing: that it comes from a source and bears affinities in form and content with a culture's central traditions. Yet the first term is pejorative and the second laudatory; the first implies a regrettable absence of originality while the second implies simply that the writing belongs. Fortunately, we no longer deplore the literature of the Restoration and eighteenth century in general as being slavishly neoclassical, as merely derivative. We recognize the period's own concern with the critical issues of tradition and originality, and we recognize the brilliance with which both are fused in the work of the giants and demi-giants who compose the canon. They and their work belong. They are the mainstream.

Reading only the giants, however, we are in danger of overpraising their originality, of failing to recognize their innumerable links with and dependencies on the whole stream of literature of which they are a part. And we are also in danger, when we do look at the other writers in the stream, of regarding them as merely derivative, as only drawing from rather than also contributing to, nourishing, the canonized giants and the stream as a whole. Such criticism is often directed at women writers, especially in the periods before the nineteenth century. When their work is called "derivative," the term seems to mean two things: that they are doing the same things as the men and that they are doing them without originality. At least, that is what the term properly implies. When it is used as broadly condemnatory, simply to dismiss women's writing because it is by women, it is not worth serious refutation. But the proper meaning of the term should be examined.

Frequently, though not always, women in fact were doing the same things as men, who were doing the same things as each other and as their immediate and more remote predecessors had done. In this period deeply marked by reverence for the ancients and respect for traditional forms, however variable and qualified these feelings were, writing by both men and women was in a sense "unoriginal." No stigma attached to using conventional genres or expressing traditional truths. Anne Killigrew, like Dryden, used the Pindaric ode; Mrs. Barbauld, like Pope, wrote in the mock heroic mode. Lady Winchilsea, like Crashaw and Philips, dipped into the traditions of nightingale poetry; together, Lady Mary Wortley Montagu and Gay developed the oddities of a kind of eclogue. And while they shared the same forms, the same universal questions and traditional truths also occupied men and women writers. Addison, Steele, and Mrs. Haywood pondered the problem of how to conduct one's life. Johnson and Miss Knight asked if it is given to man to be happy. Pope and Mrs. Brooke considered what it means to be young and beautiful, while Mrs. Behn and Southerne addressed the fate of the idealist in a corrupt world. Neither the men nor the women in these pairings originated the topics or the forms. They were all doing what their predecessors had done; that is, they all belong.

Participation in the tradition does not preclude originality. But originality became increasingly a desideratum as the eighteenth century went along, while the traditions of both form and content continued to be revered. This combination of values created a problem under which artists have labored ever

since: how to deal with the burden of the past, how to cope with
the anxiety of influence.[1] Here, women writers had the advantage over men, the possibility of being more original rather than
less.

Almost always less well educated, especially in the classics,
women could be said to have carried a lighter burden, to have
been freer to invent, than their highly indoctrinated brothers.
They could think beyond the ode and epic to the novel, the
freest form and one of their greatest strengths; they could ring
new changes on the lyric and the essay. And they did. They
could also bend the more traditional forms to the expression of
their own truths. Women's truths, women's points of view, had
not been expressed, re-expressed, worn out over hundreds and
thousands of years. As literary expression, they were relatively
new. Perhaps this is why Dr. Johnson, monumentally bored
with common maxims and familiar images but still wanting literature to be a faithful mirror of manners and of life, spent so
much time and energy encouraging women to write. They
stood a better chance of being both new and true.

Of course, the potential for greater originality brought with
it counterbalancing disadvantages. If less education freed
women to be more original, it also created an intense anxiety of
authorship as they contemplated publishing and submitting
their work to the judgment of their well-trained brothers. If
their points of view were fresh and new, they could be—and
were—dismissed as trivial and invalid because feminine. Small
wonder that they often clung to the most common conventions
and filled their prefaces with humble apologies. So their position in the world of letters was not the same as the men's, despite their sharing of forms and themes.

That sharing is one of the women writers' two principal
claims to belong to the mainstream. The other is, paradoxically,
their very differentness. To adopt a phrase from a most unlikely
source, Harold Bloom, acts of "creative correction" can be seen
to constitute the mainstream of literature. He limits his argument to men, the "strong poets" who create by "misinterpret-

ing" their fathers (p. 30), but he has inadvertently described a great deal of what women writers do. Although women did innovate and men did follow in their paths, it is true that in this period women more often claimed their membership in literature by adopting traditional forms and dealing with topics of central concern to humanity—but from their own point of view; that is, they creatively corrected, or re-viewed, the concerns central to both halves of the human species. That they so often perceived those concerns rather differently does not make them outsiders.

Literature written by women is not derivative in the pejorative sense, nor is it peripheral to the mainstream. It belongs. And we are only now beginning to discover, and rejoice in the discovery, that the main stream is wider and deeper and richer than we had thought.

SELECTED POEMS

The poems reprinted below have been partially modernized in punctuation for ease of reading and therefore do not always accord with the poems as cited in my text, where I quote the poems as printed in the original or in scholarly editions.

Anne Killigrew (1660-1685)

The Discontent

I

Here take no Care, take here no Care, my *Muse,*
　　Nor ought of Art or Labour use:
　　But let thy Lines rude and unpolisht go,
Nor equal be their Feet, nor Num'rous let them flow.
　　The ruggeder my Measures run when read,
They'l livelier paint th'unequal Paths fond Mortals tread.
　　Who when th'are tempted by the smooth Ascents,
　　　　Which flatt'ring Hope presents,
　　Briskly they clime, and Great Things undertake;
　　But Fatal Voyages, alas, they make:

For 'tis not long before their Feet,
Inextricable Mazes meet,
Perplexing Doubts obstruct their Way,
Mountains with-stand them of Dismay;
Or to the Brink of black Dispaire them lead,
Where's nought their Ruine to impede,
In vain for Aide they then to Reason call,
Their Senses dazle, and their Heads turn round,
The sight does all their Pow'rs confound,
And headlong down the horrid Precipice they fall:
Where storms of Sighs for ever blow,
Where rapid streams of Tears do flow,
Which drown them in a Briny Floud.
My Muse, pronounce aloud, there's nothing Good,
Nought that the World can show,
Nought that it can bestow.

II

Not boundless Heaps of its admired Clay,
Ah, too successful to betray,
When spread in our fraile Vertues way:
For few do run with so Resolv'd a Pace,
That for the Golden Apple will not loose the Race.
And yet not all the Gold the Vain would spend,
Or greedy Avarice would wish to save,
Which on the Earth refulgent Beams doth send,
Or in the Sea has found a Grave,
Joyn'd in one Mass, can Bribe sufficient be,
The Body from a stern Disease to free,
Or purchase for the Minds relief
One Moments sweet Repose, when restless made by grief.
But what may Laughter, more than Pity, move:
When some the Price of what they Dear'st Love
Are Masters of, and hold it in their Hand,
To part with it their Hearts they can't command:

But chose to miss, what miss't does them torment,
And that to hug, affords them no Content.
Wise Fools, to do them Right, we these must hold,
Who Love depose, and Homage pay to Gold.

III

Nor yet, if rightly understood,
Does Grandeur carry more of Good;
To be o'th'Number of the Great enroll'd,
A Scepter o're a Mighty Realm to hold.
        For what is this?
        If I not judge amiss,
But all th'Afflicted of a Land to take,
And of one single Family to make?
    The Wrong'd, the Poor, th'Opprest, the Sad,
    The Ruin'd, Malcontent, and Mad?
    Which a great Part of ev'ry Empire frame,
    And Interest in the common Father claime.
    Again what is't, but always to abide
    A Gazing Crowd? upon a Stage to spend
    A Life that's vain, or Evil without End?
And which is yet nor safely held, nor laid aside?
And then, if lesser Titles carry less of Care,
Yet none but Fools ambitious are to share
Such a Mock-Good, of which 'tis said, 'tis Best,
When of the least of it Men are possest.

IV

But, O, the Laurel'd Fool! that doats on Fame,
Whose Hope's Applause, whose Fear's to want a Name;
    Who can accept for Pay
    Of what he does, what others say;
Exposes now to hostile Arms his Breast,
To toylsome Study then betrays his Rest;
    Now to his Soul denies a just Content,

Then forces on it what it does resent;
And all for Praise of Fools: for such are those,
Which most of the admiring Crowd compose.
O famisht Soul, which such Thin Food can feed!
O Wretched Labour crown'd with such a Meed!
Too loud, O Fame! thy Trumpet is, too shrill,
  To lull a Mind to Rest,
  Or calme a stormy Breast,
Which asks a Musick soft and still.
'Twas not *Amaleck's* vanquisht Cry,
Nor *Israels* shout of Victory,
That could in *Saul* the rising Passion lay,
'Twas the soft strains of *David*'s Lyre the Evil Spirit chace't
 away.

V

But Friendship fain would yet it self defend,
  And Mighty Things it does pretend,
To be of this Sad Journey, Life, the Baite,
The sweet Refection of our toylsome State.
 But though True Friendship a Rich Cordial be,
  Alas, by most 'tis so alay'd,
  Its Good so mixt with Ill we see,
  That Dross for Gold is often paid.
 And for one Grain of Friendship that is found,
 Falshood and Interest do the Mass compound,
Or coldness, worse than Steel, the Loyal heart doth wound.
 Love in no Two was ever yet the same,
 No Happy Two ere felt an Equal Flame.

VI

Is there that Earth by Humane Foot ne're presst?
That Aire which never yet by Humane Breast
Respir'd, did Life supply?
  Oh, thither let me fly!

Where from the World at such a distance set,
All that's past, present, and to come I may forget:
The Lovers Sighs, and the Afflicteds Tears,
What e're may wound my Eyes or Ears,
The grating Noise of Private Jars,
The horrid sound of Publick Wars,
Of babling Fame the Idle Stories,
The short-liv'd Triumphs Noysy-Glories,
The Curious Nets the subtile weave,
The Word, the Look that may deceive.
No Mundan Care shall more affect my Breast,
My profound Peace shake or molest:
But *Stupor,* like to Death, my Senses bind,
That so I may anticipate that Rest,
Which only in my Grave I hope to find.

Cloris Charmes Dissolved by Eudora

I

Not that thy Fair Hand
Should lead me from my deep Dispaire,
Or thy Love, *Cloris,* End my Care,
And back my Steps command:
But if hereafter thou Retire,
To quench with Tears, thy Wandring Fire,
This Clue I'll leave behinde,
By which thou maist untwine
The Saddest Way,
To shun the Day,
That ever Grief did find.

II

First take thy Hapless Way
Along the Rocky Northern Shore,
Infamous for the Matchless Store

Of Wracks within that Bay.
None o're the Cursed Beach e're crost
Unless the Robb'd, the Wrack'd, or Lost,
    Where on the Strand lye spread
    The Sculls of many Dead.
        Their mingl'd Bones,
        Among the Stones,
    Thy Wretched Feet must tread.

III

The Trees along the Coast,
Stretch forth to Heaven their blasted Arms,
As if they plaind the North-winds harms,
    And Youthful Verdure lost.
There stands a Grove of fatal Ewe,
Where Sun nere pierc't, nor Wind ere blew.
    In it a Brooke doth fleet,
    The Noise must guide thy Feet,
        For there's no Light,
        But all is Night,
    And Darkness that you meet.

IV

Follow th'Infernal Wave,
Until it spread into a Floud,
Poysoning the Creatures of the Wood;
    There twice a day a Slave,
I know not for what Impious Thing,
Bears thence the Liquor of that Spring.
    It adds to the sad Place,
    To hear how at each Pace,
        He curses God,
        Himself, his Load,
    For such his Forlorn Case.

V

Next make no Noyse, nor talk.
Until th'art past a Narrow Glade,
Where Light does only break the Shade;
'Tis a Murderers Walk.
Observing this thou need'st not fear,
He sleeps the Day or Wakes elsewhere.
Though there's no Clock or Chime,
The Hour he did his Crime,
His Soul awakes,
His Conscience quakes
And warns him that's the Time.

VI

Thy Steps must next advance,
Where Horrour, Sin, and Spectars dwell,
Where the Woods Shade seems turn'd [to] Hell;
Witches here Nightly Dance,
And Sprights joyn with them when they call;
The Murderer dares not view the Ball,
For Snakes and Toads conspire,
To make them up a Quire,
And for their Light,
And Torches bright,
The Fiends dance all on fire.

VII

Press on till thou descrie
Among the Trees, sad, gastly, wan,
Thinne as the Shadow of a Man,
One that does ever crie,
"She is not; and she ne're will be;
Despair and Death, come swallow me";
Leave him; and keep thy way,

No more thou now canst stray;
    Thy Feet do stand,
    In Sorrows Land,
It's Kingdomes every way.

VIII

Here Gloomy Light will shew
Reard like a Castle to the Skie,
A Horrid Cliffe there standing nigh
    Shading a Creek below,
In which Recess there lies a Cave,
Dreadful as Hell, still as the Grave.
    Sea-Monsters there abide
    The coming of the Tide.
      No Noise is near
      To make them fear;
God-sleep might there reside.

IX

But when the Boysterous Sea
With Roaring Waves resumes this Cell,
You'd swear the Thunders there did dwell,
    So lowd he makes his Plea;
So Tempests bellow under ground,
And Ecchos multiply the Sound!
    This is the place I chose,
    Changeable like my Woes,
      Now calmly Sad,
      Then Raging Mad,
As move my bitter Throwes.

X

Such Dread besets this Part,
That all the Horrour[s] thou hast past,

Are but Degrees to This at last.
　　The sight must break thy Heart.
Here Bats and Owles that hate the Light
Fly and enjoy Eternal Night.
　　Scales of Serpents, Fish-bones,
　　Th'Adders Eye, and Toad-stones,
　　　　Are all the Light
　　　　Hath blest my Sight,
　　Since first began my Groans.

XI

　　When thus I lost the Sense
Of all the healthful World calls Bliss,
And held it Joy, those Joys to miss,
　　When Beauty was Offence:
Celestial Strains did rend the Aire,
Shaking these Mansions of Despaire;
　　　A Form Divine and bright,
　　　Stroke Day through all that Night,
　　　　As when Heav'ns Queen
　　　　In Hell was seen,
　　With wonder and affright!

XII

　　The Monsters fled for fear,
The Terrors of the Cursed Wood
Dismantl'd were, and where they stood,
　　No longer did appear.
The Gentle Pow'r, which wrought this thing,
Eudora was, who thus did sing:
　　"Dissolv'd is Cloris *spell,*
　　From whence thy Evils fell;
　　　Send her this Clue,
　　　'Tis there most due
　　And thy Phantastick Hell."

Anne Finch, Countess of Winchilsea (1661-1720)

To the Nightingale

Exert thy Voice, sweet Harbinger of Spring!
    This Moment is thy Time to sing,
    This Moment I attend to Praise,
And set my Numbers to thy Layes.
    Free as thine shall be my Song;   5
    As thy Musick, short, or long.
Poets, wild as thee, were born,
    Pleasing best when unconfin'd,
    When to Please is least design'd,
Soothing but their Cares to rest;   10
    Cares do still their Thoughts molest,
    And still th'unhappy Poet's Breast,
Like thine, when best he sings, is plac'd against a Thorn.
She begins. Let all be still!
    Muse, thy Promise now fulfill!   15
Sweet, oh! sweet, still sweeter yet
Can thy Words such Accents fit,
Canst thou Syllables refine,
Melt a Sense that shall retain
Still some Spirit of the Brain,   20
Till with Sounds like these it join.
    'Twill not be! then change thy Note;
    Let division shake thy Throat.
Hark! Division now she tries;
Yet as far the Muse outflies.   25
    Cease then, prithee, cease thy Tune;
    Trifler, wilt thou sing till *June?*
Till thy Bus'ness all lies waste,
And the Time of Building's past!
    Thus we Poets that have Speech,   30
Unlike what thy Forests teach,
    If a fluent Vein be shown

That's transcendent to our own,
Criticize, reform, or preach,
Or censure what we cannot reach.   35

Lady Mary Wortley Montagu (1689-1762)

Friday
The Toilette
Lydia

Now twenty Springs had cloath'd the Park with Green
Since Lydia knew the blossom of Fiveteen.
No Lovers now her morning Hours molest
And catch her at her Toilette halfe undrest;
The thundering Knocker wakes the street no more,   5
Nor Chairs, nor Coaches, croud the silent door;
Now at the Window all her mornings pass,
Or at the dumb Devotion of her Glass.
Reclin'd upon her Arm she pensive sate,
And curst th'Inconstancy of Man, too late.   10
        "Oh Youth! Oh spring of Life, for ever lost,
No more my Name shall reign the fav'rite Toast,
On Glass no more the Di'mond grave my Name,
And Lines mispelt record my Lovers Flame,
Nor shall side boxes watch my wand'ring Eyes,   15
And as they catch the Glance in rows arise
With humble Bows, nor white Glov'd Beaux incroach
In crouds behind to guard me to my Coach.
        "What shall I do to spend the hatefull Day?
At Chappel shall I wear the Morn away?   20
Who there appears at these unmodish hours,
But ancient Matrons with their frizled Tours,
And grey religious Maids? My presence there
Amidst that sober Train, would own Dispair;
Nor am I yet so old, nor is my Glance   25
As yet fix'd wholly on Devotion's Trance.

"Strait then I'll dress and take my wonted Range,
Through India shops, to Motteux's, or the Change,
Where the Tall Jar erects his stately Pride
With Antick Shapes in China's Azure dy'd;   30
There careless lyes a rich Brocard unroll'd,
Here shines a Cabinet with burnish'd Gold;
But then, Alas! I must be forc'd to pay,
Or bring no Pen'norths, not a Fan away.
    "How am I curs'd! unhappy and forlorn,   35
My Lover's Triumph, and my Sexes Scorn!
False is the pompous Greife of youthfull Heirs,
False are the loose Coquettes inveigling airs,
False is the crafty Courtier's plighted word,
False are the Dice when Gamesters stamp the Board,   40
False is the sprightly Widow's public Tear,
Yet these to Damon's Oaths are all sincere.
    "For what young Flirt, Base Man! am I abus'd?
To please your Wife am I unkindly us'd?
'Tis true her Face may boast the Peaches bloom,   45
But does her nearer whisper breathe Perfume?
I own her taper Shape is form'd to please,
But don't you see her unconfin'd by Stays?
She doubly to fiveteen may claim pretence,
Alike we read it, in her Face, and sense.   50
Insipid servile Thing! whom I disdain,
Her Phlegm can best support the Marriage Chain.
Damon is practis'd in the modish Life,
Can Hate and yet be Civil to his Wife.
He Games, he drinks, he swears, he fights, he roves,   55
Yet Cloe can beleive he fondly Loves;
Mistriss and Wife by turns supply his need,
A Miss for pleasure and a Wife for breed.
Powder'd with Di'monds, free from Spleen or Care
She can a sullen Husband's humour bear;   60
Her Credulous Freindship, and her Stupid Ease,
Have often been my Jest in happier Days.
Now Cloe boasts and triumphs in my Pains,

To her he's Faithfull, 'tis to me he feigns.
Am I that stupid Thing to bear Neglect   65
And force a smile, not daring to Suspect?
No, perjur'd Man! a Wife may be content,
But you shall find a Mistriss can resent—"
　　Thus Lovesick Lydia rav'd; her Maid appears,
And in her faithfull Hand, the Band box bears,   70
(The Cestos that reform'd Inconstant Jove,
Not better fill'd with what allures to Love).
"How well this Riband's Gloss becomes your Face,"
She cries in Rapture! "Then so sweet a Lace!
How charmingly you look! so bright! so fair!
'Tis to your Eyes the Head dress owes its Air!"   75
　　Strait Lydia smil'd; the Comb adjusts her Locks
And at the Play House, Harry keeps her Box.

John Gay (1685-1732)

The Toilette
A Town Eclogue
Lydia

Now twenty springs had cloath'd the Park with green,
Since *Lydia* knew the blossom of fifteen;
No lovers now her morning hours molest,
And catch her at her Toilette half undrest;
The thund'ring knocker wakes the street no more,   5
No chairs, no coaches croud her silent door;
Her midnights once at cards and *Hazard* fled,
Which now, alas! she dreams away in bed.
Around her wait Shocks, monkeys and mockaws,
To fill the place of Fops, and perjur'd Beaus;   10
In these she views the mimickry of man,
And smiles when grinning *Pug* gallants her fan;
When *Poll* repeats, the sounds deceive her ear,

For sounds like his, once told her *Damon's* care.
With these alone her tedious mornings pass;   15
Or at the dumb devotion of her glass,
She smooths her brow, and frizles forth her hairs,
And fancys youthful dress gives youthful airs;
With crimson wooll she fixes ev'ry grace,
That not a blush can discompose her face.   20
Reclin'd upon her arm she pensive sate,
And curs'd th'inconstancy of youth too late.
    "O Youth! O spring of life! for ever lost!
No more my name shall reign the fav'rite Toast,
On glass no more the di'mond grave my name,   25
And rhymes misspell'd record a lover's flame:
Nor shall side-boxes watch my restless eyes,
And as they catch the glance in rows arise
With humble bows; nor white-glov'd Beaus encroach
In crouds behind, to guard me to my coach.   30
Ah hapless nymph! such conquests are no more,
For *Chloe's* now what *Lydia* was before!
    "'Tis true, this *Chloe* boasts the peach's bloom.
But does her nearer whisper breathe perfume?
I own her taper shape is form'd to please.   35
Yet if you saw her unconfin'd by stays!
She doubly to fifteen may make pretence,
Alike we read it in her face and sense.
Her reputation! but that never yet
Could check the freedoms of a young Coquet.   40
Why will ye then, vain Fops, her eyes believe?
Her eyes can, like your perjur'd tongues, deceive.
    "What shall I do? how spend the hateful day?
At chappel shall I wear the morn away?
Who there frequents at these unmodish hours,   45
But ancient matrons with their frizled tow'rs,
And gray religious maids? My presence there
Amid that sober train would own despair;
Nor am I yet so old; nor is my glance

As yet fixt wholy to devotion's trance.   50
    "Strait then I'll dress, and take my wonted range
Through ev'ry *Indian* shop, through all the *Change;*
Where the tall jarr erects his costly pride,
With antic shapes in China's azure dy'd;
There careless lies the rich brocade unroll'd,   55
Here shines a cabinet with burnish'd gold;
But then remembrance will my grief renew,
'Twas there the raffling dice false *Damon* threw;
The raffling dice to him decide the prize.
'Twas there he first convers'd with *Chloe's* eyes;   60
Hence sprung th'ill-fated cause of all my smart,
To me the toy he gave, to her his heart.
But soon thy perj'ry in the gift was found,
The shiver'd *China* dropt upon the ground;
Sure omen that thy vows would faithless prove;   65
Frail was thy present, frailer is thy love.
    "O happy *Poll,* in wiry prison pent;
Thou ne'er hast known what love or rivals meant,
And *Pug* with pleasure can his fetters bear,
Who ne'er believ'd the vows that lovers swear!   70
How am I curst! (unhappy and forlorn)
With perjury, with love, and rival's scorn!
False are the loose Coquet's inveigling airs,
False is the pompous grief of youthful heirs,
False is the cringing courtier's plighted word,   75
False are the dice when gamesters stamp the board,
False is the sprightly widow's publick tear;
Yet these to *Damon's* oaths are all sincere.
    "Fly from perfidious man, the sex disdain;
Let servile *Chloe* wear the nuptial chain.   80
Damon is practis'd in the modish life,
Can hate, and yet be civil to a wife.
He games; he swears; he drinks; he fights; he roves;
Yet *Chloe* can believe he fondly loves.
Mistress and wife can well supply his need,   85

A miss for pleasure, and a wife for breed.
But *Chloe*'s air is unconfin'd and gay,
And can perhaps an injur'd bed repay;
Perhaps her patient temper can behold
The rival of her love adorn'd with gold,   90
Powder'd with di'monds; free from thought and care,
A husband's sullen humours she can bear.
   "Why are these sobs? and why these streaming eyes?
Is love the cause? no, I the sex despise;
I hate, I loath his base perfidious name.   95
Yet if he should but feign a rival flame?
But *Chloe* boasts and triumphs in my pains,
To her he's faithful, 'tis to me he feigns."
   Thus love-sick *Lydia* rav'd. Her maid appears;
A band-box in her steady hand she bears.   100
"How well this ribband's gloss becomes your face,"
She crys, in raptures! "Then, so sweet a lace!
How charmingly you look! so bright! so fair!
'Tis to your eyes the head-dress owes its air."
Strait *Lydia* smil'd; the comb adjusts her locks,   105
And at the Play-house *Harry* keeps her box.

Anna Laetitia Barbauld (1743-1825)

The Groans of the Tankard

Dulci digne mero! (Horat.)

Of strange events I sing, and portents dire;
The wondrous themes a reverent ear require:
Though strange the tale, the faithful Muse believe,
And what she says, with pious awe receive.

'Twas at the solemn, silent, noon-tide hour,   5
When hunger rages with despotic power,

When the lean student quits his Hebrew roots
For the gross nourishment of English fruits,
And throws unfinished airy systems by
For solid pudding and substantial pie;   10
When hungry poets the glad summons own,
And leave spare Fast to dine with Gods alone:
Our sober meal dispatched with silent haste,
The decent grace concludes the short repast:
Then, urged by thirst, we cast impatient eyes   15
Where deep, capacious, vast, of ample size,
The Tankard stood, replenished to the brink
With the cold beverage blue-eyed Naiads drink.
But lo! a sudden prodigy appears,
And our chilled hearts recoil with startling fears: 20
Its yawning mouth disclosed the deep profound,
And in low murmurs breathed a sullen sound;
Cold drops of dew did on the sides appear;
No finger touched it, and no hand was near.
At length th'indignant vase its silence broke,   25
First heaved deep hollow groans, and then distinctly spoke.
    "How changed the scene!—for what unpardoned
        crimes
Have I survived to these degenerate times?
I, who was wont the festal board to grace,
And 'midst the circle lift my honest face   30
White o'er with froth, like Etna crowned with snow,
Which mantled o'er the brown abyss below,
Where Ceres mingled with her golden store
The richer spoils of either India's shore,
The dulcet reed the Western islands boast,   35
And spicy fruit from Banda's fragrant coast.
At solemn feasts the nectared draught I poured,
And often journeyed round the ample board:
The portly Alderman, the stately Mayor,
And all the furry tribe my worth declare;   40
And the keen Sportsman oft, his labours done,

To me retreating with the setting sun,
Deep draughts imbibed, and conquered land and sea,
And overthrew the pride of France—by me.
Let meaner clay contain the limpid wave,   45
The clay for such an office nature gave;
Let China's earth, enriched with coloured stains,
Penciled with gold, and streaked with azure veins,
The grateful flavour of the Indian leaf,
Or Mocho's sunburnt berry glad receive: 50
The nobler metal claims more generous use,
And mine should flow with more exalted juice.
Did I for this my native bed resign
In the dark bowels of Potosi's mine?
Was I for this with violence torn away,   55
And dragged to regions of the upper day?
For this the rage of torturing furnace bore,
From foreign dross to purge the brightening ore?
For this have I endured the fiery test,
And was I stamped for this with Britain's lofty crest?   60
Unblest the day, and luckless was the hour,
Which doomed me to a Presbyterian's power:
Fated to serve the Puritanic race,
Whose slender meal is shorter than their grace;
Whose moping sons no jovial orgies keep;   65
Where evening brings no summons—but to sleep;
No Carnival is even Christmas here,
And one long Lent involves the meagre year.
Bear me, ye powers! to some more genial scene,
Where on soft cushions lolls the gouty Dean,   70
Or rosy Prebend with cherubic face,
With double chin, and paunch of portly grace,
Who lulled in downy slumbers shall agree
To own no inspiration but from me.
Or to some spacious mansion, Gothic, old,   75
Where Comus' sprightly train their vigils hold;
There oft exhausted, and replenished oft,

O let me still supply th'eternal draught,
Till Care within the deep abyss be drowned,
And thought grows giddy at the vast profound!"   80
    More had the goblet spoke; but lo! appears
An ancient Sibyl, furrowed o'er with years.
Her aspect sour and stern ungracious look
With sudden damp the conscious vessel struck:
Chilled at her touch its mouth it slowly closed,   85
And in long silence all its griefs reposed:
Yet still low murmurs creep along the ground,
And the air vibrates with the silver sound.

Washing-Day

> . . . and their voice,
> Turning again towards childish treble, pipes
> And whistles in its sound.

The Muses are turned gossips; they have lost
The buskined step, and clear high-sounding phrase,
Language of gods. Come then, domestic Muse,
In slipshod measure loosely prattling on
Of farm or orchard, pleasant curds and cream,   5
Or drowning flies, or shoe lost in the mire
By little whimpering boy, with rueful face;
Come, Muse, and sing the dreaded Washing-Day.
Ye who beneath the yoke of wedlock bend,
With bowed soul, full well ye ken the day   10
Which week, smooth sliding after week, brings on
Too soon;—for to that day nor peace belongs
Nor comfort;—ere the first gray streak of dawn,
The red-armed washers come and chase repose.
Nor pleasant smile, nor quaint device of mirth,   15
E'er visited that day: the very cat,
From the wet kitchen scared and reeking hearth,

Visits the parlour,—an unwonted guest.
The silent breakfast-meal is soon dispatched;
Uninterrupted, save by anxious looks   20
Cast at the lowering sky, if sky should lower.
From that last evil, O preserve us, heavens!
For should the skies pour down, adieu to all
Remains of quiet: then expect to hear
Of sad disasters,—dirt and gravel stains   25
Hard to efface, and loaded lines at once
Snapped short,—and linen-horse by dog thrown down,
And all the petty miseries of life.
Saints have been calm while stretched upon the rack,
And Guatimozin smiled on burning coals;   30
But never yet did housewife notable
Greet with a smile a rainy washing-day.
—But grant the welkin fair, require not thou
Who call'st thyself perchance the master there,
Or study swept, or nicely dusted coat,   35
Or usual 'tendance;—ask not, indiscreet,
Thy stockings mended, though the yawning rents
Gape wide as Erebus; nor hope to find
Some snug recess impervious: shouldst thou try
The 'customed garden walks, thine eye shall rue   40
The budding fragrance of thy tender shrubs,
Myrtle or rose, all crushed beneath the weight
Of coarse checked apron,—with impatient hand
Twitched off when showers impend: or crossing lines
Shall mar thy musings, as the wet cold sheet   45
Flaps in thy face abrupt. Woe to the friend
Whose evil stars have urged him forth to claim
On such a day the hospitable rites!
Looks, blank at best, and stinted courtesy,
Shall he receive. Vainly he feeds his hopes   50
With dinner of roast chicken, savoury pie,
Or tart or pudding:—pudding he nor tart
That day shall eat; nor, though the husband try,

Mending what can't be helped, to kindle mirth
From cheer deficient, shall his consort's brow   55
Clear up propitious:—the unlucky guest
In silence dines, and early slinks away.
I well remember, when a child, the awe
This day struck into me; for then the maids,
I scarce knew why, looked cross, and drove me from
      them: 60
Nor soft caress could I obtain, nor hope
Usual indulgencies; jelly or creams,
Relic of costly suppers, and set by
For me their petted one; or buttered toast,
When butter was forbid; or thrilling tale   65
Of ghost or witch, or murder—so I went
And sheltered me beside the parlour fire:
There my dear grandmother, eldest of forms,
Tended the little ones, and watched from harm,
Anxiously fond, though oft her spectacles   70
With elfin cunning hid, and oft the pins
Drawn from her ravelled stocking, might have soured
One less indulgent.—
At intervals my mother's voice was heard,
Urging dispatch: briskly the work went on,   75
All hands employed to wash, to rinse, to wring,
To fold, and starch, and clap, and iron, and plait.
Then would I sit me down, and ponder much
Why washings were. Sometimes through hollow bowl
Of pipe amused we blew, and sent aloft   80
The floating bubbles; little dreaming then
To see, Mongolfier, thy silken ball
Ride buoyant through the clouds—so near approach
The sports of children and the toils of men.
Earth, air, and sky, and ocean, hath its bubbles,   85
And verse is one of them—this most of all.

NOTES

INTRODUCTION
RESTORING THE PICTURE

1. Cheri Register, "Bibliographical Introduction," in *Feminist Literary Criticism: Explorations in Theory,* ed. Josephine Donovan (Lexington: Univ. Press of Kentucky, 1975), p. 10. Other surveys include Elaine Showalter, "Towards a Feminist Poetics," in *Women Writing and Writing About Women,* ed. Mary Jacobus (London and New York: Croom Helm, Barnes & Noble, 1979), pp. 22-41; Nina Auerbach, "Feminist Criticism Reviewed," in *Gender and Literary Voice,* ed. Janet Todd (New York and London: Holmes & Meier, 1980), pp. 258-68; Cheri Register, "Literary Criticism," *Signs* 6 (Winter 1980): 268-82; Elaine Showalter, "Feminist Criticism in the Wilderness," *Critical Inquiry* 8 (Winter 1981): 179-205. (Notes 1 through 12 give only a few of many possible references.)

2. Showalter, "Feminist Criticism in the Wilderness," pp. 197-205.

3. Virginia Woolf, *A Room of One's Own* (1929; rpt. London: Hogarth, 1954), especially pp. 148ff.; special issue of *Women's Studies* 2 (Winter 1974); *Gender and Literary Voice,* ed. Todd.

4. Showalter, "Feminist Criticism in the Wilderness," pp. 190-93; Anne Stevenson, "Writing as a Woman," in *Women Writing and Writing About Women,* ed. Jacobus, pp. 174-75.

5. Lawrence Lipking, "Aristotle's Sister: A Poetics of Abandonment," *Critical Inquiry* 10 (Sept. 1983): 61-81.

6. Sandra M. Gilbert and Susan Gubar, *The Madwoman in the Attic: The Woman Writer and the Nineteenth-Century Imagination* (New Haven and London: Yale Univ. Press, 1979), pp. 71-83 et passim.

7. Cheri Register, "Bibliographical Introduction," in *Feminist Literary Criticism: Explorations in Theory,* ed. Donovan, p. 2; Annette Kolodny, "Literary Criticism," *Signs* 2 (Winter 1976): 413.

8. Auerbach, pp. 259-60.

9. Sandra Gilbert, "Life Studies, or, Speech After Long Silence: Feminist Critics Today," *College English* 40 (1979): 862-63.

10. Lillian S. Robinson, "Treason Our Text: Feminist Challenges to the Literary Canon," *Tulsa Studies in Women's Literature* 2 (Spring 1983): 86-87.

11. Register, "Literary Criticism," p. 274 ("distinctly female"); Myra Jehlen, "Archimedes and the Paradox of Feminist Criticism," in *Feminist Theory: A Critique of Ideology*, ed. Nannerl O. Keohane et al. (Chicago: Univ. of Chicago Press, 1982), pp. 189-215, especially pp. 199-200. This stimulating essay presents a solid theoretical rationale for comparative study. See also Ruth Perry, Introduction to *Mothering the Mind: Twelve Studies of Writers and Their Silent Partners*, ed. Ruth Perry and Martine Watson Brownley (New York and London: Holmes & Meier, 1984): "It is time to reinstate the value of connectedness—of the artist to his or her family, to personal history, and to the person or persons who supported the work and encouraged its free expression" (p. 22)—and to other artists, I would add.

12. Rogers, "Opportunities for Scholarship in Eighteenth-Century British Literature," in *Women in Print*, ed. Joan E. Hartman and Ellen Messer-Davidow, vol. 1 (New York: Modern Language Association, 1982), p. 193.

13. Showalter, "Feminist Criticism in the Wilderness," p. 203.

14. Annette Kolodny, "Dancing Through the Minefield: Some Observations on the Theory, Practice, and Politics of a Feminist Literary Criticism," *Feminist Studies* 6 (Spring 1980): 20, makes a similar point.

15. Register, "Literary Criticism," p. 281, acknowledges this "norm."

16. This common notion is disputed by John Sitter in *Literary Loneliness in Mid-Eighteenth-Century England* (Ithaca and London: Cornell Univ. Press, 1982). I agree that the foundations for such isolation were laid in the middle of the eighteenth century, as he argues. Yet much sense of community and of public voice remained throughout the century.

17. Robinson, p. 91, documents nineteenth-century life with evidence from New England. The parallel picture and its changes in England are complex. Lawrence Stone, *The Family, Sex and Marriage in England 1500-1800* (London: Weidenfeld and Nicholson, 1977), gives evidence for some division of the sexes, including the custom of the ladies retiring after dinner, that prevailed in the eighteenth century as well as some evidence for integrated social life (pp. 400-3); his discussion of post-1800 family types (pp. 666ff.) and his statement that the status of women declined after 1800 (p. 667) support the idea of increasing limitation to the domestic scene and hence the increasingly "homosocial" culture of women. The isolation from the public world of the Victorian "perfect lady" is also emphasized in Martha Vicinus, "Introduction: The Perfect Victorian Lady," in *Suffer and Be Still: Women in the Victorian Age*, ed. Martha Vicinus (Bloomington and London: Indiana Univ. Press, 1972), pp. vii-xv.

18. Stone, *The Family, Sex and Marriage*; Keith Thomas, *Man and the Natural World: A History of the Modern Sensibility* (New York: Pantheon, 1983).

19. Virginia Woolf, thinking back to Coventry Patmore's poem *The Angel in the House*, found that the first adventure of her professional life was the nec-

essary murder of that angel of Victorian "purity" ("Professions for Women," in *The Death of the Moth and Other Essays* [New York: Harcourt, Brace, 1942], pp. 235-42).

20. Myra Jehlen and Rachel Blau Duplessis, "'The Tongue of Power,'" review of *The Madwoman in the Attic, Feminist Studies* 7 (Fall 1981): 542-43.

21. Pilkington, *Memoirs,* 3 vols. (1748; rpt. New York: Garland, 1975), 2:295. Page numbers in text refer to this edition.

22. Barbauld is quoted in Miss [Anne Isabella] Thackeray, *A Book of Sibyls* (London: Smith, Elder, 1883), p. 41.

23. "The Circuit of Appollo," in *The Poems of Anne Countess of Winchilsea,* ed. Myra Reynolds (1903; rpt. New York: AMS Press, 1974), p. 92.

24. Robert von Hallberg, "Editor's Introduction," *Critical Inquiry* 10 (Sept. 1983): iii. Terry Eagleton takes the same stance in *Literary Theory: An Introduction* (Oxford: Blackwell, 1983).

25. Robinson, "Treason Our Text: Feminist Challenges to the Literary Canon," *Tulsa Studies in Women's Literature* 2 (Spring 1983): 83-98.

26. Lady Winchilsea and Lady Mary Wortley Montagu have been granted some status; see the fourth edition of *The Norton Anthology of English Literature,* vol. 1.

27. Josephine Donovan, "Afterword," *Feminist Literary Criticism: Explorations in Theory,* predicts that a feminine aesthetic may be "less 'criticism' and more 'appreciation'" (p. 79). See also Paul Fussell, *The Boy Scout Handbook and Other Observations* (New York and Oxford: Oxford University Press, 1982), Preface: ". . . a thing is literature if it's worth reading more than a couple of times for illumination or pleasure" (p. vii).

28. Lady Mary Wortley Montagu has been well served by her editors, Robert Halsband and Isobel Grundy, as has Frances Brooke's *The History of Emily Montague* by its editor, Mary Jane Edwards of the Centre for Editing Early Canadian Texts. The remaining six women represented in this book can be read only in outdated nineteenth- and early twentieth-century editions, facsimile reprints, or original editions. I hope the slender appendix in this book will help.

ONE

A PROBLEM OF PRAISE
John Dryden and Anne Killigrew

1. *Poems (1686) by Mrs. Anne Killigrew,* facsimile edition with introduction by Richard Morton (Gainesville, Fla.: Scholars' Facsimiles and Reprints, 1967), p. 84. Page numbers in text refer to this edition.

2. Anthony Wood, *Athenae Oxoniensis* (1721), c. 1036; the same sentiments appear in biographical notes by T. Cibber and G. Ballard.

3. Wallerstein, "On the Death of Mrs. Killigrew: The Perfecting of a Genre," *Studies in Philology* 44 (1947): 519-28. Jerome, "On Decoding Humor," *Antioch Review* 20 (Winter 1960-61): 486-87. Hoffman, *John Dryden's Imagery* (Gainesville, Fla.: Univ. of Florida Press, 1962), pp. 98-119, especially p. 101. Vieth, "Irony in Dryden's Ode to Anne Killigrew," *Studies in Philology* 62 (January 1965): 91-100; "Divided Consciousness: The Trauma and Triumph of Restoration Culture," *Tennessee Studies in Literature* 22 (1977): 53. (The argument is developed further, in a somewhat different direction, in C. Anderson Silber, "Nymphs and Satyrs: Poet, Readers, and Irony in Dryden's Ode to Anne Killigrew," in *Studies in Eighteenth-Century Culture,* vol. 14, ed. O. M. Brack, Jr. [Madison: Univ. of Wisconsin Press, 1985], pp. 193-212.) Daly, "Dryden's Ode to Anne Killigrew and the Communal Work of Poets," *Texas Studies in Literature and Language* 18 (1976): 184-97.

4. *The Poems of Anne Countess of Winchilsea,* ed. Myra Reynolds (1903; rpt. New York: AMS Press, 1974), p. xxiii. Hampsten, "Petticoat Authors: 1660-1720," *Women's Studies* 7, nos. 1/2 (1980): 31-32.

5. Two poems commemorate the same boy: Martial, *Epigrams,* trans. Walter C. A. Ker, Loeb Classical Library (1919; rpt. London: Heinemann, 1930), 1:373 (book 6, number 28, which I quote here); the epigram on Anne Killigrew's title page is on p. 375 (book 6, number 29).

6. *Poems by the Incomparable Mrs. K. P.* (London, 1664), p. 28, "On the 3. of September, 1651." William George Smith and Janet E. Heseltine, eds., *The Oxford Dictionary of English Proverbs* (Oxford: Clarendon Press, 1936), p. 103.

7. Translations of this line vary; I quote the Authorized Version. Commentators disagree on why Araunah is described "*as* a king"; he was not, but the gesture of offering the gift is kingly. It is worth noting too that Araunah is a Jebusite and thus has other gods than David's; the queen was Catholic and Anne Killigrew was Anglican.

8. *The Poetical Works of John Dryden,* ed. George R. Noyes (Boston: Houghton Mifflin, 1950), p. 213 (ll. 71-74). References in text below are to this edition.

9. Martial, 2: 99 (book 9, number 37). As noted earlier, the epigram on the title page is also from Martial. Perhaps Anne Killigrew could read Latin. She clearly had some acquaintance with Martial, as the name "Galla" indicates, and the epigram on the title page could have been chosen because she particularly liked Martial. *The New Cyclopedia of Names* (1954) lists her as "poet, painter, and scholar" but cites no source for the last epithet.

10. Anne Killigrew alludes to Orinda and her fame again in "Upon the saying that my Verses were made by another" (p. 46); Dryden compares the two women poets in his ode as having "equal souls" and equal fates, both having died of smallpox (ll. 162-64).

11. Aphra Behn, "To my Lady Morland at Tunbridge," in *Works,* ed. Montague Summers (1915; rpt. New York: Blom, 1967), 6:175-77, maintains a

single standard when she says that "Cloris" deserves a male "Virgin-Heart" (p. 177), which is partly a compliment to Lady Morland and partly an attempt to keep "Amyntas" for herself.

12. Vieth, "Irony in Dryden's Ode to Anne Killigrew," p. 95. Dryden's editors note this allusion. See *The Works of John Dryden*, vol. 3: *Poems 1685-1692*, ed. Earl Miner et al. (Berkeley and Los Angeles: Univ. of California Press, 1969), p. 322.

13. Fussell, *The Rhetorical World of Augustan Humanism* (Oxford: Clarendon Press, 1965), chap. 11.

14. Matthew Prior, *Poems on Several Occasions*, ed. A. R. Waller (Cambridge: Cambridge Univ. Press, 1905), p. 322.

15. I will concentrate on landscape images in the following paragraphs. A few of the other echoes: after the Nymph is beaten, "Vertue darts forth a Light'ning 'bove the Skin" (p. 98); Orinda too glowed with virtue: "It was her Radiant Soul that shon With-in, / Which struk a Lustre through her Outward Skin" (p. 46); another nymph also "shine[s]" with grace (p. 67). "Monsters" and "poison" are closely associated in "An Invective against Gold" (p. 30); both appear in "Cloris Charmes" (pp. 87, 91). Noise is undesirable: Eudora is praised as "Noyseless" (p. 100), and the poet shuns the world's "Noysy-Glories" (p. 56). Both the Nymph in "The Miseries of Man" and the speaker in "Cloris Charmes" "chose" the cave for her "Woes" (pp. 32, 90), with identical ideas and rhyme words; the cave is "fit" for and "like" the woes (pp. 33, 90). "Motion" is part of beauty (pp. 36, 99). George Ballard, *Memoirs of Several Ladies of Great Britain, Who Have Been Celebrated for Their Writings or Skill in the Learned Languages, Arts, and Sciences* (London, 1775), pp. 240-41.

16. Marina Warner, *Alone of All Her Sex: The Myth and the Cult of the Virgin Mary* (New York: Knopf, 1976), pp. 321-22, discusses Mary's visit to hell as familiar in Eastern Christianity but probably unknown in the West. But somehow Anne Killigrew seems to have known about it.

17. E.g., Thomas Shadwell, *The Virtuoso* (1676), ed. Marjorie Hope Nicholson and David Stuart Rodes (Lincoln: Univ. of Nebraska Press, 1966), p. 93, speaks of "disciplining" old gentlemen with rods.

18. Eric Partridge, *A Dictionary of Slang and Unconventional English*, 8th ed. (New York: Macmillan, 1984); Partridge lists the first known use of "tune" in this sense as 1780, however. Anthony Hamilton, *Memoirs of the Count de Grammont*, trans. Horace Walpole, notes by Sir Walter Scott and Mrs. Jameson (1890; rpt. London: Allen & Unwin, 1926), pp. 251-52. Lawrence Stone, *The Family, Sex and Marriage*, p. 732, n. 93.

19. Charles E. Ward, *The Life of John Dryden* (Chapel Hill: University of North Carolina Press, 1961), p. 216. Other references to this biography appear in the text. Anne Killigrew is not mentioned in Dryden's extant letters.

20. Ward examines the criteria of art and morality in *The Life of John Dryden*, p. 22.

TWO
NOVEL INTO PLAY
Aphra Behn and Thomas Southerne

1. Thomas Southerne, *Oroonoko,* ed. Maximillian E. Novak and David Stuart Rodes (Lincoln: Univ. of Nebraska Press, 1976), Dedication, p. 4. My text below refers to this edition.

2. Robert Jordan, "Mrs. Behn and *Sir Anthony Love,*" *Restoration and Eighteenth-Century Theater Research* 12 (May 1973), 58-59. Southerne, Epistle Dedicatory, *The Fatal Marriage* (London, 1694), n.p. The comic plot has no connection with Mrs. Behn's novel, though Southerne has devised some neat parallels which unite it to the tragic plot. Montague Summers prints thirteen novels in *The Works of Aphra Behn* (1915; rpt. New York: Blom, 1967), vol. 5. He does not reprint the partially epistolary novel *Love-Letters Between a Nobleman and His Sister,* 3 vols. (London, 1684). Allardyce Nicoll lists and classifies twenty-one plays in *A History of English Drama 1660-1900,* vol. 1, *Restoration Drama 1660-1700,* 4th ed. (Cambridge: Cambridge Univ. Press, 1961), pp. 390-93. Aphra Behn has attracted much biographical attention but relatively little critical attention. See, e.g., George Woodcock, *The Incomparable Aphra* (London and New York: Boardman, 1948); Frederick M. Link, *Aphra Behn* (New York: Twayne, 1968); Maureen Duffy, *The Passionate Shepherdess: Aphra Behn 1640-89* (London: Cape, 1977); Angeline Goreau, *Reconstructing Aphra: A Social Biography of Aphra Behn* (New York: Dial, 1980). The proportion of fact to romantic speculation varies in these and other studies. See also the brief but useful introduction by Lore Metzger in Aphra Behn, *Oroonoko or the Royal Slave* (New York: Norton, 1973).

3. Works, ed. Summers, 5:349-98.

4. Robert L. Root, Jr., *Thomas Southerne* (Boston: Twayne, 1981), p. 45. Regarding the Shakespearean echo, consider, for instance, Rosalind and Celia in *As You Like It* and Beatrice and Hero in *Much Ado About Nothing.*

5. Southerne, *Sir Anthony Love* (London, 1691), p. 69.

6. Root, *Thomas Southerne,* p. 45, uses the term "worldly"; his brief discussion of the similarities and differences between Southerne's play and Mrs. Behn's novel is accurate and useful.

7. John Wendell Dodds, *Thomas Southerne Dramatist* (1933; rpt. Hamden, Conn.: Archon, 1970), p. 73; Root, *Thomas Southerne,* pp. 50-51; see also pp. 51-52 for a brief survey of other critical opinion.

8. *The History of the Nun: or, The Fair Vow-Breaker,* in *Restoration Prose Fiction 1666-1700,* ed. Charles C. Mish (Lincoln: Univ. of Nebraska Press, 1970), pp. 97-99.

9. Perhaps the brevity of these passages explains Larry Carver's curious contention that Isabella murders her two husbands because she cannot "cope with the guilt that comes from breaking vows to father and church" ("Aphra Behn: The Poet's Heart in a Woman's Body," *Papers on Language and Literature*

14 [1978]: 421). Her reasons for the murders are complex but do not include these broken vows.

10. Staves, *Players' Scepters: Fictions of Authority in the Restoration* (Lincoln and London: Univ. of Nebraska Press, 1979), pp. 191-251.

11. Quoted in Staves, *Players' Scepters,* p. 215.

12. Dunton, in *The Athenian Mercury,* deplored "violations of contractual obligations," even those much misunderstood contracts known as verbal spousals, but such a stance was "fairly austere" in the late seventeenth century, says Lawrence Stone in *Marriage, Sex and the Family,* p. 34.

13. See the title page reproduced in *The History of the Nun,* ed. Mish, p. 94.

14. Preface to *Don Sebastian,* in *The Works of John Dryden,* vol. 15, ed. Earl Miner, George R. Guffey, and Franklin B. Zimmerman (Berkeley, Los Angeles, and London: Univ. of California Press, 1976), p. 66. Rich, "Isabella of Southerne's *The Fatal Marriage* (1694): Saint or Sinner," *Restoration* 5, no. 2 (Fall 1981): 90, 95, et passim. *The Spectator,* ed. Donald F. Bond (Oxford: Clarendon Press, 1965), 4:205. Addison also speaks of the "noble Perplexity" of the play. Root, *Thomas Southerne,* pp. 83-86, outlines the critical responses to the play and its stage history.

15. John Harold Wilson, *A Preface to Restoration Drama* (Boston: Houghton Mifflin, 1965), finds that "The play has neither social nor moral purpose" (p. 117), nothing to offer but sentimentalism.

16. E.g., H. A. Hargreaves, "New Evidence of the Realism of Mrs. Behn's *Oroonoko,*" *Bulletin of the New York Public Library* 74 (1970): 437-44; B. Dhuicq, "Further Evidence on Aphra Behn's Stay in Surinam," *Notes & Queries* 224, n.s. 26 (1979): 524-26; Goreau, *Reconstructing Aphra,* pp. 41-69.

17. Mary Ann O'Donnell, "Experiments in the Prose Fiction of Aphra Behn: Behn's use of narrational voice, character, and tone" (Ph.D. diss., Fordham University, 1979); Carver (see note 9 above).

18. E.g., Novak and Rodes, Introduction to *Oroonoko;* Root, *Thomas Southerne;* Dodds, *Southerne Dramatist;* Laurie P. Morrow, "Marriage à la Melpomene: Husbands and Wives in Eighteenth-Century Tragedy" (paper read at the American Society for Eighteenth-Century Studies, New York, April 1983).

19. Dodds, *Southerne Dramatist,* p. 137.

20. Behn, *Works,* ed. Summers, 5:129. Page numbers in text below refer to this edition.

21. But perhaps pregnancy was not a deterrent. Pepys reports going to visit a Mrs. Martin for some unspecified degree of dalliance but having his visit forestalled by the news that she had just given birth (*The Diary of Samuel Pepys,* ed. Robert Latham and William Matthews, vol. 6 [Berkeley and Los Angeles: Univ. of California Press, 1972], 52-53 [March 9, 1665]).

22. Hottman has no counterpart in the novel; Aboan has no exact parallel, but minor characters fulfill some of his functions.

23. The stage directions are not entirely clear; Southerne seems to want to have it both ways: "She lays her hand on his in order to give the blow" and "Stabs herself" (pp. 122-23); the action seems to be either primarily or entirely hers.

24. Thematic plot connections are discussed by Laurie P. Morrow; Novak and Rodes, Introduction to *Oroonoko,* pp. xli-xlii; Michael M. Cohen, "'Mirth and Grief Together': Plot Unity in Southerne's *Oroonoko,*" *Xavier University Studies* 11, no. 3 (Winter 1972): 13-17; Julia A. Rich, "Heroic Tragedy in Southerne's *Oroonoko* (1695): An Approach to Split-plot Tragicomedy," *Philological Quarterly* 62 (1983): 187-200.

25. Hume, *The Development of English Drama in the Late Seventeenth Century* (Oxford: Clarendon Press, 1976), p. 426; Hagstrum, *Sex and Sensibility: Ideal and Erotic Love from Milton to Mozart* (Chicago and London: Univ. of Chicago Press, 1980), p. 81.

26. Mrs. Evelyn is quoted in Hume, *Development of English Drama,* p. 273.

27. Southerne's Oroonoko too is a slave trader. The Captain mentions the fact once, very briefly (I.ii.147-49), but we hear no more about it and certainly never see him offering to sell people.

28. Wylie Sypher, "A Note on the Realism of Mrs. Behn's *Oroonoko,*" *Modern Language Quarterly* 3 (1942): 404-5; this article authenticates this and many other additional details but concludes cautiously that Mrs. Behn could have used published sources for such information.

29. Martine Watson Brownley, "The Narrator in *Oroonoko,*" *Essays in Literature: Western Illinois University* 4 (1977): 176. For Behn's claim to have been an eyewitness in *The Fair Jilt,* see *Works,* 5:74.

30. Mish, *Restoration Prose Fiction,* pp. vii, ix, 37.

31. *Congreve: "Incognita" and "The Way of the World,"* ed. A. Norman Jeffares (London: Arnold, 1966), pp. 32-33.

32. *The Novels of Mary Delariviere Manley,* ed. Patricia Köster, vol. 1: *The Secret History of Queen Zarah* (Gainesville, Fla.: Scholars' Facsimiles and Reprints, 1971), "To the Reader" (unpaginated).

33. Although the point may be too obvious to need documentation, see Hagstrum *Sex and Sensibility,* p. 66 and note 23.

34. Rich, "Heroic Tragedy"; see also Staves, *Players' Scepters,* p. 187 and chap. 1, passim.

35. Hume, *Development of English Drama,* pp. 351, 177; see also Hagstrum, *Sex and Sensibility,* p. 65.

36. Dodds, *Southerne Dramatist,* p. 138.

37. Dryden, Preface to *Don Sebastian,* p. 65; Root, *Thomas Southerne,* p. 87.

38. See Brownley, "The Narrator," pp. 178-79, for a different interpretation of these crucial absences; her analysis is provocative, but I disagree with it. George Guffey, "Aphra Behn's *Oroonoko:* Occasion and Accomplishment," in *Two English Novelists: Aphra Behn and Anthony Trollope* (Los Angeles: William

Andrews Clark Memorial Library, 1975), shows that *Oroonoko* is not an abolitionist tract, though it deals with the topic of slavery (pp. 20-24); he argues for the story's political meaning (p. 8 et passim).

THREE
SELECTED NIGHTINGALES
Anne Finch, Countess of Winchilsea, et al.

1. *The Poems of Anne Countess of Winchilsea,* ed. Myra Reynolds (1903; rpt. New York: AMS Press, 1974). The volume does not include the poems in the Wellesley manuscript, which have never been published. My discussion of the poems draws on this edition; page numbers appear in the text. For Wordsworth's praise, see "Essay, Supplementary to the Preface," *The Poetical Works of Wordsworth,* ed. Thomas Hutchinson, rev. Ernest de Selincourt (London: Oxford Univ. Press, 1956), p. 747, col. 1. Also see Brower, "Lady Winchilsea and the Poetic Tradition of the Seventeenth Century," *Studies in Philology* 42 (1945): 61-80, and Riedenauer, "Die Gedichte der Anne Finch, Countess of Winchilsea" (Ph.D. diss., University of Vienna, 1964), passim, especially pp. 347-51.

2. Rogers, *Feminism in Eighteenth-Century England* (Urbana: Univ. of Illinois Press, 1982), pp. 85-92. Some of the analysis is slanted; for example, Rogers claims (p. 88) that Lady Winchilsea's sex isolated her from "the fashionable world," when it was in fact her nonjuring politics that did so. Also see Hampsten, "Petticoat Authors: 1660-1720," *Women's Studies* 7, nos. 1/2 (1980): 34-38, and my own "Lady Winchilsea and Twice-Fallen Woman," *Atlantis* 3, no. 2, pt. 1 (Spring 1978): 82-98, and "Publishing Without Perishing: Lady Winchilsea's *Miscellany Poems* of 1713," *Restoration* 5, no. 1 (Spring 1981): 27-37.

3. E.g., she suffered, genuinely, from "spleen" and from her loyalty to the Stuart cause after 1688; see Reynolds's introduction, pp. xxviii-xxx and xlii-xliii.

4. Brower, "Lady Winchilsea," p. 66.

5. Albert R. Chandler, "The Nightingale in Greek and Latin Poetry," *Classical Journal* 30 (1934-35): 78.

6. *The Complete Poetry of Richard Crashaw,* ed. George Walton Williams (New York: New York Univ. Press, 1972), p. 535, line 6. My citations of Crashaw in text below refer to this edition.

7. *The Poems of Ambrose Philips,* ed. M. G. Segar (Oxford: Blackwell, 1937), p. 66, l. 19. Line numbers in text below refer to this edition.

8. This clear statement of the dualism of art and nature comes from the 1748 version of the Pastorals; the 1709 version is less explicit.

9. Dichotomy or dualism is not the whole story, though Philips did not go beyond this concept. Lawrence Manley, *Convention 1500-1750* (Cambridge,

Mass., and London: Harvard Univ. Press, 1980), especially chap. 1, adds the idea of convention to the ideas of nature and art and explores the complex relationships among the three; his discussion illuminates the metaphysical sense of the oneness of man and nature and the later sense of separateness.

10. David A. Bannerman, *The Birds of the British Isles* (Edinburgh and London: Oliver and Boyd, 1954), 3:298-302. By the nineteenth century, the notion that the female bird sang had been corrected. See W. Swaysland, *Familiar Wild Birds* (London: Assell, 1883), 1:132.

11. See, e.g., "Song: If for a Woman I wou'd dye," in *The Poems,* ed. Reynolds, p. 133.

12. Lady Winchilsea, "The Introduction," in *The Poems,* ed. Reynolds, p. 5.

13. Keith Thomas, *Man and the Natural World: A History of the Modern Sensibility* (New York: Pantheon, 1983), pp. 90-91, 93, 127-29, 137, 139.

14. Ray, Jonson, and Wilkins are quoted in Thomas, *Man and the Natural World,* p. 32.

15. One is tempted here into a digression comparing this line with Wordsworth's "thoughts that do often lie too deep for tears," with the intriguing differences between high and deep, syllables and thoughts. But one will resist the temptation.

16. For a feminist reading of the poem which focuses on the female sex of the bird, see Lucy Brashear, "Finch's 'The Bird and the Arras,'" *Explicator* 39, no. 3 (1981): 21-22. The notion that women had no souls persisted on the fringes of eighteenth-century thinking, but Lady Winchilsea's conventional Christianity obviously did not embrace that notion.

17. "An Invitation to Dafnis," in *The Poems,* ed. Reynolds, pp. 28-30.

FOUR

TOWN ECLOGUES
Lady Mary Wortley Montagu and John Gay

1. Robert Halsband, *The Life of Lady Mary Wortley Montagu* (1956; rpt. London: Oxford Univ. Press, 1961), pp. 45-58, covers the period January 1715 through July 1716. Isobel Grundy, "'The Entire Works of Clarinda': Unpublished Juvenile Verse by Lady Mary Wortley Montagu," *Yearbook of English Studies,* vol. 7 (1977), 91, 93-95, 101; in her imitation of Virgil, Lady Mary changed the forsaken shepherd to a forsaken shepherdess.

2. John Gay, *Poetry and Prose,* ed. Vinton A. Dearing with Charles E. Beckwith (Oxford: Clarendon Press, 1974), 2:508 (notes); all references to Gay's works in text below refer to this edition, the most complete available for the poetry despite its limitations; see the review by H. Bunker Wright, in *Modern Philology* 76 (1978-79): 89-94.

3. Forsgren, *John Gay, Poet "of a Lower Order,"* vol. 2 : *Comments on His Urban and Narrative Poetry* (Stockholm: Natur och Kultur, 1971), pp. 135-39, 193-95, 199-205.

4. Lady Mary Wortley Montagu, *Essays and Poems and "Simplicity, a Comedy,"* ed. Robert Halsband and Isobel Grundy (Oxford: Clarendon Press, 1977), p. 182. All references to her poems and to editorial notes on her poems are to this edition.

5. Dearing and Beckwith, in Gay, *Poetry and Prose,* 2:572 (notes), summarize the story of publication.

6. Quoted in ibid., p. 573.

7. Halsband and Grundy, p. 182. Walpole noted, however, that Lady Mary was "a little apt" to claim as hers poems by other people (*Correspondence,* ed. W. S. Lewis, vol. 14 [New Haven: Yale Univ. Press, 1948], p. 246, note; for his preference for Lady Mary's eclogues, see pp. 242-43).

8. Robert Halsband, "Pope, Lady Mary, and the *Court Poems* (1716)," *PMLA* 68 (1953): 242.

9. The mutual respect between Lady Mary and Gay as poets did not last; twenty-odd years later, she referred to him dismissively as "a good-natured man, and a little poet" (Joseph Spence, *Anecdotes, Observations, and Characters of Books and Men,* ed. Samuel Weller Singer and Bonamy Dobrée [Carbondale, Ill.: Southern Illinois Univ. Press, 1964], p. 146).

10. Halsband and Grundy, p. 198, following Walpole, identify Lydia as Mrs. Mary Coke (d. 1724); Dearing and Beckwith make no identification. Gay rarely satirized identifiable people (William Henry Irving, *John Gay: Favorite of the Wits* [Durham: Duke Univ. Press, 1940], p. 151). For the purposes of my analysis, the existence and identity of a real-life model is irrelevant and, if Mrs. Coke is the person, even misleading, since Lydia in both poems is unmarried.

11. Halsband, "Pope, Lady Mary, and the *Court Poems* (1716)," p. 242.

12. See Lady Mary's "Saturday: The Small Pox: Flavia," in Halsband and Grundy, pp. 201-4, especially l. 27: "Now Beautie's Fled, and Presents are no more."

13. *The Poems of Alexander Pope,* vol. 2: *The Rape of the Lock and Other Poems,* ed. Geoffrey Tillotson (London and New Haven: Methuen and Yale Univ. Press, 1962), 197; the note to line 166 quotes Warton: "Nothing is more common in poets, than to introduce omens as preceding some important and dreadful event."

14. *The Complete Letters of Lady Mary Wortley Montagu,* ed. Robert Halsband, vol. 1. *1708-1720* (Oxford: Clarendon Press, 1965), p. 78.

15. *Letters,* vol. 1, contains frequent charges of Wortley Montagu's "ill usage"; a particularly poignant letter is dated November 1714, complaining of his neglect after two years of marriage (pp. 236-37). Also see *Letters,* 1: 105.

16. Patricia Meyer Spacks, *John Gay* (New York: Twayne, 1965), p. 80.

17. Spacks, *John Gay,* pp. 98-101, sees limitation of perspective and lack of self-knowledge as the central theme of Gay's first collection of fables.

18. Lady Winchilsea, for example, in "The Unequal Fetters," describes the "chain" as binding to both partners in marriage but shorter for the woman (*The Poems of Anne Countess of Winchilsea,* ed. Myra Reynolds [1903; rpt. New York: AMS Press, 1974], pp. 150-51).

19. This passage makes it sound as if Damon is married. He is, in Lady Mary's version. Gay's version is unclear on this point, perhaps indicating insufficient revision of the lines he shared with Lady Mary.

20. Chudleigh, *Poems on Several Occasions* (1703), 3d ed. (London, 1722), pp. 45-46.

21. Although in this analysis I have for the most part followed the organization of Lady Mary's poem, a line-by-line comparison shows the rearrangement of some passages in Gay's version to produce the effect of a disorganized mind.

22. *John Gay,* p. 83; I disagree, however, with Spacks's contention that Lydia has "a weak but real desire to find alternatives" to the superficial standards of her society (p. 83). Other critics follow Spacks in identifying "ambiguity" as a frequent characteristic of Gay's poetry; see, for example, Harold E. Toliver, *Pastoral Poems and Attitudes* (Berkeley: Univ. of California Press, 1971), pp. 191-94; Christine Rees, "Gay, Swift, and the Nymphs of Drury Lane," *Essays in Criticism* 23 (Jan. 1973): 11-13.

23. Spacks, *John Gay,* p. 82.

24. Dearing and Beckwith, 1:83.

25. Martin C. Battestin finds the "ideal" in Gay's poetry to lie in "that curious discrepancy between his subject matter, which can be gross and sordid enough, and his elegant, witty manner" ("Menalcas' Song: The Meaning of Art and Artifice in Gay's Poetry," *JEGP* 65 [1966]:665); his argument for the ultimate value of form works well for "The *Tea-Table*" though less well for Gay's other poems.

26. For example, in "Tuesday," "Wednesday," and "Friday" of the *Shepherd's Week.*

27. Dearing and Beckwith, 2:591-92 (notes), compare this poem to other, more vicious, anti-Quaker satires.

28. Spacks, *John Gay,* passim, especially p. 84.

29. James Sutherland, "John Gay" (1949), in *Eighteenth-Century English Literature: Modern Essays in Criticism,* ed. James L. Clifford (New York: Oxford Univ. Press, 1959), p. 133.

30. Even the relatively gentle Lady Winchilsea reserved her sharpest satire for her own sex; see "Ardelia's Answer to Ephelia," pp. 38-46.

31. Grundy in Halsband and Grundy, headnotes to the six eclogues, pp. 182-201.

32. Halsband, "Pope, Lady Mary, and the *Court Poems* (1716)," pp. 243-44.

33. Halsband and Grundy print the variants, pp. 192-93.

34. It is perhaps significant that Dancinda is the only protagonist in the town eclogues with no identifiable real-life model.

35. Halsband and Grundy, p. 193; pp. 35, 201.

36. The Twickenham edition of Pope's works (vol. III.i, ed. Maynard Mack [London and New Haven: Methuen and Yale Univ. Press, 1950], pp. 31-32), notes various models for this passage, but not Lady Mary's poem.

FIVE

EDUCATIONAL *SPECTATORS*

Richard Steele, Joseph Addison, and Eliza Haywood

1. Eliza Haywood, *The Female Spectator,* 4 vols. (London, 1775). The twenty-four books were collected into four volumes, which were reissued in at least seven editions; the bibliographical history is confused. Pagination differs in the different editions, and the only one available to me is the 1775 edition (microfilm). Page numbers therefore seem pointless; I will cite only the book numbers. *The Spectator,* ed. Donald F. Bond, 5 vols. (Oxford: Clarendon Press, 1965), 1:21 (Number 4). All references are to this edition and will appear in the text. To avoid peppering my text with figures, I will cite only *Spectator* numbers and then only for major references; minor references may easily be found using Bond's splendid index, which is virtually a concordance.

2. Whicher, *The Life and Romances of Mrs. Eliza Haywood* (New York: Columbia Univ. Press, 1915), p. 144; Marr, *The Periodical Essayists of the Eighteenth Century* (London: Clark [1923]), p. 107.

3. Walter and Clare Jerrold, *Five Queer Women* (London, New York, and Paris: Brentano's, 1929), p. 262.

4. Robert D. Mayo, *The English Novel in the Magazines, 1740-1815* (Evanston, Ill.: Northwestern Univ. Press, 1962), p. 85.

5. Cynthia Leslie White, *Women's Magazines, 1693-1968* (London: Joseph, 1970), p. 28. Alison Adburgham, *Women in Print* (London: Allen & Unwin, 1972), surveys the contents of the *Female Spectator* (pp. 95-103) and says, rather oddly, that it has "much the same format" as the *Spectator* (p. 95); otherwise, she makes no comparisons.

6. Einhoff, *Emanzipatorische Aspekte im Frauenbild von "The Review," "The Spectator" und "The Female Spectator"* (Frankfurt, Bern, and Cirencester: Lang, 1980), pp. 84-139. Macaree, "A *Trimulierate* of Eighteenth-Century Periodical Editresses," in *Transactions of the Samuel Johnson Society of the Northwest,* vol. 12, ed. Ann Messenger (Burnaby: [SJSNW], 1981), 110, 108.

7. *The Female Spectator, Being Selections from Mrs. Eliza Heywood's periodical (1744-1746),* ed. Mary Priestley, intro. J. B. Priestley (London: Bodley Head,

1929). It is unfortunate that this book is the only readily available *Female Spectator*. The selections are not edited to show that they are selections and seem to have been chosen to show that Mrs. Haywood was an eccentric who loved snails and that she reveled in risqué stories. J. B. Priestley's introduction barely conceals a sneer at this "book to smile over," and he finds "splendid" the line drawings by Constance Rowlands, which are oppressively cute. The *Female Spectator* is far more worth reading than this edition indicates.

8. Hodges, "The *Female Spectator*, a Courtesy Periodical," in *Studies in the Early English Periodical*, ed. Richmond P. Bond (Chapel Hill: Univ. of North Carolina Press, 1957), p. 154. One of the earliest commentators, writing in *The Gentleman's Magazine* (Dec. 1744), also recognized Mrs. Haywood's practicality:

> On the FEMALE SPECTATOR,
>   now publishing monthly.
> Ye fair philosophers in virtue's cause,
> Conspicuous merit claims a just applause!
> Thrice worthy league! your gen'rous plan pursue,
> And take this tribute to your labours due:
> Were your great predecessor yet on earth,
> He'd be the first to speak your page's worth:
> There all the foibles of the fair you trace;
> There do you shew your sex's truest grace;
> There are the various wiles of man display'd,
> In gentle warnings to the cred'lous maid;
> Politely pictur'd, wrote with strength and ease,
> And while the wand'rer you reclaim, you please:
> Whether the fair, yet glows the blooming maid,
> Or a gay bride to hymen's porch is led
> Or matron busy'd with domestick cares,
> Or as a widow for her loss despairs,
> Learn'd in the weaker sex in every state,
> *You* shew a *judgment* more than *man*'s complete.
> Women, the heart of women best can reach;
> While men from maxims—you from practice teach.

9. "Eliza Haywood and the *Female Spectator*," *Huntington Library Quarterly* 42 (Winter 1978): 45, 46. Whicher sees something like the survival message in Mrs. Haywood's *A Present for a Servant-Maid: or, the Sure Means of gaining Love and Esteem . . .* (1743) but finds the "considerations of self-interest" to be not "edifying" (p. 147).

10. Mrs. Haywood's novels sometimes serve a similar purpose; her "stories attempt to rouse their female readers from lethargy and urge them to become active participants in and controllers of their fate" (Mary Anne Schofield,

Quiet Rebellion: The Fictional Heroines of Eliza Fowler Haywood [Washington, D.C.: Univ. Press of America, 1982], p. 122). Schofield deals only briefly with the *Female Spectator* in this survey of the novels.

11. Donald F. Bond's note on the character of Mr. Spectator is succinct and helpful 1:1n).

12. Critics of Addison and Steele, especially of Steele, usually say something about this topic. See, e.g., Rae Blanchard, "Richard Steele and the Status of Women," *Studies in Philology* 26 (1929): 325-55; Richard H. Dammers, *Richard Steele* (Boston: Twayne, 1982), pp. 70-74, 98-102; Robert M. Otten, *Joseph Addison* (Boston: Twayne, 1982), p. 93; Eberhard Einhoff, *Emanzipatorische Aspekte im Frauenbild.*

13. Whicher and the Jerrolds trace her career as she leaves her husband and struggles to win a place for herself in the world of letters. They agree, as does Schofield, that Mrs. Haywood's work took a somewhat different turn after she was pilloried by Pope in the *Dunciad.* Whether she herself "reformed" or adapted her stories to the taste of a less gallant age is arguable. I would suggest that her accumulated experience taught her the strength of the social, moral, and literary forces she was up against, hence her advice to her readers in the *Female Spectator* not to engage in battles they would inevitably lose. Mayo sees her "reformation" as "only a matter of emphasis" in her fiction (p. 92).

14. Bond cites the *Oxford English Dictionary*'s definition of "rotonda," which uses this line as the first known example, as "simply 'a round or circular object'" (2:7n). But surely the overtones of its usual meaning, the Pantheon, remained, especially as Addison continues the comparison with reference to "an *Egyptian* Temple."

15. Mrs. Haywood occasionally deals with topics which were of so much less importance in 1711-14 that Addison and Steele passed over them lightly, e.g., gambling and pleasure gardens.

16. In *Tatler* No. 84, a woman's reading, if not accompanied by modesty, is said to appear "masculine."

17. The eighteenth-century "microscope" could be a single lens; the Female Spectator probably carried a magnifying glass on her field trip.

18. Keith Thomas surveys a range of theories on what distinguishes man from beast, reason being central to the mainstream of the argument (*Man and the Natural World: A History of the Modern Sensibility* [New York: Pantheon, 1983], pp. 30-36).

19. The *Female Spectator*'s short fiction would be a study in itself. I say "sixty-odd" because the mixture of stories, anecdotes, letters, and character sketches, with all the problems of overlapping genres, makes a strict count impossible. Donald Kay has surveyed the short fiction in the *Spectator* (*Short Fiction in "The Spectator"* [University, Ala.: Univ. of Alabama Press, 1975]).

20. Schofield makes a similar point about the heroines in the novels (*Quiet*

Rebellion, p. 110). She alters her emphasis, wrongly I think, in her introduction to *Four Novels of Eliza Haywood* (Delmar, N.Y.: Scholars' Facsimiles and Reprints, 1983), when she finds a disguised "revolutionary plea" in Haywood's urgings that her readers become "more assertive" (p. 15).

SIX

ARABELLA FERMOR, 1714 and 1769

Alexander Pope and Frances Moore Brooke

1. Lorraine McMullen, "Moore, Frances (Brooke)," in *Dictionary of Canadian Biography*, vol. 4: *1771-1800*, ed. Francess G. Halpenny (Toronto: Univ. of Toronto Press, 1979), 553-56. All biographical data come from this source. For her historical importance, see, e.g., C. S. Blue, "Canada's First Novelist," *Canadian Magazine* 58 (1921-22): 3-12; Desmond Pacey, "The First Canadian Novel," *Dalhousie Review* 26 (1946-47): 143-50.

2. [Frances Moore Brooke], *The History of Julia Mandeville*, By the Translator of Lady Catesby's Letters. A new edition (London: Dodsley, 1788), 2: 47-49. Frances Brooke, *The History of Emily Montague*, ed. Mary Jane Edwards ([Ottawa:] Carleton Univ. Press, 1985). All page numbers in text below refer to this edition. The accuracy of Mrs. Brooke's depiction of social life is confirmed in *Canada Home: Juliana Horatia Ewing's Fredericton Letters 1867-1869*, ed. Margaret Howard Blom and Thomas E. Blom (Vancouver: Univ. of British Columbia Press, 1983). Although these letters were written a century after the novel, the picture of colonial life they contain is remarkably similar. Travel letters of the period also document that way of life. For a discussion of *The History of Emily Montague* as travel literature, see Janet Giltrow, "North American Travel Writing" (Ph.D. diss., Simon Fraser University, 1979), pp. 164-74.

3. For an analysis of the novel's political and religious elements, see Mary Jane Edwards, "Frances Brooke's *The History of Emily Montague*: A Biographical Context," *English Studies in Canada* 7, no. 2 (Summer 1981): 171-82. For an analysis of the novel as reflecting a specifically Canadian mode of thinking, "a duality [which] is a fundamental characteristic of garrison life," see John Moss, *Patterns of Isolation in English Canadian Fiction* (Toronto: McClelland and Stewart, 1974), pp. 30-33; one can, however, see the duality as a common habit of eighteenth-century thinking rather than specifically Canadian. For a more balanced Canadian view, see William H. New, "Frances Brooke's Chequered Gardens," *Canadian Literature*, no. 52 (Spring 1972), pp. 24-38.

4. "To Mrs. ARABELLA FERMOR," in *The Rape of the Lock and Other Poems*, ed. Geoffrey Tillotson, *The Poems of Alexander Pope*, vol. 2, Twickenham Edition (London and New Haven: Methuen and Yale Univ. Press, 1962), p. 143. References in text below refer to this edition.

5. *The History of Emily Montague,* ed. Carl Klinck, New Canadian Library (Toronto: McClelland and Stewart, 1961), p. ix; in a review of *Dictionary of Canadian Biography,* vol. 4, in *English Studies in Canada* 7 (1981): 499. Most of the few scholars who discuss the novel simply assume the connection between Arabella and Belinda. See, e.g., Paula R. Backscheider, "Woman's Influence," *Studies in the Novel* 11 (1979): 11; Katharine M. Rogers, "Sensibility and Feminism: The Novels of Frances Brooke," *Genre* 11 (1978): 164.

6. In *The History of Julia Mandeville,* Lady Anne Wilmot (a vivacious young widow and Arabella's predecessor as a wise and witty coquette) has both direct quotations from and allusions to *The Rape of the Lock* in her letters; see, e.g., 1:70; 1:121; 2:35.

7. Rogers, "Sensibility and Feminism," makes a similar point, that Arabella is "seen from the inside as a thinking human being" (p. 164), but obviates the point when she goes on to say that Arabella is "too frivolous" to "articulate ideas" (p. 165). The inconsistency vanishes when one considers the frivolity to be role-playing, as I am arguing that it is.

8. The *locus classicus* for discussion of the poem's mixed attitudes is Cleanth Brooks, "The Case of Miss Arabella Fermor," in *The Well Wrought Urn* (New York: Harcourt, Brace, 1947), pp. 80-104. I see a somewhat harsher tone than Brooks does in the mixture of feelings about Belinda, however.

9. Richetti, "The Portrayal of Women in Restoration and Eighteenth-Century English Literature," in *What Manner of Woman: Essays on English and American Life and Literature,* ed. Marlene Springer (New York: New York Univ. Press, 1977), p. 83.

10. Pope, *Poems,* 2:372.

11. Shohet, "An Essay on *The History of Emily Montague,*" in *The Canadian Novel,* vol. 2: *Beginnings,* ed. John Moss (Toronto: New Canada Publications, 1980), p. 32. For a clear statement about "the voice of the Brooke coquette: superficially frivolous but assertive and acute," see W. H. New, *"The Old Maid: Frances Brooke's Apprentice Feminism," Journal of Canadian Fiction* 2, no. 3 (Summer 1973): 9-12, especially p. 9.

12. McMullen, *An Odd Attempt in a Woman: The Literary Life of Frances Brooke* (Vancouver: Univ. of British Columbia Press, 1983), p. 108.

13. Some other tributes to Arabella are listed in Pope, *Poems,* 2: 373-74.

SEVEN

HEROICS AND MOCK HEROICS
John Milton, Alexander Pope, and Anna Laetitia Barbauld

1. Knox is quoted in Stuart Tave, *The Amiable Humorist* (Chicago: Univ. of Chicago Press, 1960), p. 34.

2. Chudleigh, "The Ladies Defence," in *Poems on Several Occasions,* 3d ed. (London, 1722), p. 253; the Parson is the object of Lady Mary Chudleigh's satire.

3. *The Poems of Anne Countess of Winchilsea,* ed. Myra Reynolds (1903; rpt. New York: AMS Press, 1974), p. 44. Page numbers in text below refer to this edition.

4. For Mrs. Haywood, see chapter 5 above. Elizabeth Montagu, quoted in "Bibliographical Note," *The Memoirs of Mrs. Laetitia Pilkington, Written by Herself,* ed. Iris Barry (London: George Routledge and Sons, 1928), pp. 471-72; Fanny Burney, *Evelina* (1778; rpt. New York: Norton, 1965), p. 254; [Ellis Cornelia Knight], *Dinarbas; A Tale: Being a Continuation of Rasselas, Prince of Abissinia,* 2d ed. (London: Dilly, 1792), pp. 310-11.

5. Betsy Rodgers, *Georgian Chronicles: Mrs. Barbauld and her Family* (London: Methuen, 1958), pp. 29-82. Most but not all of her writing and some of her letters are collected in *The Works of Anna Laetitia Barbauld,* ed. and with a "Memoir" by Lucy Aikin, 2 vols. (London: Longman et al., 1825). Page numbers in text below refer to this edition.

6. *Monthly Review,* January 1773, p. 57.

7. *Critical Review,* March 1773, p. 193.

8. *The Odes of Horace,* trans. Helen Rowe Henze (Norman: Univ. of Oklahoma Press, 1961), p. 144; the translator explains that "Wine was poured into the fountain with the flowers" (note, p. 144).

9. John Bickerdyke, *The Curiosities of Ale and Beer* (1889; rept. London: Spring Books, 1965), chap. 14, describes the history of and various recipes for lambswool and other wonderfully named similar drinks. Mrs. Barbauld was not a teetotaller. In a letter dated "Marseilles, Dec. 1785," she lists "Advantages of Travelling," which include inexpensive wine (2:37).

10. Philippa Pullar, *Consuming Passions: Being an Historic Inquiry into Certain English Appetites* (Boston and Toronto: Little, Brown, 1970), pp. 174-75, describes the usual scene.

11. Rodgers, pp. 110-19.

12. Donald McCormick, *The Hell-Fire Club,* Dennis Wheatley Library of the Occult (1958; rpt. London: Sphere Books, 1975), pp. 60-76 and 141-48. Page numbers in text below refer to this edition. McCormick throughout his book denies that the society practiced Satanism, but Dennis Wheatley, in the introduction, calls the denial "whitewash" (pp. 7-9).

13. Dashwood was a student of Rosicrucianism and might have used some of its symbols in his rituals; it is known that he did display a lamp with Rosicrucian symbols of serpent and doves (McCormick, pp. 62-63). *The Rape of the Lock,* Mrs. Barbauld's principal model for "The Groans of the Tankard," draws on Rosicrucianism for the machinery of the sylphs, as Warburton's note explains. But this is probably coincidence.

14. Oskar Seyffert, *Dictionary of Classical Antiquities,* rev. ed. (New York: Meridian Books, 1956), "Sibyl."

15. Some of the essays are dated, but most are not. Lucy Aikin, editor of the *Works* and Mrs. Barbauld's niece, has arranged the poems as nearly chronologically as possible (1:lxii).

16. Aikin places "The Rights of Woman" immediately after "To Dr. Priestley," which is dated December 29, 1792.

17. The tone of the poem is complex. Some readers have taken the claims to sovereignty and to possession of "sacred mysteries" as simultaneously ironic and not ironic. But I question that degree of complexity and the concomitant sense of the superiority of women, which I do not find borne out elsewhere in her writing.

18. *The Diary of Samuel Pepys,* ed. Robert Latham and William Matthews, II (Berkeley and Los Angeles: Univ. of California Press, 1970), 31 (Feb. 5, 1661), etc. All references are to this edition; publication dates of volumes vary. In Mrs. Barbauld's day, washing was done about every five weeks (Exhibition Guide to "An Elegant Art: Fashion and Fantasy in the Eighteenth Century," Los Angeles County Museum of Art, March-June 1983).

19. Guatimozin, or Cuauhtémoc, was a sixteenth-century Aztec emperor who was tortured by Spanish invaders.

20. Addison's and Johnson's objections appear in the *Spectator* and *Lives of the Poets,* cited and discussed by Christopher Ricks, *Milton's Grand Style* (Oxford: Clarendon Press, 1963), p. 27.

21. "Aeronautics," *Encyclopaedia Britannica,* 11th ed. (1910). The allusion helps to date the poem. Aikin places it third after "To the Poor," which is dated 1795. It is not in the 1792 collection.

22. She mentions meeting "one of the first who ascended in a balloon" in a letter dated "Besançon, Oct. 9th, 1785," and calls this M. de Morveau "a man of great merit" (2:29). See also 2:22-23, 56-57, 147.

23. Other changes in the quotation are not significant. "Towards" for "toward" is a slight error; "its" for "his" probably represents an accidental modernizing of the pronoun.

24. Anna Laetitia Barbauld, *The British Novelists* (London, 1810), Preface to Fanny Burney, pp. x, iii. (I have not seen this collection of novels, but I have seen a microfilm of a single volume in which are collected the introductory essay and the several prefaces.) Also see in this volume the introductory essay, "On the Origin and Progress of Novel Writing," which mentions Cervantes, pp. 12-13; and the Preface to Charlotte Lennox, pp. i, iii.

25. Ibid., Preface to Fanny Burney, p. ii.

26. Rodgers, *Georgian Chronicles,* pp. 108-10.

27. The reviewer is quoted in Rodgers, *Georgian Chronicles,* pp. 140-41. Rodgers mentions only one more publication, a short memoir of Dr. Estlin prefixed to an edition of his work. Mrs. Barbauld continued to write verse, however, which Lucy Aikin collected and published after her death.

EIGHT
CHOICES OF LIFE
Samuel Johnson and Ellis Cornelia Knight

1. Conant, *The Oriental Tale in England in the Eighteenth Century* (1908; rpt. London: Frank Cass, 1966), chapter titles et passim; Devendra P. Varma, *The Gothic Flame* (London: Barker, 1957), pp. 132ff. The term "horror-romanticism" is used throughout Eino Railo, *The Haunted Castle: A Study of the Elements of English Romanticism* (London: Routledge, 1927); Railo discusses very briefly the orientalism of Beckford, Byron, and Southey.

2. For "absurdist," see Charles E. Pierce, Jr., "The Conflict of Faith and Fear in Johnson's Moral Writing," *Eighteenth-Century Studies* 15, no. 3 (Spring 1982): 317-38, especially pp. 334-37; most other points of view are summarized in Carey McIntosh, *The Choice of Life: Samuel Johnson and the World of Fiction* (New Haven and London: Yale Univ. Press, 1973), pp. 163ff.

3. Rawson, "The Continuation of *Rasselas*," in *Bicentenary Essays on "Rasselas,"* ed. Magdi Wahba, Supplement to *Cairo Studies in English* (1959), pp. 92-94. Luttrell, *The Prim Romantic: A Biography of Ellis Cornelia Knight, 1738-1837* (London: Chatto and Windus, 1965), p. 86. Also see McIntosh: "*Dinarbas . . .* is the result of one reader's total inability to live with the ending as written" (p. 198).

4. Knight, *Dinarbas; A Tale: Being A Continuation of Rasselas, Prince of Abissinia,* 2d ed. (London: Dilly, 1792), Preface, p. viii. Page numbers in my text below refer to this edition.

5. Samuel Johnson, *The History of Rasselas, Prince of Abyssinia,* ed. George Birkbeck Hill (1887; rpt. Oxford: Clarendon Press, 1954), p. 42. Page numbers in text below refer to this edition.

6. Hawkins, *Life of Johnson,* 2d ed. (1787; rpt. New York: Garland, 1974), p. 372.

7. James Boswell, *Life of Johnson* (London, New York, and Toronto: Oxford Univ. Press, 1953), pp. 548, 601, e.g.

8. Knight, *Dinarbas,* p. 298; Boswell, *Life of Johnson,* p. 662.

9. Boswell, *Life of Johnson,* p. 28.

10. Luttrell, *The Prim Romantic,* pp. 41-115 passim, 157-99, 200-22.

11. Ibid., pp. 87, 115. I have not seen all of Miss Knight's diaries, but Luttrell, *The Prim Romantic,* cites them frequently. Her description is for the most part confirmed by *The Autobiography of Miss Cornelia Knight . . . With Extracts from her Journals and Anecdote Books,* ed. J. W. Kaye, 2 vols. (London: W. H. Allen, 1861). Written in her last years, this book describes her youth (without mentioning *Dinarbas*) quite dispassionately, with a purely formal tribute to her mother on that lady's death (1:138). Miss Knight expresses strong feeling only in the immensely detailed accounts of her relationships with Queen

Charlotte and her granddaughter, Princess Charlotte, especially when she had been slighted or otherwise hurt (see, e.g., 1:189, 260-62).

12. Alice C. C. Gaussen, *A Woman of Wit and Wisdom: A Memoir of Elizabeth Carter* (London: Smith, Elder, 1906), p. 26, quotes a letter: "To look gay when one is really unhappy is a duty society has the right to demand"; only a particularly intimate friend was allowed to know how miserable Elizabeth Carter really felt.

13. Such imagery, and such sentiments, occur in Isaac Watts's "True Monarchy" and "True Courage," though Miss Knight was probably not directly influenced by the enthusiasms of that nonconformist divine.

14. Luttrell, *The Prim Romantic*, p. 80 (quoting Mrs. Piozzi), p. 139 et passim.

15. See also pp. 290-91 on the necessity of satire in an imperfect world.

16. Riches create similar insecurity; see chap. 20.

17. Miss Knight knew some minor royal persons before writing *Dinarbas;* her more intimate acquaintance with royalty, not always happy, came later. See Luttrell *The Prim Romantic*, pp. 78-79, 157ff.

18. Miss Knight herself, the orphan of a military man, suffered permanent financial hardship as a result of the government's failure to provide for the dependents of its heroes. See Luttrell, *The Prim Romantic*, pp. 38, 48, etc.

19. Luttrell, *The Prim Romantic*, pp. 17-99 passim.

20. Johnson, *Ramblers* 38, 65, 120, 190, 204, 205; *Idlers* 75, 99, 101.

21. E.g., McIntosh, *The Choice of Life*, pp. 186-93.

AFTERWORD
WOMEN'S WRITING:
DERIVATIVE OR MAINSTREAM?

1. I take these phrases from Walter Jackson Bate, *The Burden of the Past and the English Poet* (New York: Norton, 1970); Harold Bloom, *The Anxiety of Influence: A Theory of Poetry* (New York: Oxford Univ. Press, 1973); and the related "anxiety of authorship" below, from Sandra Gilbert and Susan Gubar, *The Madwoman in the Attic: The Woman Writer and the Nineteenth-Century Literary Imagination* (New Haven: Yale Univ. Press, 1979), in the title of chap. 2 et passim.

INDEX